NEVER ENOUGH

THE REMARKABLE FRAUDS OF
JULIUS MELNITZER

NEVER ENOUGH

BRIAN MARTIN

Stoddart

First published in 1993 by
Stoddart Publishing Co. Limited
34 Lesmill Road
Toronto, Canada
M3B 2T6
(416) 445-3333

Canadian Cataloguing in Publication Data

Martin, Brian
Never enough: the remarkable frauds of Julius Melnitzer

Includes index.
ISBN 0-7737-2688-8

1. Melnitzer, Julius.   2. Swindlers and swindling —
Ontario — Biography.   3. Fraud — Ontario — Case
studies.   I. Title.

HV6699.C32056 1993   364.1′63′092   C93-093068-1

Cover design by Brant Cowie/ArtPlus
Typesetting by Tony Gordon Ltd.
Printed and bound in Canada

Stoddart Publishing gratefully acknowledges the
support of the Canada Council, Ontario Ministry of
Culture and Communications, Ontario Arts Council
and Ontario Publishing Centre in the development of
writing and publishing in Canada.

For Kay, Lindsey and Scott

Contents

Acknowledgments   ix

  1 The Banker   1
  2 The Mountie and Dreams
     of Singapore   17
  3 Beginnings   34
  4 Career Building   46
  5 Grand Bend and Glory   65
  6 Women and Ego   90
  7 Money and Ego   106
  8 Never Enough   121
  9 Forging On   142
 10 A Question of Trust   161
 11 Hot July   179
 12 Collapse   194
 13 An Empty Cookie Jar   217
 14 Fallout   243

Epilogue   261

Appendix   269

Index   273

Acknowledgments

THIS IS A WORK of nonfiction. The material for this book is derived from documents filed in criminal, civil and bankruptcy courts and from extensive research, interviews and previously printed material. No pseudonyms have been used.

A project of this kind cannot be accomplished without the help of many people, and I was extremely fortunate in the cooperation I received, on many fronts.

Among the many individuals deserving of special thank-yous are David Reich in Montreal for his assistance in matters of geography, culture and history in that vibrant community. In New York City, where crooked lawyer Alvin Ashley practiced his frauds, David Margolick of the *New York Times* and Clinton Calhoun, chief of frauds in the district attorney's office, were of great help. Lawyers Christopher Osborne and Jennifer Badley of McMillan Binch in Toronto provided assistance compatible with their obligations to the National Bank of Canada and to Coopers and Lybrand.

In London, Ontario, Brian Cunliffe, of RBG Dominion Securities, was an invaluable resource person on matters of securities and the intricacies of the stock market. John Everett, senior bankruptcy officer with Consumer and Corporate Affairs Canada, was extremely patient and helpful providing information on bankruptcy and insolvency. Rick Jackson, a vice-president at Peat Marwick Thorne, provided much help and insight into matters of insolvency. Sergeant Ray Porter, of the commercial-crime section of the London RCMP detachment, was most cooperative and shared the author's interest in accuracy. Kelley Teahen was of considerable help on several fronts. Also in London, I am indebted to the photographic department of the *London Free Press* and to the D. B. Weldon Library at the University of Western Ontario for access to its *Free Press* photo negatives.

In the publishing field, novelist, colleague and friend Joan Barfoot was at her supportive best. Thanks also to Beth Martin in Toronto for her help at the formative stages of this project. And at Stoddart Publishing, Angel Guerra lived up to his first name.

Much appreciated assistance came from my first-line editors Susan Greer and Helen Wigle, whose tireless efforts and thoughtful ideas helped make this book a reality. In Toronto, my editor Anne Holloway did a wonderful job of urging further improvements with her sensitive and intelligent pencil, and copy editor Maryan Gibson deserves thanks for her insightful suggestions and fierce attention to detail.

And finally, I must thank the many friends, associates and others whose lives were touched by Julius Melnitzer for sharing their stories with me. Most of them asked for anonymity, saying it was more important that a true portrait emerge of the man they knew than that they see their names appear in print.

BRIAN "CHIP" MARTIN
London, Ontario

1

The
Banker

"You've really helped me out here."

J OHN GRAHAM SQUINTED into the bright sunshine
that greeted his eyes as the revolving door
ejected him onto Fullarton Street.

It was just after 10:15, and the 36-year-old banker set off
on what he knew would be a pleasant walk this fine midsummer morning. There was a bounce in his step as he
strolled eastward toward busy Richmond Street, the main
north-south artery leading to London's city core. Behind
him, on the second floor of the glass-sided Talbot Centre, was
his desk, covered with the work that had piled up during his
vacation. He'd get back to it soon enough, he thought.

He was on a priority mission, carrying an important document in his black leather portfolio. The date was Wednesday, July 31, 1991.

Graham handled millions of dollars every year as an
account manager with the commercial banking centre of the
National Bank of Canada in London, Ontario. Responsible for
the financial dealings of more than 20 good-sized companies

and their principals, he had to stay abreast of interest rates and the latest investment products offered by his steadily growing bank, the sixth-largest in the country.

Short and slight, with salt-and-pepper hair and a neatly trimmed mustache, Graham possessed a soft-spoken style, good people skills, a ready smile and a preference for informality. A native of Orillia, a small city about 275 kilometres northeast of London, he had been in banking for 15 years, the last six with the National. He had a knack for making his clients feel at ease and was more than happy to leave the stuffed-shirt-banker atmosphere as often as possible, preferring to see his customers where they lived and worked.

At Richmond Street, beside the Art Deco federal government building, he turned left, walked north a short block to the stoplight at Dufferin Avenue and stopped. Looking east on Dufferin as he waited for the light to change, he could see St. Peter's Basilica, the city's largest Roman Catholic Church, to the left. Ahead on the right were several office buildings partly hidden by huge maple trees.

The banker couldn't help but wonder what lay in store for him a couple of blocks away. He was meeting Julius Melnitzer, one of London's most prominent lawyers, a man with whom he had been dealing for several years. Every couple of months the two men spoke on the telephone and once a year they met for lunch.

Melnitzer was quite a client, Graham mused. The lawyer was a wealthy man, worth some $77 million by the National Bank's last calculation. Described as a tiger in court, he was also aggressive in business with no shortage of investment schemes — or demands on his banker. Graham admired Melnitzer for his intelligence and his drive, and he had always sought to maintain a good relationship with him. It had been a strain at times, for the senior partner of Cohen, Melnitzer, the city's fourth-largest law firm, was prone to significant mood swings. When he didn't get what he wanted, he was known to display fearsome outbursts of temper, and his frequently gruff manner and loud voice were intimidating; he could alternately threaten or cajole, act petulant or be utterly charming and magnanimous. The banker was also well aware of Melnitzer's philanthropy, exercised through his law firm's support of the local theatre and symphony orchestra.

Melnitzer's reputation was considerable in London and growing across Canada. When Graham first met him, the lawyer boasted he had virtually authored Ontario's rent-review legislation. He had won several big cases, including a precedent-setting one involving property rights on a public beach, and his firm had drawn widespread attention for its use of billboards to promote its services. His financial statement showed he earned $360,000 a year from his law practice, had $30 million in offshore investments and controlled $15 million in family holdings. In addition, he was becoming a leading spokesperson for a province-wide landlord-rights group and was regularly quoted in the Toronto media. He lived in a fine neighborhood and had an art collection said to be valued at more than $2 million. A few months earlier, Melnitzer's face had graced the cover of a weekend magazine in which an article saluted his legal victories and predicted great things for his future. He had both profile and promise.

It had been four years since Melnitzer had come to the National Bank of Canada, which prided itself on personal service and its reputation as an entrepreneur's bank. Graham, who'd just been posted to London, was assigned to the account. The lawyer had been looking for a substantial personal line of credit, saying it was to enable him to purchase controlling interest in his family's real estate investment firm, Melfan Investments Ltd. Melnitzer already held some shares but needed help to gain control of the multimillion-dollar operation.

That was July 1987, and the bank extended Melnitzer a credit line of $2 million, taking as collateral a demand promissory note, a guarantee in the same amount from Melfan, and power of attorney over the shares to be purchased. In reviewing the files recently, Graham concluded that the line of credit was operating well and that Melfan had proven to be a good investment. The bank had obtained financial statements showing that Melfan's retained earnings stood at nearly $15 million. Melnitzer still owed $1.6 million on the line of credit but had fulfilled his obligations, and the bank was earning its prime plus three-quarters percent.

As Graham approached Clarence Street, he left the roar of traffic from Richmond behind. He enjoyed London for its clean environment and slower pace, but so far he'd resisted living in the city. Instead, home was 100 kilometres to the east, in Cambridge, halfway to Toronto. As a banker, Graham knew his lifestyle might become somewhat nomadic because of job postings, so he chose to continue commuting on a daily basis. Besides, his wife was a physiotherapist in the Cambridge area. If his career took the path he hoped, his commute would be in the opposite direction, to Toronto, the Ontario nerve centre of the National Bank. That would mean one less move for his wife and three children. The call for promotion had not yet come, so Graham was content to do his best where he was.

Directly ahead stretched the fortresslike headquarters of the London Life Insurance Company. Occupying nearly an entire city block, the home of the corporate giant looked out across Victoria Park, the city's central green oasis. Built in the 1920s, the building had lost none of its imposing character despite several modern additions. When London Life had reorganized internally a few years earlier, it had rented out some of its quarters to prestigious clients. This part of the building was renamed the Victoria Park Executive Centre. There, on the second floor, Cohen, Melnitzer was accommodated in a lavish suite of offices.

Graham had made this trip often in recent months, as Melnitzer sought to obtain more money from the National Bank. In March, the lawyer had requested that his line of credit be bumped back up to $2 million (at the time, the line had been reduced to $1.6 million). Graham and his superiors had approved the plan but demanded several restrictions and additional documentation, which Melnitzer ultimately rejected as unacceptable. The balance remained at $1.6 million, but at the lawyer's insistence the bank agreed to waive a pay-down of $200,000 that had been due in February, the same month Melnitzer said he had just purchased a big new home in Toronto.

Melnitzer had made a number of additional requests for funds since the first of the year. The lawyer said he was seeking money for real estate transactions but for reasons of confidentiality wouldn't provide details. He'd seemed annoyed at being pressed for the information and refused to pledge any further security. The bank had rejected all his requests.

"I'm a wealthy man, you know that," Melnitzer had complained with his customary bluster. "There are plenty of other bankers in this town who'd love to have the business I'm doing with you. If you people don't start being reasonable I'm going to take my business elsewhere. I'll write you a cheque to clear off my balance right now and we're history. And I'll smear your name all over London — in Toronto, too. You guys will never be any more than a two-bit outfit if you don't get with it."

It wasn't the first time Melnitzer had threatened to move to the competition. That diatribe and variations on it annoyed Graham every time he heard them. He was a professional money lender and he wanted to do business with Melnitzer, but he had to protect the bank's interests and comply with its policies. Graham wasn't accustomed to hearing his clients react this way. But with a reassuring smile and promises that he'd see what he could do, he had always been able to calm Melnitzer and retain the moody client. He came to dismiss the outbursts as those of a man on the move who was merely expressing his impatience with a banking system that didn't operate at his preferred pace. His approach was quite different from Graham's, the banker thought, but it obviously worked. The lawyer had become an extremely wealthy man and he was only 43.

As Graham waited for Melnitzer in the lushly appointed rose-and-gray reception area of the law firm, he hoped the lawyer would be in good spirits. He should be, the banker thought; he was getting a lot of money from the bank. In his portfolio was a letter of commitment for Melnitzer to sign. It spelled out the terms of a new credit line totalling $15 million that the National Bank had already authorized. The bank had agreed to provide the money to help Melnitzer fund unspecified personal investments and to consolidate the earlier $1.6 million still outstanding. Interest would be prime plus a half percent. In addition to Melnitzer's signature, Graham was to collect some blue-chip shares the lawyer had pledged as collateral. The shares, he understood, had a face value of nearly $25 million.

Graham was somewhat puzzled by the new loan and the shares that would support it. His senior manager, David Renwick, had told him that Melnitzer was seeking a $20-million line of credit and had pledged shares in such corporate giants as IBM, Exxon and Canadian Pacific. Renwick had handled the request while Graham was on holiday. The bank had agreed to accept the shares, but limited the credit line to $15 million, about 60 percent of the current face value of the stocks. In all Graham's dealings with Melnitzer, the lawyer had never mentioned holdings such as these. That struck him as odd, because with this kind of asset at his disposal, Melnitzer could easily have obtained the line-of-credit increase he'd sought in March — and saved himself a lot of shouting. Graham wondered if the holdings were new, or something Melnitzer had merely chosen to keep quiet about. He wondered if the lawyer didn't trust him for some reason. He would have liked to ask Melnitzer about it, but didn't want to risk a confrontation and the possibility of alienating a big customer.

"Hi, John, come on in," Melnitzer boomed, snapping Graham out of his reverie.

The lawyer, casually dressed in brown slacks, beige short-sleeved shirt and brown-and-white striped tie, smiled broadly and held out a beefy hand that engulfed the banker's slender one. Melnitzer led the visitor down a hall past three doorways before ushering him into his private office. While not a particularly big man, Melnitzer was massive compared to the banker. At five nine, he was five inches taller and, at about 190 pounds, outweighed his visitor by nearly 60 pounds. His short neck and broad shoulders made the square-built lawyer seem much larger than he was.

Melnitzer and Graham settled on opposite sides of the lawyer's virtually barren desk, custom made of pine and measuring nearly eight feet by four feet. Its natural finish matched the cubbyhole credenza behind, which stretched the width of the office, and the tongue-and-groove wood on the walls. Aside from the telephone and a picture of his young wife, the only thing on the desk was a brown leather portfolio.

"Sorry about moving the meeting up a half hour," Melnitzer began, settling into his chair. "I'm off to Singapore on the, ah, a week today. Should be gone for three or four weeks in all. The first week or so is business, then we're on to Europe to do the tourist thing. Some cycling, see the sights, you know. I really need a break, but I've got a million things to clear up before then. It just worked out better if you could come over a little earlier."

Graham said it had been no problem and he could understand the need for a holiday, still feeling refreshed from two weeks of lounging around the backyard pool with his family. He sensed Melnitzer was in one of his good moods and felt relieved.

"You're just back from the Middle East, aren't you?" Graham asked. "Taking it easy this summer and keeping the travel agents hopping, I see," he teased.

"Deena and I had a great time," Melnitzer said. "It was one of those Discovery Tour package things. We toured the Holy Land, Jerusalem, then over to Egypt, a cruise on the Nile and explored the pyramids. Man, did those guys ever move a lot of rock! Only two weeks, but the weather was great. I could've stayed another month, but there's too much to do here."

Melnitzer tugged at his wide mustache and allowed a flicker of a smile, then abruptly turned to the business at hand. As usual, he was never much for small talk.

"So, you've brought the acceptance, have you? Just before we do this, let me show you something."

He pulled a piece of paper out from beneath the portfolio and flashed it at Graham. It was correspondence on the letterhead of the Toronto Dominion Bank. Graham had only a brief look.

"That's a commitment from the TD for a line of $21 million," Melnitzer said. "They're prepared to take the same security I'm giving you and let me have $6 million more than you guys. And they're willing to do it at prime plus a quarter, not prime plus a half. Just thought you'd like to know what the competition is up to."

Graham started to say that share valuations can differ and no two banks have identical policies about the margining of such holdings.

"Save your breath, John," the lawyer interrupted. "I'll stick with our deal. It's obviously not the best I can get, but I gave my word to Renwick. And my word is my bond. You know that. When I make a commitment, that's it. It's the only way to do business."

With that, Melnitzer slipped a series of share certificates out from under the slim leather case.

"Well, here we are," the lawyer said, placing them in front of him. "Let's see, I've got to come up with enough of these to make you comfortable with the margin, right? A little over $20 million worth should do the trick, if my numbers are correct."

Graham, slightly unnerved at this rather casual approach to such a major transaction, agreed.

Melnitzer spread the share certificates out in front of him and reached for a calculator. Graham could see they were the promised blue-chip holdings.

"That's impressive, Julius," Graham said, noting several were for nearly 100,000 shares. "What do you put the total value at?"

"Not really sure today," the lawyer replied. "It's got to be over $30 million." He pulled them together, like a card dealer preparing to shuffle, and handed them to the banker. There were two certificates for IBM, two for Exxon, one for McDonald's, one for Canadian Pacific and one for BCE Inc., the parent company of Bell Canada.

Graham was astonished at the size of the holdings. As a banker, it was rare for him to actually see such documents, although he had been involved in many transactions involving them. Usually customers with substantial stock holdings felt safer leaving their certificates in the hands of brokers, transfer agents or in safety-deposit boxes. As he held them, Graham noticed the banknote-type texture of the paper and the elaborate detail work aimed at foiling counterfeiters. He studied them while, across the desk, Melnitzer was stabbing away at the calculator, talking to himself as he consulted a list.

"Let's see now, IBM, 98,435 at 101 and a quarter, hmm, nearly $10 mill . . . Okay, Exxon, 96,998 at, say, 59, is, ah, just shy of $6 mill. There's $15 million. No, no, better the other Exxon for 50,412, that's, ah, $3 mill, for sake of argument . . . Now, McDonald's, 95,193 at 32.75, hmm, just over $3 mill . . ."

Graham marvelled at the speed with which Melnitzer worked and his apparent nonchalance toward the big numbers he was crunching. The whole scene seemed unreal, like a game of Monopoly.

Melnitzer completed his calculations and reached for the certificates. "It looks like I'll make you happy if I give you these five and keep these two," he said, sorting through them.

He gave Graham the IBM certificate for 98,435 shares, the Exxon certificate for 50,412 shares, the McDonald's for 95,193 shares, one BCE for 71,628 shares and one Canadian Pacific for 94,622 shares. "I put the total at about $22 million, give or take a bit," Melnitzer said. "That should more than cover the loan with the margin you're allowing me. Am I right?"

It was Graham's turn to do some rapid calculations, and it didn't take him long to confirm the numbers. "Yes, that should do it, Julius," he agreed. "That should do it nicely."

Melnitzer smiled, placing the certificates he was keeping back beneath the portfolio. "I think I'll be taking these to the TD," he said in explanation. "I figure they should be good for another $5 million."

Graham slipped the five certificates into his case and brought out the letter of commitment. The three-page document, dated July 22, had already been signed by Graham and Renwick and laid out the terms of the $15-million credit line.

"If you'll just sign the acceptance at the bottom, Julius, we're in business, and I'll let you get back to your work."

Melnitzer scanned the letter quickly, nodded with an approving grunt, then signed the acceptance with his customary scrawl, dating it July 31, 1991. Graham also produced documentation giving the bank power of attorney over the shares, which the lawyer signed.

"So, what do you plan to do with all this?" Graham asked. "Onto something big?"

"Real estate stuff, mostly local," was the reply. "I can't really talk about it right now. We're at a tricky stage on the major part of it and I'd hate to louse it up. I'm sure you can appreciate that."

Graham wasn't surprised with the response. Melnitzer always seemed to be involved in deals he couldn't talk about. Dropping the topic, the banker turned to more comfortable conversational turf.

"How soon do you think you'll be drawing down the funds?" he asked.

"Fairly soon. Probably in a matter of days. Before I'm off for Singapore at any rate," the lawyer replied. "The first will be a cheque for $2 or $3 million either to Allan Richman or to Grand Canyon Properties, I'm not sure right now. I'll be looking for another $10 million in a few weeks."

Melnitzer said he planned to write a number of postdated cheques and agreed to provide Graham with a list of them. He busied himself with his papers and Graham sensed the meeting was over.

"I'll return your security on the old line before you leave, hopefully on Tuesday," Graham said, then paused before adding, "and do me a favor — give us a day or so notice before you write any large cheques, anything over a million or two." He gathered his papers and rose to leave.

Melnitzer agreed and walked Graham back to the reception area where the lawyer warmly expressed his gratitude. It was a marked departure from his usual perfunctory style. "John, you've really helped me out here. Thanks a lot. I really appreciate it," he said, his voice dropping, becoming almost soft.

The two men shook hands and Melnitzer placed his free hand on top of the handshake as if to emphasize its importance. "It's been good doing business. We'll see you later. Take care."

The banker wished the lawyer a good trip and began to retrace his steps to his own office building. His brow was furrowed as he replayed the encounter in his head. Although he was happy to have concluded a deal with such good security backing it, he was troubled by a few details. And he was more than a little nervous about carrying $22 million in share certificates through the streets of London.

Back at the Talbot Centre, Graham reported to Renwick. He produced Melnitzer's acceptance of the National Bank terms and the certificates.

"You know, Dave," he said, "I can't quite get over this business about his not divulging all these shares to us until now. I thought I knew this guy. It's not like he just bought them. As you can see, they all date back to 1987. I was tempted to ask him about it, but I didn't want to run the risk of pissing him off. You know how he can be."

Renwick was handling the certificates, noting the number of shares and inspecting them, one after another. "Hmm, hmm," he offered in agreement.

"He didn't have them when we extended that first credit line," Graham continued. "They were issued about four months later. So why didn't he put these down as an asset or offer them up earlier when we wanted better security? It doesn't figure."

Renwick looked up from the certificate he was studying. He replied that the stocks had been a major part of his discussions with Melnitzer when Graham was on holiday. "It could be that we never knew about these because we didn't have full details of his assets until he applied for this new line," Renwick said. He put the certificates down. "You know, come to think of it, Melnitzer did ask me something at one point that I thought was kind of strange. He seemed concerned we might want to register the shares under the PPSA, but I said we wouldn't bother. And he didn't want us to transfer the shares into the bank's name, but he agreed to a power of attorney."

The furrows on Graham's forehead deepened. He knew the Personal Property Security Act provided a way for lenders to formally register property they've taken as security. It was designed to help lenders check the security on a government computer to ensure it was not encumbered elsewhere. The fact that Melnitzer didn't want the shares registered added to the niggling anxiety Graham was feeling about the deal.

Graham decided to validate all the securities, and he proceeded to make some local calls to stockbrokers to verify that the certificates were worth $22 million at current share prices. The calls revealed that everything appeared to be in order. He then went a step further by calling Brad Sutcliffe at the Toronto office of the bank to see if he could further authenticate the stocks and confirm that they were still held by Melnitzer. Sutcliffe, a senior banker with the unwieldy title of Manager, Business Development Client Services, had friends in the stock business who might prove useful. By noon, Graham had relayed to Sutcliffe the dates of issue, amounts and certificate numbers of the shares. He asked that they be checked without delay, since they were being held as security for a $15-million line of credit already authorized by the London commercial banking centre.

At the Toronto end, Sutcliffe jotted down the particulars Graham provided. He knew that the transfer agent for CP and BCE was Montreal Trust. As such, the trust firm acted as registrar for the shares of those companies and maintained records of the shareholders. In many cases, an agent also retained the actual share certificates on behalf of the share-holders. Sutcliffe had a contact at Montreal Trust, and he telephoned to ask her to search the firm's records for the two certificates. He routinely made such requests, and so she readily complied when he asked her to confirm the details Graham had given him: a BCE certificate, number DC045634, issued November 19, 1987, to Julius Melnitzer; and a Canadian Pacific certificate, number CCB343826, issued November 25, 1987, to Julius Melnitzer.

Sutcliffe couldn't help but note the share amounts, which indicated that these two certificates alone were probably worth $4 to $5 million. Nice holdings, he thought, as he awaited the reply.

He wasn't prepared for the answer he received late that afternoon.

Julius Melnitzer had no shares in either company.

The certificates bearing those numbers were held by some-one else named Melnitzer, said the woman from Montreal Trust, and furthermore were only for one share each. A BCE certificate with that serial number was for a single share, issued April 26, 1991, to Melissa Melnitzer, whose mailing address was a London, Ontario, law firm — Cohen, Melnitzer. The Canadian Pacific certificate was also for a single share, issued April 26, 1991, to Melissa Melnitzer at the same address.

Sutcliffe knew it would take somewhat longer to verify the remaining three certificates, but he also knew something was terribly wrong. He tried to reach Graham in London but the banker had gone for the day. Sutcliffe sent a message by fax, asking Graham to contact him first thing the next morning.

When they heard the news, Graham and Renwick were in shock. Sutcliffe was told to keep trying to verify the remaining three certificates.

The phone lines between the London and Toronto offices buzzed. Had the unbelievable happened? Had Melnitzer, prominent citizen, wealthy lawyer and trusted customer, committed fraud? It was unthinkable. The bank had approved him for $15 million and he was going to start writing cheques immediately and leave the country in a few days. And if he had produced forged documents for the latest line of credit, what about the earlier line?

Graham was convinced that if these stocks were fake, the earlier security was probably suspect, too. The bank could freeze Melnitzer's accounts and stop his flight with the latest money, but the $1.6 million was already gone. The bankers had to get to the bottom of the situation, and fast.

They decided to take the certificates to Toronto for inspection by experts. A slim chance remained that there was some sort of misunderstanding. The bank couldn't afford to let a simple error alienate a high-profile client, who would probably sue if the bank's suspicions proved groundless. Jobs could be on the line.

There was no time to waste. Graham and Renwick drove immediately to Toronto with the certificates, which gave them about two and a half hours to ponder the possibility that their banking careers might be in jeopardy.

In Toronto, Graham, Renwick and Sutcliffe took the certificates to the Front Street offices of Montreal Trust where they met Ed Shea, manager of the firm's corporate services division, and his assistant, Diethard Polzl. The trust firm executives compared Melnitzer's Canadian Pacific share certificate with a legitimate one and pronounced the Melnitzer one a fake.

Melnitzer's had blue borders instead of green; it had an incorrect style of dating; the asterisks had six instead of five points; the paper was different; a Montreal Trust official whose signature appeared on the certificate wasn't with the firm in 1987. And the certificate contained a copyright date of 1990, an impossibility on a share supposedly issued in 1987. The bankers kicked themselves for not having spotted that. Finally, nowhere in Montreal Trust's records did Julius Melnitzer appear as a CP shareholder.

Turning to the BCE certificate, Shea and Polzl noted similar discrepancies: compared with a legitimate share, its colors were subdued; the paper quality was inferior; the asterisks different; and the signature was wrong for 1987.

The bankers and trust executives immediately contacted a representative of Royal Trust, Canadian transfer agent for McDonald's Corporation. He confirmed that this certificate was a fake, particularly easy to spot because Melnitzer's document had been computer-generated and back in 1987, McDonald's certificates were still being typed.

Sutcliffe contacted the U.S. transfer agent for McDonald's and learned that Melnitzer's certificate number was for a single share, also issued to Melissa Melnitzer in April, 1991. He checked out the IBM certificate number P318900 and discovered it was not registered to either Julius or Melissa Melnitzer; however, the next number in sequence to it, P318901, was registered in April to Melissa. For one share. The Exxon certificate number was also for a single share issued in April to Melissa Melnitzer.

By late afternoon the bankers' worst fears were confirmed. All five certificates were forgeries. Instead of holding nearly $25 million in security, they had worthless pieces of paper. With $15 million at risk, of which $1.6 million was gone, they knew they were the victims of one of the largest frauds ever perpetrated on a Canadian bank.

They had to move quickly. The Mounties would have to be brought in.

But first they called their lawyers.

2

The Mountie and Dreams of Singapore

"Something big is happening."

R AY PORTER HAD BEEN looking forward to this outing and he wasn't disappointed. He hadn't played golf for six years and here he was knocking balls around Westminster Trails almost as though he knew what he was doing. His foursome had teed off about noon and it promised to be a fun day. It was the Friday afternoon before

Ontario's 1991 civic-holiday long weekend in August and two weeks of vacation lay ahead.

To an outsider, Porter and his companions, Al MacDonald, Henry Thompson and Joe Peel, looked like businessmen who had decided to goof off early on a warm midsummer afternoon. In fact, they were, respectively, a sergeant, two corporals and a constable in the Royal Canadian Mounted Police. They were among 20 members of the London detachment taking part in an office golf tournament, whacking their way around the course located just minutes south of the city.

Porter's dapper appearance particularly belied his profession. At five eight, the 40-year-old sergeant looked more like an accountant or a salesman, nothing like the scarlet-tunic-clad hero of old movies chasing his man across the frozen tundra. Porter and his foursome were members of a new breed of Mountie, who more frequently follow paper trails than dogsleds. Five months earlier, Porter, a 19-year veteran of the federal force, had been promoted to the rank of sergeant and placed in charge of the five-member commercial-crime section in London. Officers in the section are button-down nine-to-fivers. Their prime job is to track down bad actors in the corporate world and to investigate suspicious bankruptcies, national and international frauds and counterfeiting.

With the first eight holes behind them, Porter, MacDonald, Thompson and Peel were midway up the ninth fairway, an undulating par four with a slight dogleg to the left. It was almost three o'clock and all were thinking about their next shots and the cool beer waiting just beyond the green. Porter was mulling over his irons when someone hollered, "Here comes trouble." He looked up to see a golf cart approaching, bouncing along from an unexpected direction.

The cart driver was unfamiliar, but Porter recognized the passenger, Constable Steve Gorman, one of the handful of officers who had been left at the detachment that afternoon to mind the shop. Porter glanced around and saw behind him a foursome of drug-squad officers, who had just teed off. For a moment, he felt sorry for the drug boys. Middle of the afternoon and they're going to be called away to take part in some drug bust. Those guys in narcotics never get a rest, he thought. Surveillance, nighttime and weekend raids; it seldom let up. Not like commercial crime. The commercial crime busters liked to joke, "There's a bankruptcy going down."

To Porter's surprise, the cart came right up to him. Gorman quickly hopped out and said, "Call the office. Something big is happening. Toronto is looking for you."

Porter's mind began to race. What in the world was up? Must be important to track him down here. Nevertheless, he finished selecting his iron as Gorman sped off. After all, he reasoned, he was heading in the right direction for the clubhouse and telephone. No need to be too hasty. But his concentration was off. He double-bogeyed the hole.

At the clubhouse, he phoned the office and was told that Inspector Dave Shewchuk of the Toronto detachment wanted him to call. Patched through, Porter learned Toronto was investigating a big case involving a London lawyer and forged documents. He should be on alert. London might be needed to arrest the man, whose whereabouts were currently unknown. Porter fetched a pager, shared the information with his curious colleagues and headed back to the course. If anything happened he'd hear about it immediately. Besides, there was a game to finish.

Despite the interruption, Porter collected himself and picked up the pace on the back nine. When the scores were tallied, he had a 97. Pretty good, he congratulated himself. Haven't played in six years and broke a hundred. Must celebrate with a beer. But first call Toronto again.

Not much new; investigation just under way. Suspect has homes in Toronto and London and still can't be found. May have fled the country. Toronto was waiting for a lawyer with the National Bank to pull together some paperwork that would help with a search warrant. People were being interviewed.

Porter and the other officers returned home to pick up their spouses and attend a pool party at Constable John

Henderson's. The evening had turned cloudy and it had begun to rain. Porter made several more calls and learned the suspect was a lawyer named Julius Melnitzer, who lived on fashionable Tallwood Road in the northern section of the city. At the party, other officers recognized the name. Some of the drug-squad boys jokingly offered to help in any arrest or search; several of them had been stung over the years while prosecuting cases in which Melnitzer or one of his partners had appeared for the defence. They felt no real grudge, just a kick at seeing a guy who defends the bad guys possibly become a defendant himself.

About 9 p.m., Ray Porter and Al MacDonald took a drive past Melnitzer's house. Outside lights were on at the single-storey executive home but there was no sign of life. Nice area, Porter thought, as he peered over the steering wheel and into the nighttime drizzle. Having moved to London less than five months before, Porter wasn't familiar with the secluded crescent of about 20 homes tucked between two ravines, although it was less than a mile from his own new home. Porter, still attuned to real estate prices from his move to the city, figured the Melnitzer house was probably worth at least $350,000, maybe $400,000.

"Nice digs," MacDonald offered from the passenger seat.

Porter agreed. "The folks around here have a few dollars. Guess we'll have to drop by again." He pulled away slowly, checking out the neighboring homes. The Mounties returned to the party and Porter made another call.

Because he was on standby, the sergeant made sure his drinks were soft. He might have to spring into action at any time, and he'd need to have all his wits about him. On the way home about midnight, Porter and his wife, Nancy, drove past 19 Tallwood. Still nothing.

In the morning on what was supposedly the first day of his annual vacation, Porter warned Nancy that if the case was really big, it might eat into their holiday plans. They had hoped to get some work done around the house and perhaps engage in some cross-border shopping. Good thing they hadn't planned to take their annual trip to visit family in Nova Scotia, they agreed.

Porter, a man who believes in physical fitness, was restless. The rain had stopped, so he and Nancy varied their usual Saturday-morning walk to include a stroll past the Melnitzer home. Still no sign of life.

Checking with Toronto, Porter learned that during the night Sergeant George Gunn had formally seized the five forged stock certificates from the National Bank of Canada offices. Melnitzer could not be found at his Toronto address in the swank Rosedale area, either.

Based on information received from National Bank officials, the Toronto detachment was convinced more phoney certificates would be found in Melnitzer's London office. A search warrant was being prepared. On this Saturday of a long weekend, a judge would have to be found and persuaded to authorize the search.

It appeared the investigation would be shifting from Toronto to London, the scene of the crime. "Don't make any plans," Gunn told him. "It looks like you may inherit this." Porter's holiday was definitely at risk.

Ray Porter was eminently capable. A native of Kentville, Nova Scotia, he had wanted to be a member of the Royal Canadian Mounted Police all his life. He tried to join the force after graduating from high school but was told he was too young. He attended Acadia University where he took a bachelor's degree in sociology and psychology, thinking both disciplines would help him in police work.

It turned out the force was starting to look for recruits with degrees. And in 1972, when he was 21, Porter signed on as a Mountie in Halifax. After the mandatory six months of basic training in Regina, Porter was posted to Ontario headquarters in Toronto for recruit field training. For six months he learned the basics of customs and excise matters before being assigned to the force's customs and excise section in Toronto.

From 1973 to 1977, the young Mountie helped uncover and investigate smuggling cases. The work involved reviewing shipments of jewelry and other products undervalued by the shippers to avoid taxes; he also looked into moonshine-liquor operations, and much of his time was spent on paperwork. Porter, who proved to be thorough and a quick study, was marked for promotion. He was soon transferred to nearby Oakville, where he opened a new customs and excise section.

In 1979, it was back to Toronto to join the commercial-crime section. Much of the work was investigating frauds, many against the federal government. In September 1981, he was promoted to the rank of corporal and moved again, this time to Hamilton to work in a smaller commercial-crime section. The posting lasted six years, in the course of which he was assigned a sensitive and high-profile case.

There were allegations that Liberal member of Parliament Sheila Copps had breached the Canada Elections Act by spending more than she was entitled to in her successful 1984 campaign in the Hamilton East riding. Federal elections commissioner Joseph Gorman claimed Copps spent $2,007.93 more than the legal limit of $35,598.58, an amount determined by the number of electors in her riding. If the allegation proved to have merit, Copps could be charged and face a penalty ranging from a $1,000 fine to a seven-year exclusion from the House of Commons. Copps was viewed by many observers as a potential future prime minister, so the case made national headlines. Her supporters were outraged, but those who opposed the ambitious young parliamentarian were hoping for a charge, conviction and exile. Banishment from the House of Commons would have made a significant dent in her upward ascent.

Gorman turned the investigation over to the Mounties, who handed it to the bright young investigator then working in Copps's hometown. It was a career case for Porter. The young corporal and his staff studied every aspect of the spending by the Copps election team. During the six-month investigation, no stone was left unturned. Sloppy work would be rewarded with an uproar in the House of Commons and the force would suffer major embarrassment.

In the end, Porter recommended no charge be laid. He found that Copps had included expenditures in her report to Gorman that had nothing to do with her campaign. When the figures were adjusted, she was actually $1,340 below her spending limit.

In late 1987, Porter was transferred to the federal enforcement section of the Hamilton detachment, where he faced considerable challenge. Officers in this section dealt with a veritable grab bag of offences under federal law, with the exception of drugs and commercial crime. Cases included passport and immigration matters, customs, copyright, excise, applications for criminal pardons, frauds against the family allowance, old-age security and unemployment insurance plans, and even Migratory Birds Act cases. Porter broadened his horizons in ways he'd never imagined.

Before long, he landed another major case that would hit the front pages. This one involved a businessman charged with infringing a copyright held by the huge computer games firm Nintendo. The computer wizard had been copying Nintendo games and selling them without authorization. The man was convicted, fined and jailed for six months, the first jail sentence ever imposed under the ancient Copyright Act.

In March 1991, Porter made sergeant and was transferred to the London detachment to run the commercial-crime section. By now a seasoned officer who constantly took courses to upgrade his skills, Porter would head a group whose major work was looking into bankruptcy cases where individuals or businesses were suspected of attempting to hide their assets from creditors. The Mounties were authorized to track down those assets in conjunction with federal bankruptcy officials. Two members of Porter's team were also assigned to work with Revenue Canada in investigating individuals and businesses, including organized crime, for income-tax evasion.

The commercial-crime office at the London detachment was always busy. By 1991, as the recession deepened, countless new bankruptcy-related cases were springing up. Porter and his crew didn't really need more work.

While the Mounties waited, lawyers for the National Bank were preparing to go before a judge in Toronto with an application for an injunction that would freeze all of Melnitzer's assets and appoint a receiver to determine, locate and manage those assets. The bank was launching a lawsuit against Melnitzer in a bid to recover the $1.6 million.

Meanwhile, the Toronto detachment, handling the criminal aspects of the case, was still trying to locate Melnitzer. A search warrant for the London law firm was being prepared. Late in the day, the application for the warrant was transmitted to London.

In Toronto, Justice H.J. Keenan of the general division of Ontario Court had granted the National Bank's injunction on an *ex parte* basis, which meant Melnitzer, wherever he was, didn't know his financial affairs were being frozen and that a receiver was being appointed to control them. The action, extraordinary on the face, is permitted in law when one party can convince a judge that another party against whom it has an action is about to flee the jurisdiction. In its motion, the National Bank noted that Melnitzer had advised them he planned to leave for Singapore on Wednesday, August 7, for three to four weeks and that he would begin drawing down on his newly negotiated $15-million line of credit during that time. A bank official swore in an affidavit that Melnitzer's action "causes the bank serious apprehension that Melnitzer may intend to leave the jurisdiction permanently."

The meticulous Porter found some minor errors in the warrant application he received from Toronto to search the Cohen, Melnitzer offices. Nothing significant, but he was going to be dealing with lawyers, and Porter knew he had to have every *t* crossed and every *i* dotted. If any flaws were uncovered in the warrant, a judge could later rule that the proceeds seized in the search were collected illegally and could not be used as evidence. Porter knew forged stock certificates were crucial to the case against Melnitzer.

Then there was the logistical problem of finding a judge to sign the warrant. As Saturday slipped into evening, Porter consulted London Crown Attorney Jerry Buchanan, and by 8:50 p.m. obtained the signature of Judge Douglas Walker, of Ontario Court, provincial division, for the amended search warrant.

Investigations into the activities of lawyers come with a unique set of problems. Lawyers claim that many of their actions and most of their files are covered by lawyer-client confidentiality. Even though the Mounties were now armed with a valid search warrant, they would have to tread carefully. Porter and Gunn knew they couldn't go pawing through the filing cabinets and desks at the law firm without running into files the lawyers would claim were confidential.

The best way to proceed was to let the firm's lawyers know what was being sought and why, Porter decided. Show them the application for the warrant, which spelled out in detail that the Mounties were looking for forged stock certificates like the ones Melnitzer had presented to the National Bank. Porter contacted senior law partner Fletcher Dawson, who handled the firm's major criminal cases. Dawson was told what had happened and that Porter and Gunn wanted to search the firm's offices immediately.

"You've got to be kidding," said a disbelieving Dawson, a serious, academic lawyer not known for his sense of humor. "There's some sort of terrible mistake. This isn't possible. Not with Julius." Dawson had worked with Melnitzer for 14 years. Who had authorized the search warrant and when? he demanded. The senior partner took some convincing, but he reluctantly agreed to call other partners and meet the Mounties at the law office to monitor the search and ensure that no lawyer-client confidentiality was breached.

Shortly before 11 p.m., a meeting took place at the offices of Cohen, Melnitzer. Dawson was there with his wife, Janine, who was a law clerk at the firm, and senior partner Ron Delanghe, a specialist in real estate and development work. Michael Epstein, a well-respected London criminal lawyer who was a friend of both Dawson and Melnitzer, was present to act as outside counsel to the law firm to protect its interests this night. Joining the group later was Russell Raikes, a junior member of the firm who had worked closely with Melnitzer. Porter and Gunn were assisted by RCMP corporals Mike Hubley and Al Tutt, the latter an identification officer able to help with fingerprints and photography as needed.

The lawyers were skeptical. They pored over the search warrant and the application that supported it. Dawson and Epstein respected Judge Walker, one of the finer minds on the local bench when it came to criminal law. They knew he wouldn't have signed a document containing any irregularities, but they wanted to assure themselves that everything was correct.

After considerable discussion, it was decided that Dawson and Delanghe would first scan the contents of filing cabinets and drawers in full view of the officers. Then they would pass nonsensitive material to an officer to be viewed.

Dawson, with Gunn at his elbow, went into Melnitzer's office; Delanghe, accompanied by Porter, took the office of Helen Pollock, Melnitzer's longtime secretary. The rest of the group stood by, conversing in hushed tones.

Dawson headed straight for Melnitzer's massive desk and began opening drawers, checking files, inspecting their contents carefully before handing them to Gunn. In the next office, Delanghe did likewise with Porter at his side. It was a slow process and the lawyers were convinced it was pointless, despite the apparently well-documented suspicions of the officers. Among the items found was a memo indicating Melnitzer had flown to Montreal two days before and was expecting to return Sunday evening. That explained the lack of activity around his London and Toronto homes. And it meant he hadn't fled the country.

About midnight Dawson pulled open a lower drawer in

his partner's desk and began thumbing through some files. He came across five identical manila envelopes and pulled out the first. On the outside was marked "BCE." Inside were two BCE share certificates, identically numbered, each issued to Julius Melnitzer for 71,628 shares.

"Bingo," called out Gunn as the rest of the group gathered around the desk.

Dawson gasped. "Oh, shit."

Quickly he pulled out another envelope. This one was marked "IBM." It contained seven IBM Corporation share certificates, all bearing the same serial numbers and issued to Melnitzer for 25,806 shares.

Dawson repeated, "Oh, shit," his voice rising.

Another envelope. This time six Exxon Corporation certificates, all identical, for 50,412 shares.

Dawson, breathing quickly, repeated his expletive and pulled out another envelope.

Two Canadian Pacific Limited certificates, for 94,622 shares.

Dawson was ashen, his colleagues silent.

The fifth envelope. More certificates. Two for McDonald's Corporation: 95,193 shares.

"This can't be," Dawson croaked. The Mounties pounced on the envelopes to compare them with the list of certificates they were seeking. They'd found what they were looking for.

But were there more? The 19 certificates had a face value of about $100 million, about four times the value of the five presented to the National Bank. And they looked good. No wonder it had taken experts to determine they were fakes.

After a brief pause while the lawyers whispered among themselves, the search resumed. Dawson, Delanghe and the others were no longer as skeptical or as reluctant to cooperate. Another hour of searching, however, failed to turn up any more evidence.

"So, how do we reach Julius?" Gunn wanted to know. It was a question already on the minds of Melnitzer's colleagues. The lawyers expected Melnitzer would have some

sort of explanation to prove this was all a colossal misunderstanding. He'd always been able to explain things before. If
he heard what the Mounties had been saying about him, and
that they'd been going through his office, he'd hit the roof,
they thought.

It was now almost 2 a.m. Gunn pressed the issue. If
Melnitzer was in Montreal, where would he be staying? The
lawyers huddled again.

"Let me try something," Epstein said to the Mounties after
a moment, and he and Delanghe went into an office. A few
phone calls later, they had tracked Melnitzer to Montreal's
Four Seasons Hotel. Melnitzer was in his hometown on a
family matter.

Delanghe went straight to the point with the partner he'd
roused from sleep.

"Julius. Ron here. The Mounties have been searching your
office and they've found some stock certificates they say are
forged. They say you've used them to get a line of credit at
the bank. It looks bad. What's going on?"

There was a pause at the Montreal end. Delanghe had
expected fireworks, was sure his trusted partner would erupt
in rage.

"How many did they get?" Melnitzer asked.

"Nineteen, I think," Delanghe said, shocked at Melnitzer's
muted response.

"So why did they search?"

"They said the National Bank checked the certificates you
gave them and they didn't check out. They were forgeries.
The same sort of stuff they found in your desk. What gives?"

"Well . . . " Melnitzer paused. "I guess they got me. They
were fakes."

"What?" Delanghe exploded. "What are you talking about?
How could you?"

There was silence at the Montreal end of the line. Then
Melnitzer said, "It's a long story." The line went silent again
for a moment. "Who's there with you?"

Delanghe recited the names of the lawyers and Melnitzer

asked him to put Epstein on the line. They spoke for a few minutes, then Epstein emerged from the office to tell the Mounties that Melnitzer would talk to them. The call was put on a speaker phone.

Gunn and Porter told Melnitzer about the allegations against him and the evidence that had been found. They said the investigation was still at an early stage but charges of fraud and forgery would be laid against him, and Porter would arrest him. The lawyer said there was no sense making a big deal out of it. He'd be returning to London about 4 p.m. Sunday. He wanted to go home, settle a few things and talk to Epstein; he promised to turn himself in shortly afterward.

It was now the Mounties' turn to huddle. Melnitzer seemed co-operative, Porter and Gunn felt, but wasn't there a chance he might flee? Already short-staffed, the officers needed further assurances. When Epstein, who had agreed to act for Melnitzer for the time being, promised to make the lawyer's surrender his personal undertaking, that clinched it. Melnitzer would come to the London detachment and turn himself in around 9 p.m. Sunday.

At 3:20 a.m., the Mounties departed and the dazed lawyers headed home. Delanghe, who seemed the most upset of the group, had the longest trip. He lived with his family about 25 kilometres northwest of the city. Fortunately there was no traffic on London streets at this time of the morning, because Delanghe's mind was not on his driving. It was thousands of miles away — in Singapore.

Delanghe was one of 11 of Melnitzer's friends and associates who had invested in what had become known as the "Singapore Deal."

Delanghe had been with Cohen, Melnitzer a little more than a year when Melnitzer told him and the other partners about an irresistible opportunity in the Southeast Asian city-state of Singapore.

He had often previously talked about various successful investments, and occasionally his partners had participated in them. Melnitzer seemed to have a Midas touch and the return he promised was usually delivered. Fellow lawyers were impressed with the apparent business acumen that seemed to match his skill at law. Melnitzer bragged about his far-flung investments, primarily in real estate, which included ventures in Utah, Washington state and the Far East.

Melnitzer said that the Singapore opportunity was safer than Canada Savings Bonds and would yield an annual return of 40 to 50 percent. He told his listeners he was involved in a company that had "pioneer status" under Singapore law, giving it certain tax advantages. The company owned land the government of Singapore wished to acquire, but because the government could not run deficits, it had to purchase the land over a period of years. It would pay Melnitzer's group a certain amount up front, then make regular payments and not close the deal until it could afford to do so. Melnitzer said one of his co-shareholders in the company that owned the land wanted out of the deal and had offered Melnitzer the chance to acquire his interest.

Because he was barred by law from increasing his share of the company, Melnitzer said he was offering his friends and associates a chance to join the scheme. He said the entire venture would be concluded in two and a half years and would produce a total return of 125 percent for participants. Melnitzer said the matter was one of his better deals and investors should act quickly. If they needed to borrow funds to invest, they shouldn't mention his name. Melnitzer said he didn't want the whole world to know what he was doing for fear it might jeopardize the deal.

Many of the partners liked what they heard. They created a numbered company as their investment vehicle, but asked Melnitzer for no documentation, aside from the promissory note and shares he held in a photochemical company. Melnitzer had earned their trust, and it was apparent he was onto something really big this time.

Delanghe, in his early 40s, had quietly built a reputation in London as a first-rate real estate and development lawyer since establishing his practice in 1974. His clients included Sifton Properties, one of the city's largest property-development firms. Glen Sifton, company president, was so impressed with Delanghe that the pair had made several personal investments together over the years.

Melnitzer, with a variety of inducements, had lured Delanghe to Cohen, Melnitzer. Delanghe had been with a larger, older firm where he didn't feel he was given sufficient recognition for his work. Melnitzer promised he would be one of the top dogs in what would soon be the largest law firm in town. Delanghe liked the innovation and aggressiveness of Cohen, Melnitzer. He joined up and brought many of his clients with him.

When Melnitzer proposed the Singapore Deal, Delanghe enthusiastically embraced it. He borrowed heavily, mortgaged his property and scraped up every cent he could find. He and his wife, Bonnie, put together $925,000. Of course he told Sifton about the opportunity, and the wealthy developer provided $1.5 million.

Other partners came aboard, and then several outside the firm. The total investment from the members of the law firm, friends and associates stood at $5.55 million.

All of them received quarterly interest payments amounting to 10 percent in February and May of 1991. Then in July, Melnitzer announced he'd just learned the Singapore Deal was closing early and payouts of about 100 percent were forthcoming. He told some of the investors they would have their cheques in August. Delanghe was presented with two cheques, one for $1.6 million payable to him personally, and another for $5 million made out to the numbered company. They were postdated August 31.

Delanghe and the others were making plans for their windfalls and already worrying about tax implications.

A far greater worry than taxes now faced Delanghe as he steered his car along the deserted streets. If Melnitzer had used forged documents to obtain lines of credit, what sort of guy was he anyway? If Melnitzer would defraud banks, why not his friends, his partners? How about the cheques? And the freeze placed on his assets? What the hell was going on here?

The questions produced a terrible, tight feeling in the pit of Delanghe's stomach. If Melnitzer goes down he'll bring all of us down with him, he thought. How could this ever happen? How could I have been so incredibly stupid?

Delanghe reached for his car phone as darkened farm fields sped by. He dialed the Montreal hotel and pulled over to the side of the road. It was now almost 4 a.m. Melnitzer seemed irritated to be bothered again.

"Is the Singapore Deal for real?" Delanghe demanded.

"No, it's not," came the heart-stopping reply.

A wave of nausea swept over Delanghe. He had been delivered a body blow from which he felt he'd never recover. He couldn't find his voice.

"Well," Delanghe stumbled, groping for words, "I guess . . . there's nothing more . . . to talk about." He hung up. The betrayal felt worse than a death in the family. Delanghe needed several minutes to compose himself before completing the journey home, where he broke the news to his wife.

Many hours later that same day, exactly as promised, Melnitzer flew back to London and surrendered to Porter. He was charged with one count of uttering five forged stock certificates in his attempt to arrange the $15-million line of credit at the National Bank of Canada.

A day later, Porter and his men found another billion dollars' worth of identical certificates at a London print shop Melnitzer had hired to produce them. The Mounties now had considerable paperwork to sort out. Helped by a co-operative Melnitzer, they spent the next few weeks unravelling his complex dealings. Another 56 charges were laid within a month: forgery, fraud and attempted fraud in connection with several lines of credit, and fraud in the Singapore Deal and other private investment schemes.

Melnitzer's victims included four of the country's six largest banks. The dollar value of the frauds topped $100 million, for a total actual loss to the banks of $12.35 million. Twenty of the charges were for defrauding individuals, including Ron Delanghe, for a further actual loss of $14.7 million. Julius Melnitzer had ripped off some of his best friends and closest associates for millions of dollars — apparently without even a twinge of conscience.

3

Beginnings

"The idea was to win . . ."

A S THE 1950S BEGAN, Montreal reigned as Canada's major metropolis. In the early post-war years, it was a bustling, cosmopolitan, outward-looking community. In contrast, Ontario's Toronto the Good was known as a city of fine redbrick homes where they rolled up the sidewalks by 9 p.m. and where there was little to do on a Sunday but attend church.

Montreal, on the other hand, was alive with action. Montrealers cheered their beloved Canadiens at the Forum and tolerated political patronage, bottle clubs known as "blind pigs," brothels and the occasional revelations of police corruption.

Aside from its economic dominance, Montreal was a thriving cultural centre with French and English cultures coexisting more or less comfortably. The province of Quebec was in its third decade of rule under Premier Maurice Duplessis, whose autocratic hand kept a lid on English-French tensions. It was not until after his departure in 1959 and the coming of a new leader that long silent stirrings of French-Canadian nationalism were heard.

Canada had the second-highest standard of living in the world, and at the midpoint of the century it appeared the country would live up to former prime minister Wilfrid Laurier's prediction that the twentieth century would be Canada's. Seen from abroad, especially from the ashes of Europe, Canada represented prosperity, a fine place to start a new life. Immigration was booming and the main recipient of newcomers was Montreal. In many areas of the city, the language of the street was neither French nor English. A visitor could travel for blocks hearing nothing but Yiddish, Polish or Hungarian.

It was to Montreal that Alexander and Fanny Melnitzer came with their two young sons in 1950. Their eldest, Herman Julius, had been born October 5, 1947, in Munich, Germany. A little less than three years later, Rudy was born. Alexander and Fanny decided shortly after Rudy's arrival that it was time for a major change. As Jews from Russia and Poland, the Melnitzer family had been persecuted by the Nazis, and Alexander felt uncomfortable remaining in Germany. In addition, the war-ravaged country was on the front lines of the developing Cold War and was taking a long time to get back on its economic feet. Alexander, a meat cutter by trade, saw a long, hard struggle ahead if he and his family remained in Germany. Like so many other survivors of the Holocaust, the Melnitzers opted for a complete break from the past. A new land with less history was appealing.

Arriving in Canada by ship, the family settled into a modest tenement in the area of St. Urbain and Rachel streets, an ethnic, mostly Jewish area. Within a few years, the family had prospered, moving northwest to another predominantly Jewish neighborhood in Montreal's Van Horne district, just off Côte des Neiges Boulevard and south across the railway tracks from Mount Royal. Strictly middle-class and full of small businesses and big dreams, the area was considered an economic stopover on the way to the more fashionable neighborhoods of Hampstead or Côte Saint-Luc, to the south and west. Not long after their arrival, the Melnitzers welcomed their last child and only daughter, Roslyn.

The family moved into the right half of a modest, two-floor, redbrick fourplex at 4841 Kent Avenue. Just up and across the street was the Brown Derby restaurant, the unofficial community centre where gossip flourished and friendships were cemented. At one time or another, nearly everyone in the community dropped by the Derby for a chat over a cup of coffee. Talk would range from the latest news from Europe to the most recent accomplishments of their offspring. Within a few blocks were several synagogues. The neighborhood, centred on Van Horne and Victoria streets, was primarily Jewish, but there were pockets of francophones and a good number of black families living along Barclay Avenue.

Alexander Melnitzer found a position as a meat cutter with Polonsky Brothers, a butcher shop specializing in kosher products. The language of the trade was Yiddish, which was welcomed by Alexander, who wasn't comfortable with the intricacies of English. The new meat cutter was industrious and not without ambition. He soon became a partner in the thriving business.

At home, Alexander and Fanny ruled their brood with a firm hand. The couple preached the work ethic and would not tolerate laziness. Alexander also insisted that while hard work was of prime importance, his children should always obey the rules and play fair. He considered the Sabbath holy and never transacted business or rode in an automobile or other mechanical conveyance on a Saturday. He forbade his children to ride their bicycles or tricycles on that day.

Any contravention of Alexander's rules brought swift retribution. The offending child was slapped or struck with the nearest object at hand. He loved his sons and daughter, but demanded absolute obedience and believed physical punishment was essential to enforce it. Years later, when Roslyn married outside the Jewish faith, he angrily cut her out of the family investment firm he had created. It took a decade of cajoling by other family members before he relented and reinstated her.

A high-strung man, prone to shouting at his offspring

when they failed to meet his lofty expectations, Alexander seldom praised them. No matter how well they had done, Alexander constantly pushed them to do better. He could always point to someone else who had.

Like many of those who had fled the hopelessness of postwar Europe, the Melnitzers put much faith in their children. This new generation, freed from the constraints of persecution, deprivation and war, was expected to flower and live up to its full potential. Children being raised in a land of relative milk and honey would not be permitted to coast through life after the sacrifices their parents had made. This was the generation that had to succeed. There was no other option.

Contemporaries of the Melnitzer children would later say theirs was an acutely competitive neighborhood. "There was no such thing as a game for the sake of the game," one recalls. "The idea was to win. The goal was always to win." But unfair play was unacceptable. Full mental and physical exertion was the only route to success.

Julius was an exceptionally bright child, and Alexander had great expectations for his firstborn. Rudy was more rebellious by nature, and Roslyn, as a girl, wasn't expected to be a superachiever. Julius proved amenable and tried to live up to his father's standards. When he fell short, he received a beating and was sent to his room, where he picked up a book and shoved the incident to the back of his mind. He loved board games, especially chess and Monopoly, and mastered both at an early age. Julius showed a flair for thinking several moves in advance and anticipating the opposition. Always scrupulously honest, he didn't need to cheat. His analytical mind made it unnecessary. In Monopoly, he enjoyed playing the banker because it gave him a form of control and ensured he could easily monitor every player's change in fortunes. He was aggressive, instantly mortgaging or dealing away marginal properties to develop his real estate acquisitions quickly. He loved erecting the first hotels, especially on the board's prime properties. He delighted in concocting deals that his opponents couldn't resist but that would invariably come back to haunt them.

Mrs. Melnitzer was just as demanding as her husband, but with a softer side. She instilled in her children a love of music, including opera and ballet. She saw to it that they took piano lessons. But she left disciplinary matters to her husband.

Meanwhile, Alexander's hard work was beginning to pay off. He assumed control of Polonsky Brothers, expanding it and transforming it into Champlain Meat Packers Ltd. He used his business success to teach his children that hard work paid dividends. As he prospered, Alexander Melnitzer's reputation as a shrewd businessman grew in the community. He increased his donations to Jewish charities and to the synagogue. Some of his neighbors felt he was a bit showy about his religion and wondered if he was trying to buy influence. But perhaps it was a means of compensating for his lack of formal education and difficulty adjusting to a new language. Nevertheless, he became a leading figure in the Jewish community and his entire family was respected.

As the children of the Van Horne area progressed through school, their parents made it clear they wanted much for them. Aspiring to take over the family business was not enough. Education was the key to success. Use of the mind to earn a respectable living was preferable to manual labor.

David Byer was one of hundreds of Julius Melnitzer's contemporaries reared in the shadow of Mount Royal. Years later he recalled that there was never any question of joining his family's business, a lamp factory. "There was no way my father wanted me to get into that," he said. "Parents insisted their children had to be professionals: doctors, lawyers, accountants, that sort of thing." Byer forsook lamps for education. Today he is a lawyer with Agriculture Canada in Ottawa.

Indeed, a large percentage of graduates from the neighborhood's Northmount High School are currently listed in the medical and legal directories of Quebec and

Ontario. The "baby boom" children from Van Horne have gone on to make considerable marks on Canadian society.

Through the 1960s, the Melnitzers chose to maintain a modest lifestyle despite increasing family fortunes. While some of their neighbors opted to move to more affluent sections of Montreal, they stayed on Kent Avenue. They were comfortable, had good friends and were well thought of. Even when the neighborhood slipped into a decline for a few years, the family remained. Money was put into savings and real estate. After Alexander's death in November 1990, Fanny continued to live in the modest duplex down the street from the Brown Derby.

Julius and the other kids in the neighborhood attended Northmount High, at Lavoie and Brochette avenues. A large school operated by the Protestant school board of Montreal, it had a student population of 1500, of which about 75 percent was Jewish. Julius applied himself to his studies, earning top marks throughout his high school years. Some of his fellow students saw him as a bit of a smart alec, and his teachers found it a challenge to keep him stimulated. Several teachers took a strong liking to the young man, who seemed so far ahead of many of his classmates. He took part in the chess club, United Nations and public-speaking clubs, as well as basketball, football and other sports.

Melnitzer had an eye for the attractive young women in his classes and competed for their attention, often relying on his penchant for mischief. He would tell a girl a story he had fabricated about one of her rivals and then enjoy sitting back to watch the fur fly when the inevitable confrontation occurred. Overall, Melnitzer was a popular student and became class vice-president. Among the many girls who caught his eye was the shy, dark-haired Katalin (Catherine) Szirt, who harbored ambitions to become a nurse. Szirt, born in Budapest nine months before Melnitzer, would later become his wife. His parents approved of her family, who were hardworking and doing well financially.

By his graduating year, the young Melnitzer had also

discovered a talent for shooting pool, another pastime that rewarded those who thought ahead. In Grade 11, he began cutting classes on Friday afternoons to hone his skills. His weekly habit was frowned upon by school officials who viewed him as the ringleader of half a dozen of his truant classmates. Years later, Peter Klym, Melnitzer's homeroom teacher that year, remembered the vice-principal's determined plan to stamp out this kind of truancy. He organized a posse of five or six teachers, including Klym, to raid a pool hall at Côte des Neiges and Linton Avenue, where Melnitzer and his shooters were found. The pool players were suspended for varying terms, but the vice-principal wanted to make an example of the group's well-known leader. Melnitzer received the strap in a hallway within earshot of his class. "We could hear him outside, just wailing," one of his classmates recalls.

Melnitzer's lengthy suspension didn't harm his prospects for graduation. He studied by himself and still received top marks. His high school yearbook reveals that Melnitzer was thinking of medicine as a career. Beside his picture was his favorite motto: "Neither a borrower nor a lender be, just help yourself." Twenty-seven years later, the inscription proved to be a fine irony.

Upon graduation, Melnitzer attended Montreal's McGill University where he studied philosophy, enjoying the mental exercise offered by the subject. He thought long and hard about his future, alternately considering medicine or law. He opted for law and, armed with top marks, applied to the University of Toronto law school. Like many of his classmates, Melnitzer felt his career prospects were better in Ontario. While he loved Montreal, he preferred to operate in the English language and Ontario offered greater opportunities and challenges. Toronto was no longer the stodgy Toronto the Good. It had overtaken Montreal in population and become the economic hub of the country. It was where the action was, and furthermore was free of the simmering English-French tensions and calls for Quebec sovereignty beginning to be heard in Montreal.

The U of T law school was considered one of the best. Its standards were high and there was no point even applying if you weren't among the very brightest. In 1968, when Melnitzer applied, he was among 1500 hopefuls. He was one of the 120 accepted. Also in the school's favor was its close proximity to Bay Street, the developing centre of Canada's financial world. Corporate lawyers on Bay Street were among the highest paid in the country.

It was a watershed year for a young man about to turn 21. On February 18, 1968 he had married Cathy Szirt in Montreal in a traditional Jewish ceremony. The couple moved to Toronto, finding modest quarters just off Spadina Avenue, not far from the university.

The September day he registered for law school, Melnitzer and some of his new friends were hoisting draft beers at the Embassy, a Bloor Street tavern popular with the college crowd, swapping stories about their backgrounds and why they chose law school. Melnitzer, pipe in hand, was talking about his continuing interest in medicine, and his conversation turned to the intriguing world of forensic psychiatry, which probed the strange workings of the criminal mind. One of his listeners was soon-to-be-classmate Harris Cohen. The quiet and likable curly-haired Cohen was drawn to the extrovert, who seemed to know so much and could command attention.

"Yes," Melnitzer was saying, drawing on his pipe for punctuation, "psychiatry is a real challenge. And it's where the serious dough is. Law is interesting, sure, but trying to figure out what makes the bad guys tick — now, that's a challenge. I think if you took a law degree then got into psychiatry, you could really make a name for yourself."

Cohen was amazed. Here was someone about to embark on the challenge and rigors of law school and he was already talking about pursuing psychiatry, which would require a medical degree and years of specialization! Obviously this Melnitzer was a sharp cookie, certainly someone with big dreams.

Harris Cohen was a young man with dreams of his own, dreams he never doubted he would achieve. The confident young man was the eldest of four children of a prosperous furniture-retailing family from London, Ontario, about 200 kilometres southwest of Toronto. His parents, Elliot and Rose Cohen, owned and managed London Furniture with other family members. For several decades the firm was the city's pre-eminent home-furnishings store. Cohen, with his brothers Jerome and Nicky and sister Rochelle, lived in North London, a comfortable area of fine homes, parks and trees. In the late 1960s, the city had a population approaching 200,000 and was the home of several major businesses, including London Life Insurance, Labatt's Breweries, Canada Trust and General Motors Diesel Division.

While predominantly White Anglo-Saxon Protestant at the time, London also had a small but vibrant Jewish community in which the Cohens were highly regarded. Harris had many childhood friends, some Jewish, some not. He attended public and high schools in his neighborhood and enrolled at the University of Western Ontario. He was a sensible young man who never even considered cutting classes. Intelligent and rather musical, he became proficient on the saxophone. While not a leader by temperament, his innate common sense and pleasant disposition ensured he was included in all sorts of extracurricular activities. As a teenager, he was a steadying influence on some of his more flamboyant friends. When Cohen was part of a group of teens, their parents could relax; Harris Cohen would keep the kids out of trouble.

Melnitzer would also come to see Cohen as a valuable influence, a sober second opinion. The boy from Montreal couldn't understand how Cohen could be so self-assured, so calm. Why didn't a fire burn in the belly of this guy from London? Didn't he know that life was a challenge, that there was a brass ring to be grabbed?

Despite their differences in upbringing and outlook, Cohen and Melnitzer became close friends in law school.

They worked hard at their studies and were rewarded with good grades. But while Cohen was easygoing and unassuming, Melnitzer displayed one of the biggest egos in the class. He continually peppered his teachers with probing questions, sometimes annoying his peers, who saw his behavior as grandstanding. One of his female classmates would later recall visiting Melnitzer and his wife after the couple's only child, Melissa, was born. "It was a tough time for him. Law school, a wife and a child," she says. The apartment was small but the classmate will never forget something she saw there. On the wall, framed and mounted for the world to see, was Melnitzer's grade-two piano graduation certificate. "I was amazed at that. He seemed to be so proud of it. I had my Grade 10 in piano and I would never have dreamed of putting it on the wall. It seemed like such a strange thing to brag about."

Melissa was born January 16, 1970, midway through Melnitzer's U of T days. He was a man with little spare time, but somehow he managed to juggle his duties as student, husband and father. Through it all, he maintained excellent grades and still found time for the regular Friday afternoon beer-and-bull sessions, where he could talk about his grand plans.

Melnitzer and Cohen both graduated near the top of the class, and after articling, were called to the Ontario bar in 1973. Graduates from the U of T law school seldom had trouble finding jobs and they were no exception. Both accepted positions with prestigious law firms on Bay Street. Cohen joined Siegal, Fogler, a 12-member, primarily Jewish firm at 372 Bay. Melnitzer found a position at Blaney, Pasternak, Smela, Eagleson and Watson, a 30-member firm directly across the street at 365 Bay.

At the smaller firm, Cohen was able to delve into a variety of files, and he particularly liked the real estate and development work. Siegal, Fogler provided its young recruits with a broader range of experience than they might find in a larger, more specialized setting. At Blaney, Pasternak and company,

Melnitzer displayed considerable chutzpah the first time he walked in the door. While most young lawyers are content to accept a salary and worry about commissions later, Melnitzer demanded and received a contract that included commissions. "He was brazen," a fellow rookie later marvelled. "He wasn't satisfied to take a salary like the rest of us."

Melnitzer was put in the litigation department of the highly specialized firm. Several lawyers were involved in a single file, and one of his tasks was to research points of law for senior lawyers. Few lawyers remained on a case from beginning to end. The firm was more like a factory, and Melnitzer, wanting to learn all aspects of the law, felt lost in the shuffle, and he chafed at the restrictions placed on him. He was anxious to prove himself, however, and plunged into any work assigned to him. If he knew nothing about a case or the law related to it, he would roll up his sleeves and work, all night if necessary, until he felt comfortable with it. But he never got a chance to try his hand at criminal law, and his visits to a courtroom were rare.

Melnitzer was one of five just-hired rookies. He was dismayed to see nearly a dozen others ahead of him with only a few more years' seniority in the firm's hierarchy. It was becoming clear he had a long wait before reaching a position of any real power at Blaney, Pasternak.

Among the top partners was Alan Eagleson, a man Melnitzer thought was unlikely to share the spotlight with the firm's ambitious young lawyers. Executive director of the National Hockey League Players' Association, Eagleson was counsel to some of the biggest names in hockey and was just starting to roll in the early '70s as a major promoter of international hockey. Since Canada's defeat of a Soviet squad in the 1972 Canada-Soviet hockey series, Eagleson's name had been familiar to hockey fans across the country.

Melnitzer realized it could take a decade to make his mark on Bay Street and that was nearly 10 years too long. He was fast growing disenchanted with Bay Street. "I didn't get enough reward. I didn't get, I suppose, enough ego satisfaction," he said much later. He and Cohen stayed in touch, commiserating about Bay Street. Cohen missed London, where the pace was more humane and where he had friends. He felt uncomfortable with the cutthroat competition he saw around him and wasn't about to change his style. He talked of leaving Toronto and setting up a practice in London, and his friend was listening. Melnitzer knew he could work with Cohen because Cohen wouldn't challenge him. The two could work easily as a team. It was a tempting proposition. Cohen could do real estate, development, wills and related work, while Melnitzer could do criminal and civil litigation.

Melnitzer peppered Cohen with questions about London. Wasn't it a real WASP town? Well, sort of, Cohen replied, but then quickly pointed out that two of the largest law firms were mainly Jewish. Wasn't it too small to make a decent living? Cohen replied that if you could become a big fish in a smaller pond you could do very well. That struck a chord with Melnitzer, who felt like a minnow in Toronto. The two continued this debate for months, and finally Melnitzer joined Cohen for the two-hour drive to London to get a feel for the place.

Melnitzer liked what he saw. He consulted a Crown attorney to see if there was room for more defence lawyers in the London criminal field and he was assured there was plenty of work available. The lifestyle in London looked comfortable, he had to admit. And the schools came highly recommended, a fact that appealed to a father whose daughter was about to enter kindergarten. Meanwhile, if Cathy, then studying nursing, was interested in a job, she should have no problem, because the city had three major hospitals.

After about a year on Bay Street, Cohen and Melnitzer opted for a future in London. In 1974, the Cohen, Melnitzer law firm was formed. The young partners found office space in a fine old home at 572 Wellington Street, opposite the serene expanse of Victoria Park. Bay Street was already a world away.

4

Career Building

"Oh, well, that's Julius."

H ARRIS COHEN WAS THRILLED to be back in his hometown. Returning to London was like slipping back into a favorite, well-worn pair of shoes. With family, friends, a familiar environment and a wide net of connections, this was a playing field he knew. And he meant to take full advantage of his position.

Cohen knew he'd have no problem getting clients for his newly established real estate and litigation practice. The family name engendered respect. He planned to work hard to earn his own share of that respect, which would ensure clients would keep coming back.

Melnitzer, the new boy in town, preferred to take criminal cases. Since none of Cohen's family or friends were likely to need the services of a criminal lawyer, he was on his own. He felt a certain affinity for those individuals who turned to crime as an expression of their dissatisfaction with their place in society. Often people who break the law do so because they are impatient; they want something badly but are not prepared to wait or make the usual sacrifices to obtain it. They may feel they have achieved so little that they've nothing to lose by contravening society's rules. In some ways, Melnitzer sympathized with this view. He understood perfectly the drive to want more and the frustration engendered by delay. Raised on the wrong side of the tracks from Mount Royal, he identified with the underdog and was prepared to fight for him.

There was something else about criminal law the aggressive young lawyer found appealing. Compared with civil law, the turnover rate on criminal cases was quick. A lawsuit could drag on for years, with endless motions, depositions, examinations for discovery and other procedures. Only well-established clients with money could afford to underwrite such suits. But a criminal case in London could be completed in an average of about six months, perhaps less. With a brand-new courthouse and a large and efficient staff, London did not suffer the kind of backlog that plagued many other jurisdictions. The fast turnover of cases meant there was always new business coming in the door. If he worked hard, Melnitzer was sure he could achieve a name for himself fairly quickly.

His clients wouldn't be the cream of London society; instead most qualified for legal aid. The financial assistance provided by the government-and-lawyer-supported scheme to persons of limited means is a major source of income for most young lawyers. A fee paid under the plan is somewhat less than what a nonsubsidized client would be charged, but at least payment is guaranteed. No need to chase around after fees from bad actors who've already demonstrated an unconventional approach toward their obligations. That aspect alone makes legal-aid work appealing to many lawyers, especially those just getting into the business.

The 26-year-old Melnitzer discovered there were about 20 lawyers in London whose practices were primarily criminal. He spread the word that he was prepared to take cases other lawyers might not want, that he could be bothered at all hours by clients and that he was willing to work hard. He began patrolling the corridors of the Middlesex County courthouse, hobnobbing with criminal practitioners and making his presence known to courthouse staff who might be in a position to recommend a lawyer to an accused person. He found some resistance from lawyers who resented the newcomer's aggressiveness. But there was enough work for everyone and Melnitzer gradually carved himself a niche.

He began getting repeat business from clients impressed with his hard work. He never went to trial unprepared and would frequently stay up all night reading and rereading briefs, transcripts, relevant cases and the very latest criminal jurisprudence. Begrudgingly, even some of his competitors began to appreciate the bulldog who'd landed in their midst, and they started to refer cases to him. This guy Melnitzer was showing the prosecutors up, and anybody who could do that was worth having around.

At first, the cases were the usual assortment of shoplifting, thefts, robberies and drinking-and-driving offences that fill the criminal lawyer's daybook. But Melnitzer wasn't prepared to let anything become routine. He didn't mind antagonizing prosecutors, occasionally even judges, if he felt it was warranted. The plight of the little guy became *his* plight. The forces of authority, with all the advantages of police investigators, money and the weight of the law on their side, had to work very hard to convict Julius Melnitzer's clients. He saw to it.

His straight-talking style, sprinkled with the colorful language of the street, impressed his clients. He came across like an older, smarter brother, a guy who was on their side and conducted a hell of a defence. They were the first to tell their cellmates about this guy with the weird last name.

For his part, Melnitzer was pleased his game plan was paying dividends so quickly. He was off and running and there was no stopping him. In some cases he waived the fee, either because he wanted to gain valuable experience or because a case might be of interest to the media. He sought all the media attention he could get in those early years, knowing that the exposure amounted to free publicity. He saved even the tiniest press clippings.

Almost two decades later, Melnitzer, reflecting on his first days in London and his bid to crack the local legal establishment, said, "I liked criminal law the best and I felt it was the greatest opportunity [to succeed] because criminals . . . well . . . you don't have to break into their clubs." At the time Cohen and Melnitzer set up shop, Jews were just beginning to be asked to join the city's several prestigious private clubs.

While his partner was carefully tapping into the old boys' network, Melnitzer was working the street, currying favor with the dispossessed, the alienated. It was an odd mix of clients who rubbed shoulders in the waiting room at the Wellington Street offices of Cohen, Melnitzer.

The ambitious lawyers talked about someday becoming the largest firm in town, and they buckled down in the first few years to establish themselves. Overhead was kept low, vacations were few — Melnitzer delayed his first one for eight years — and workweeks of 70 or 80 hours were not uncommon. They were excited about building something of their own. There were no menial tasks handed down by senior partners they'd never met. This was their show.

In the few free hours they could find in a week, Melnitzer and Cohen socialized, and Cohen took pains to introduce his partner to his circle of friends. Melnitzer found Londoners to be as conservative as advertised, but always polite. London was not like his old neighborhood, which had embraced newcomers. He was going to have to win acceptance and it would take some time.

Melnitzer, Cathy and Melissa were living in the middle-class Orchard Park subdivision, in a modest two-storey home they rented for $350 a month. Cathy finished nursing school and went to work as a company nurse at Northern Telecom. The young lawyer didn't have much time for his neighbors.

He was busy building a career that he hoped would carry him far away from Orchard Park.

Melnitzer's habit of taking ordinary cases and putting extraordinary effort into them would soon pay off. On December 4, 1975, Frederick Lovell, a 33-year-old bouncer at the Belvedere Hotel in downtown London, was on duty keeping an eye on patrons in the hotel's Horseshoe Lounge. The ancient hotel had seen better days. Its rooms were shabby and inexpensive. Its main source of revenue was the bar, whose regular clientele consisted of pensioners, blue-collar workers and native Canadians. This night, the crowd was sizable. The Miss Nude Canada Revue, a seven-member troupe from Montreal, was a good draw and Lovell was earning his money. About six o'clock, waitress Pat Hedden learned that a group of men was drinking whisky in the washroom. She asked Lovell, a strong, well-built man, to intercede. In the washroom confrontation, which erupted in blows, Lovell prevailed and Peter Louie Nicholas was felled. The 25-year-old Nicholas left the hotel with his companions, cursing and warning Lovell he was a dead man.

An hour later, Nicholas and three companions returned to the lounge. One of them concealed a sawed-off shotgun. "He's got a gun!" a patron shouted. All eyes turned to the area of the bar. Without hesitating, Lovell jumped in and grappled with the gunman to pry away the weapon. A blast ripped through the lounge and Lovell hit the floor. The father of two young children, whose common-law wife was eight months pregnant with a third, lay dying. The four men, all natives aged 25 to 31, fled on foot. Two were arrested that night and two others, subjects of a police manhunt, turned themselves in four days later. All four were charged with noncapital murder, although the charge against one man was later dropped.

The trial was held in April, during the spring assizes of the Ontario Supreme Court in London. Melnitzer had been retained by 28-year-old Isaac William Doxtator. The two remaining accused were represented by lawyers with more experience.

Other lawyers watched the case carefully, wondering if the young Melnitzer had more than he could handle. The shooting and subsequent trial made headlines, partly because of suggestions that the hotel was the scene of racial tension and that bouncers treated natives unfairly. Melnitzer, believing the natives were at a disadvantage in white society, felt driven to give his client the best representation possible.

It was the perfect stage for Melnitzer and he vowed that no one would outwork him. The trial lasted about a month and Melnitzer worked through many nights, going over statements again and again, reviewing his notes, looking for any inconsistencies that might raise the sort of doubts that could lead to an acquittal for his client. His defence was simple. Doxtator was an innocent bystander and he would prove it.

"My client didn't know there were any guns when he went into the hotel that night," Melnitzer told the jury in his opening remarks. "He went there to have a beer and wait for his girlfriend."

Melnitzer went on to say that his client had been drinking in the lounge earlier that day, but had left by the time of the washroom scuffle. He'd gone home to take a telephone call from his girlfriend, who lived 90 minutes outside the city. In that call, she told Doxtator she'd be arriving in London that evening, and they arranged to meet at the Belvedere about seven. Doxtator was in the area of the hotel shortly before that time when he ran into his three friends and returned with them to the hotel. Melnitzer said Doxtator was unaware anyone had a gun and was merely planning to have a beer and await his girlfriend. When Doxtator testified later, he said he fled with his companions after the shooting because he was surprised by what happened and feared for his own safety.

Earlier in the trial, Melnitzer tried a stunt worthy of Perry Mason. An eyewitness to the shooting was recounting how, about an hour before, he'd seen the four men Lovell confronted in the washroom.

"I saw the same four guys there who came back later with the gun," John Allen MacDonald told the court. The prosecution was pleased with this evidence. It gave all four men a reason for being angry at Lovell and, crucially, a motive for the killing. Motive made the case a murder. Without proof of motive, the slaying would be the lesser offence of manslaughter.

Then it was Melnitzer's turn at the witness. He couldn't risk having the jurors believe MacDonald. If they did, they would reject Doxtator's insistence that he wasn't around at the time of the fight, a fact that was essential to his defence. Melnitzer was nearly abusive to the witness. He challenged the man's eyesight, his vantage point, his memory, even his character.

MacDonald took an instant dislike to the obnoxious lawyer, and under Melnitzer's withering cross-examination, became increasingly irritated. MacDonald wasn't going to let Melnitzer score any points and the exchanges grew testy. MacDonald insisted he recognized Doxtator. He said he'd known the man for two years, and despite the confusion and lighting conditions at the hotel, he knew Doxtator was one of the four in the washroom brawl.

Melnitzer then produced a photograph and showed it to MacDonald. "I suggest to you this is not a photograph of my client, Isaac Doxtator," Melnitzer said.

"Yes it is," MacDonald snarled. "It's him. I'd know him anywhere."

Melnitzer smiled. The fish had taken the bait.

"And you're sure about that? As sure as you are of the rest of your evidence?" he pressed.

"Yes," MacDonald replied confidently.

"Well, Mr. MacDonald, you're wrong," the lawyer replied,

savoring the moment. "It's not a picture of my client at all. It's one of his relatives."

MacDonald tried to regroup, but it was too late.

Melnitzer left it at that. Later in his closing argument, he reminded jurors of the misidentification and urged them to accept Doxtator's version of events. He warned them it would be dangerous to convict on the evidence of an eyewitness such as MacDonald.

The seven women and five men deliberated for 13 hours before reaching their verdicts. It was an anxious time for all the lawyers, especially Melnitzer, who so desperately wanted a victory.

The two accused represented by the other lawyers were convicted of manslaughter. Melnitzer's client was acquitted. It was the young lawyer's first big case and he was elated. He could brag that his was the only victory and he'd earned it. In less than two years, he felt, he had risen to top rank of the city's defence bar.

Lawyers intimate with the details of the case weren't quite as impressed with Melnitzer's talents. Some suggested that, of the three accused men, Doxtator was the easiest to defend. In fact, his critics said, the case against Doxtator was so weak Melnitzer should have obtained a discharge for the man following the preliminary hearing.

When he heard some of the gossip, Melnitzer promptly dismissed it as resentment at the success of the new boy in town. Still, he was angry and hurt. He would find his career in London continually plagued by similar sentiments.

Reporters who followed the Belvedere Hotel case were impressed by the newcomer, however, and he received favorable coverage. Melnitzer was obviously well prepared and he never asked a question of a witness without knowing the answer. True, at times he had looked shaky and haggard. His eyes betrayed him. With their natural propensity to dark circles because of excess pigment in the sockets, they looked even worse when Melnitzer was tired. Still, despite the pressure and the strain, Melnitzer triumphed. As his confidence grew, so did his reputation.

At Cohen, Melnitzer, the workload continued to increase. From an early stage, Melnitzer discovered that relatively few London lawyers took cases to the Ontario Court of Appeal in Toronto. He thought that was a mistake. Granted, appeal work required an inordinate amount of preparation and wasn't very lucrative, but Melnitzer believed the practitioners in London were merely worried about upsetting local judges by trying to have their decisions overturned in Toronto. He let it be known he welcomed appeal work. Aside from the obvious market for it, he liked the mental challenge it provided, the trip to Toronto to taste the legal big time, and the possibility he might get his name enshrined in a legal text.

By 1977, the partners agreed it was time to expand. Two new lawyers were added, and early in the year the firm relocated to a suite of offices in an eight-storey building on Dundas Street, the city's major east-west artery. One of the newcomers was Fletcher Dawson, a quiet, studious chap who loved criminal law and the possibility of appeal work. He had recently been called to the bar. The other was Paul Vogel, an equally serious young man who would deal with matters of family law but would later switch to civil litigation. The new arrivals were told Cohen, Melnitzer was going to be a very big and influential law firm in London. Both were pleased to find themselves on the ground floor of what they hoped would become a major enterprise. They were made partners within two years.

Dawson and Melnitzer soon combined their talents on a case that eventually propelled Melnitzer to a major victory in the Supreme Court of Canada.

In August 1977, a 57-year-old London house painter named John Elmer Boggs was convicted of driving while impaired and refusing to take a breath test, contrary to the Criminal Code of Canada. In addition to being fined, Boggs had his licence automatically suspended, under the terms of

Ontario's Highway Traffic Act. Two years later, Boggs was again stopped by police. This time he was charged with driving while disqualified, because the previous suspension was still in effect. The driving-while-disqualified charge was laid under the Criminal Code and carried with it a maximum penalty of two years in jail. Boggs was convicted of this second offence in provincial court.

Melnitzer seized on the case as one with great potential. He knew a bit about constitutional law and found the court's finding grossly unfair. He felt the federal government, through its Criminal Code, shouldn't be making it a crime to offend a provincial statute. Melnitzer noted, for instance, that a licence can be suspended for nonpayment of traffic tickets. So technically, someone caught driving while under suspension for that sort of offence could be arrested, finger-printed, put in jail and wind up with a record. Just like a common criminal.

"Take, for example, somebody who lost their licence for a parking ticket and got caught driving. Can you honestly say that is a social evil that endangers society in any way?" he asked reporters. "Because if you can't, then it's not a subject for criminal law."

Melnitzer was off and running again. He appealed the provincial court finding to the Ontario Court of Appeal on constitutional grounds and lost. At the Supreme Court of Canada, the judges found sufficient merit in Melnitzer's arguments to hear the case.

At the time, Canada's revamped Constitution, which would include the new Charter of Rights and Freedoms, had yet to be enacted. So Melnitzer relied upon such documents at the British North America Act of 1867, under which the British Parliament had established the form of government for the Dominion. Relatively few lawyers attempted constitutional arguments before the new Constitution was enacted, but Melnitzer, ever the quick study, dug into the BNA Act and all the relevant cases he could uncover to support his position.

He argued that it was outside the scope (in legal terms, *ultra vires*) of the federal government to enforce provincial laws such as the Highway Traffic Act. Melnitzer noted that Boggs had been suspended from driving in Ontario, but the federal law would make it a crime for him to be found driving anywhere in Canada.

Melnitzer handled the case personally at the Supreme Court of Canada, citing more than a dozen cases in support of his contention that this section of the Criminal Code was unconstitutional. He was opposed by Murray Segal, a top lawyer with the Ontario government. The government of Canada was sufficiently concerned by the possibility Melnitzer might win the case that it had a lawyer present, and so did the province of Alberta.

It took many months for the court to render its decision, but finally in early 1981, it sided with Melnitzer in no uncertain terms. The federal government had acted outside its powers in criminalizing a provincial statute, the court ruled. It was the first time in about 60 years that a section of the Criminal Code had been struck down on constitutional grounds.

The impact of the decision was immediate and dramatic. Hundreds, perhaps thousands, of similar cases against Ontario motorists were promptly dropped. Many of them had been adjourned pending the outcome of the Boggs case. From then on in Ontario, charges of driving while suspended would have to be filed under the Highway Traffic Act, with a maximum penalty of a $500 fine.

The case made headlines across the country, and Melnitzer revelled in the attention. He had continued pressing the case even when Boggs's funds were exhausted simply because he knew he was right. If he wasn't being paid, he was going to get as much professional mileage from the case as possible.

Asked by a CBC interviewer why Boggs had pursued what seemed like a trivial matter all the way to the top court in the land, Melnitzer replied with great delight, "Because Mr. Boggs is a very principled man."

Melnitzer's standing was enhanced and he now had his name in the law books. A major victory in the Supreme Court of Canada was every lawyer's dream. Professionally, he couldn't have been happier.

The same month that decision was released, Melnitzer was arguing yet another matter in the Supreme Court of Canada. It was the case of Yanik Szpyt (pronounced "shpit"), a man who had been charged under the Criminal Code with "directing" 10 women engaged in prostitution. Szpyt and another man had operated an escort agency in London, conducting business entirely by telephone. Police couldn't charge him with operating a bawdy house because no central premises existed, so they charged him with "directing" prostitution activities.

At his appearance in provincial court, Szpyt was asked if he wanted to have his trial before a judge sitting alone or before a judge and jury. Such a question is routine when an offence is too serious to be handled in provincial court, the lowest level of court in the country's judicial hierarchy. In Ontario at the time, a choice of judge or judge and jury meant the trial would automatically be held in the next highest level of court, county court. Only the most serious cases, such as murder and manslaughter, were tried in the court a notch above that, the Supreme Court of Ontario. When asked how he wanted to be tried, Szpyt, on Melnitzer's advice, replied, "By judge and jury. Ontario Supreme Court judge and jury."

The judge refused to accept the unexpected request, and Melnitzer promptly appealed the matter to the Ontario Supreme Court. It was a unique appeal and, if Melnitzer succeeded, one that observers predicted would have widespread impact on the justice system. Thousands of cases could suddenly be channelled to the highest courts in their provinces, overburdening and clogging the system.

On a practical level, Melnitzer was hoping that if he was permitted a trial in Ontario Supreme Court, he could transfer the case to a larger centre such as Toronto, where crimes of morality might be more easily tolerated. Otherwise, he would be stuck in Middlesex County Court, which meant a trial in London, where prostitution-related cases were not common. The stakes were high. If convicted, Szpyt faced a maximum penalty of a 10-year prison term.

Melnitzer lost his application to force the judge to accept the type of trial chosen by his client, at the Ontario Supreme Court and then at the Ontario Court of Appeal. But once again, his appeal was viewed as sufficiently novel and of potentially wide impact to permit him to pursue it at the Supreme Court of Canada.

With his usual confidence, Melnitzer argued that an accused person has the right to select not only the mode of his trial, but also the forum in which it will be heard. This time he had to place more emphasis on his powers of persuasion. Finding only one supporting criminal case to cite, he urged a new interpretation of wording in the Criminal Code to bolster his position.

After hearing Melnitzer's pitch, Chief Justice Bora Laskin was terse, but polite. "The success of this appeal must rest on finding a necessary implication to support election of the forum as well as the mode of trial." He said he could see no such implication in the Criminal Code.

Despite the loss, Melnitzer obtained considerable publicity and his name was once again in the official reports of proceedings of the highest court in the land.

As the 1980s began, Melnitzer was growing somewhat disenchanted with the tedium of criminal law. There were too many small-potatoes cases, too much repetition. He would continue to take appeals, but Dawson was proving to be an adept criminal practitioner and was handling the day-to-day work. Melnitzer thought it was time to expand his horizons, tackle new challenges and start making some serious money. There was only so much Legal Aid could do for the bottom line, he reasoned. And his dreams were infinite.

Civil litigation was alluring because clients were not likely to undertake a lawsuit if they didn't have money. And if they won, they'd have more, potentially much more. Melnitzer was becoming increasingly attuned to financial pressures. In late 1979, he and Cathy had purchased a custom-designed home in an exclusive subdivision. He was making substantial monthly payments on a mortgage of $280,000. In addition, he was dabbling in a number of personal investments, which occasionally required significant injections of cash. Many of them were real estate ventures.

Partly because of his interest in property, Melnitzer began representing landlords who were struggling with Ontario's rent-control program, enacted in 1976 as a "temporary" measure. The landlords chafed at controls that limited the annual rent increase they could charge, and they blamed the province for interfering in free market forces. In 1979, the Ontario government enacted a bill creating a Residential Tenancy Commission to administer a new rent-control program, establish obligations for landlords and tenants and arbitrate disputes between them. Howls of protest arose from landlord groups, who said these actions amounted to enshrining rent controls as a permanent fixture, which would eventually reduce apartment construction.

Late that year, the provincial government was under mounting pressure from critics who insisted the pending legislation was unconstitutional. To address that question, the government took the unusual step of referring the matter directly to the Ontario Court of Appeal for a ruling. The court was asked to consider two key questions about the proposed legislation: whether the government could empower the new commission to make orders evicting tenants, and whether the commission could order landlords and tenants to comply with obligations imposed by the act.

Melnitzer, fresh from his research into the Constitution for the Boggs case, assured his landlord clients that the proposed legislation was outside the power of the province. He said it usurped the power of county courts, to which the federal government had delegated landlord and tenant matters. That meant the province was treading on federal turf, so the commission concept was invalid. His views impressed landlords and property owners in London and elsewhere. He was retained to argue on their behalf at the Appeal Court hearing.

A five-member panel of Ontario Supreme Court judges — one of whom was John Morden, who'd presided over Melnitzer's first big victory, the Belvedere Hotel shooting — sat as the Appeal Court. Lawyers from a wide variety of landlord, tenant and other groups were heard. The Appeal Court was aware the province would be arguing that the new commission did not violate the Constitution, and to ensure a balance between the opposing sides, it appointed the most renowned constitutional lawyer in Canada, J.J. Robinette.

Robinette, 72 at the time of this appearance, was considered one of the giants of the legal profession. In 50 years of practice, the Toronto litigator had established himself as a topflight criminal lawyer. In his later years he had turned to civil law and become the country's acknowledged expert in constitutional law, invariably arguing cases from a federal perspective. At the time of his appearance on the Residential Tenancy Commission matter, he was about to begin arguments in the Supreme Court of Canada for the patriation of Canada's Constitution. As in most of his constitutional endeavors, he would prove successful.

Melnitzer was fully aware of Robinette's reputation when he appeared to present his own constitutional argument, but the young London lawyer was not one to be intimidated. When it came time to put forth the landlords' position, he made a strong pitch, arguing forcefully that not only was it unconstitutional for the commission to deal in landlord-tenant matters because of the conflict with county court, but that the provinces had no constitutional right to control rents. He sat down, spent but satisfied he'd been persuasive.

Robinette was the next to speak. The distinguished senior counsel started his submission by saying he agreed with the landlords' lawyer that it was unconstitutional for the proposed commission to delve into landlord-tenant disputes, thereby clearly infringing on county court powers. He followed that by saying that rent controls had nothing to do with the Constitution, contrary to Melnitzer's argument.

This provoked a snort from the direction of Melnitzer's table. "I don't give a fuck what Robinette says," the landlords' counsel muttered in clearly audible tones. The remark was directed toward a law student sitting beside him, but the volume was suitable for a much larger audience. Several of the justices heard it and scowled at the impertinent young lawyer. For his part, Robinette didn't miss a beat. He continued to press his position.

After all arguments were completed, and without further outbursts from the landlords' lawyer, the court reserved its decision. It eventually ruled that the proposed commission was unconstitutional. But the justices sided with Robinette — and against Melnitzer — when they declared rent controls posed no similar problem.

Back in London, Melnitzer was increasingly busy. His reputation was spreading and opposing civil counsel were developing a grudging admiration for him. With Melnitzer on the other side, it meant a real fight was ahead. Yet this bulldog of a man who seemed bent on victory was proving to be completely honest. His aggressiveness never caused him to bend professional ethics. Melnitzer's partners noted how quickly he would dissociate himself from a case if there was even a hint of potential conflicts of interest. If Julius Melnitzer gave his word to another lawyer, or made a promise in court, it was solid.

Increasingly confident in his abilities, Melnitzer believed he could make some tangible contributions to his profession. He began judging "moot courts" at the University of Western Ontario law school. This involved criticizing students on their courtroom techniques and the way they marshalled their evidence.

Melnitzer also believed he could make life easier for criminal lawyers slogging it out in the trenches. He and

Fletcher Dawson, along with new associate Christopher Bentley, began working on *The Defence Lawyer's Trial Book*, a compilation of hundreds of leading and current cases in various aspects of criminal law. The idea was to create a ready reference manual for busy defence lawyers or lawyers for whom criminal law was unfamiliar territory. The book, which took more than a year to complete, was constantly updated in new editions and remains a fixture in most law libraries.

Around the same time, Melnitzer's earlier exploits at the Supreme Court of Canada drew attention from an unexpected quarter. The Law Reform Commission of Canada, a sort of legal think tank that studies various aspects of the law and makes recommendations to Parliament on an ongoing basis for improvements, asked him to produce a study paper on the best way to dispose of goods seized by police in criminal investigations. The commission was concerned that no formalized procedures existed for presenting or returning goods that might be used as evidence in court.

Being approached by such a prestigious body was a distinct feather in Melnitzer's legal cap. He bragged about it to anyone who would listen. Responding to the invitation with his usual vigor, he enlisted the help of law students and other members of the firm. Melnitzer's main thesis was that goods seized as a result of unconstitutional searches must be returned promptly to their rightful owners and that the paperwork should be minimal. His paper resulted in the commission's recommending changes to the Criminal Code that established formal procedures for the return of goods and permitted courts to accept photographs of items as evidence. Predictably, Melnitzer crowed about his impact on the commission and the legislative changes.

His friends and associates in London noticed that the young lawyer never seemed satisfied with his growing list of accomplishments. He was constantly talking about his successes and how much more he wanted to achieve. He never seemed able to relax and enjoy life. Instead he continually drove himself in an apparent compulsion to gain more recognition, impress others with his achievements. He also was in the habit of bragging about exploits other than professional ones, including exaggerated tales about his personal life. He claimed to have written several best-selling pop tunes, including "Hotel California," recorded by the Eagles. The song, one of the most popular ever produced by the band, was credited to three of its members, Don Henley, Glen Frey and Don Felder. Melnitzer insisted that the group had stolen the song and that he had considered suing. His listeners knew Melnitzer could strum a guitar but retained doubts about the boast. Melnitzer boasted of having played hockey in the Montreal Junior Canadiens' organization and saying he'd toyed with thoughts of becoming a professional hockey player before opting for law. "He was always telling stories," a lawyer who articled with Cohen, Melnitzer said years later. "You knew some of them couldn't be true, but you said to yourself, 'Oh, well, that's Julius.'"

Melnitzer repeatedly talked about his various real estate investments. He spoke of having money in his family and how he'd become quite the shrewd businessman. There was always some brilliant deal he had just concluded.

Melnitzer was determined to be London's premier lawyer before the decade was out, and he set his sights on creating the largest law firm in town. Cohen was agreeable. He left most of the major decisions to Melnitzer, seldom opposing his friend. With Melnitzer firmly in control, Cohen, Melnitzer began to add lawyers. Bright young people were signed up and experienced lawyers from other companies were wooed. The firm began purchasing the practices of lawyers who had moved, left the profession or died. The high prices paid for such acquisitions occasionally raised eyebrows. Melnitzer wanted a diversified group, able to handle cases in nearly every aspect of the law. And he wanted lawyers from a variety of backgrounds. He didn't want Cohen, Melnitzer to be seen as an exclusively Jewish law firm.

By the mid-eighties, the firm had grown to 10 lawyers and needed larger quarters. Melnitzer wanted the new premises to reflect Cohen, Melnitzer's new stature, and in 1986, when the law firm moved into the second floor of the imposing London Life building, he saw to it that no expense was spared decorating it in tasteful shades of rose and gray. The rent was substantial: under the terms of a five-year lease, it would increase incrementally to $183,000 a year.

The operation of the law partners was becoming a big business. The overhead of rent and support staff meant the pressure was on to improve the revenue picture. Billings became substantial. Melnitzer led the way, charging amounts two or three times that of other lawyers with similar experience. Despite the large fees, he invariably collected. He had the fewest accounts receivable in the firm and was quick to complain about anyone else at Cohen, Melnitzer who couldn't match his performance. He bragged about the amount he charged and told the other lawyers he did such good work that his clients were only too happy to pay up. He was earning more than $200,000 a year from his practice.

The question of billings became a sore point between him and Cohen. Melnitzer complained that his founding partner wasn't carrying his weight.

"Come on, Harris," he would say in front of the newer partners, "we have major commitments now. You've got to get those billable hours up. And chase down those outstanding bills. Look at me. I charge plenty and collect it all. I'm not doing it just for me. I'm doing it for the firm. Get with it, man."

Cohen would promise to do better, but his heart wasn't in it. His dreams and his ego weren't as big as Melnitzer's. He didn't share the overpowering desire to get to the top of the heap. Distance between the partners grew. It was becoming clear to both of them that their once-close friendship was slowly degenerating into a marriage of convenience.

But better days were ahead. And worse ones. Much worse.

5

Grand
Bend
and Glory

"You ain't seen nothin' yet."

THE MORE MELNITZER ATTAINED, the more he
wanted. The swank new offices, the growing
staff and rising fees didn't satisfy him. He needed more
adulation, a higher profile. He tested the waters of public
opinion whenever he could and didn't like what he found.
The legal community viewed him as being too aggressive,
obnoxious and altogether arrogant. Melnitzer's insatiable
desire for recognition occasionally took bizarre twists.
Melnitzer was no stranger at the London City Press Club, the
designated watering hole for the city's journalists. At the
time, the best-known member of the local media was Del
Bell, a colorful and bombastic columnist for the *London Free
Press*. The pipe-smoking extrovert was alternately loved or
hated by his large readership, the ideal situation for any

columnist. Other media wrote about him. He had a profile. It was hard to ignore Bell. Melnitzer envied Bell's standing and viewed him as a sort of kindred spirit.

On one particular visit to the press club, Melnitzer was disappointed Bell was not around. He'd enjoyed talking politics with the columnist on earlier occasions, although their exchanges had sometimes developed into ego clashes. Still, Melnitzer respected the aggressive writer whose arrogance nearly matched his own. The lawyer began buttonholing Bell's colleagues. "What do you figure Bell earns?" he asked several patrons. "$100,000? Maybe $150,000?"

Melnitzer measured success in dollars, and he wanted assurances that even if he didn't enjoy Bell's profile, he at least earned more than the columnist. He was shocked — and pleased — to learn that the editor of the newspaper probably earned less than $100,000 and Bell about half that. Melnitzer wasn't going to worry about competition from that quarter anymore.

Still, the problem of acceptance remained. A popular lawyer in London was Gordon Cudmore, a contemporary of Melnitzer's and a man with a similar drive to succeed. Armed with an infectious sense of humor and a blindingly quick wit, Cudmore had no shortage of invitations to social events. He and a troupe of talented colleagues, calling themselves Lord Gord and the Benchwarmers, performed musical skits for legal gatherings in London, Toronto and beyond. Their scathing parodies of judges and other notables in the legal field drew rave reviews. Cudmore was also in demand as an extremely able master of ceremonies at all sorts of charitable and social functions. He appeared on television frequently, filed regular reports about legal matters to CBC Radio and became a semi-regular columnist in the local newspaper. Cudmore was a fine lawyer, he was aggressive and yet he was accepted in ways Melnitzer could only dream about. Melnitzer thought he was smarter and a better lawyer than Cudmore, but it was Cudmore who was the toast of the profession. He had to learn the secret.

One day, Melnitzer phoned Cudmore, using a legal matter as a pretext. The conversation soon took a twist that surprised Cudmore. "Gord, you're amazing," Melnitzer said. "I've got to know, Why are you so popular? I can't figure it out. Here I am, working my ass off, trying to get some profile in this town, and you're the guy everybody loves. I want to know how you do it. Let's have lunch."

The bewildered Cudmore found the request bizarre. At first he thought it was some sort of clever ploy. Then, embarrassed, he realized Melnitzer really wanted to pick his brains. He didn't know how to respond. He mumbled something about lunch being a good idea and made an uncharacteristically feeble joke to change the subject. The lunch date never materialized, and Cudmore was left puzzling over the conversation for a long time. He couldn't understand why someone as capable and successful as Melnitzer would be so interested in emulating him. The man must be plagued by some strange demons, Cudmore thought.

That an ambitious lawyer can feel frustrated by the occasionally hidebound characteristics of his profession is not unusual. The practice of law by its very nature concentrates on the past. Since law is built on precedent, the decisions in similar cases previously adjudicated, much emphasis is placed on the scene in the rearview mirror. Judges, who are in a position to effect great change, to make new law, seldom do. Their conservatism is frequently a function of their being drawn from the ranks of older, experienced lawyers, practitioners who spent careers studying precedent. It has been said that the law *evolves;* it never really changes.

The profession tends to make tradition paramount. Witness the title of the professional body that governs and disciplines the 25,000 lawyers who practise in Ontario. The Law Society of Upper Canada takes its name from the former British colony bounded by the Great Lakes. Upper Canada was renamed Canada West in 1841, then became Ontario in time for Confederation in 1867.

Among the many rules with which the law society governed the conduct of law was one that prevented any lawyer from advertising his or her services. It was seen as beneath the dignity of the profession to promote one's self. If a lawyer was an able practitioner, he or she should be able to rely on word of mouth or referrals to attract new business. Advertising was suitable only for car dealers, department stores and other mere pedlars.

With a glut of lawyers entering the profession in the 1970s and 1980s, pressure was building for a relaxation of the rules governing advertising. Young lawyers argued that the profession needed greater competition, fresh approaches and a more consumer-oriented attitude. Why should the legal community feel it must remain aloof from the reality of an increasingly competitive world and the normal rules of economics? Why shouldn't lawyers tell the public about themselves and what sort of law they specialized in? The law was increasingly complex, they noted, and not all practitioners could handle all aspects of it; it was necessary to say who was good at what.

After much debate, the law society relented and in 1985 agreed that lawyers should be able to advertise their services. Limits were placed on what could be said, and any advertising of fees was still frowned upon. But the move was dramatic.

The timing was perfect for the firm of Cohen, Melnitzer. Just when it was positioning itself to overtake the largest firms in London, the new opportunity presented itself. Melnitzer felt that advertising and promotion were keys to the future for Cohen, Melnitzer. Tradition be damned, he thought. He went at marketing with a vengeance, studying practices in the U.S., which had a much more liberal attitude toward advertising and competition.

After attending a seminar in Washington, D.C., on law marketing, Melnitzer was hooked. Cohen, Melnitzer, under his direction, was going to market itself and quickly become a household word. He convinced his partners that a small investment could pay big dividends and catapult the firm to the top of the heap. Law, he argued, was not a noble calling. It was a business, pure and simple.

At Melnitzer's urging, the partners agreed to set aside about five percent of the firm's budget for marketing and developing a promotional strategy. Cohen's wife, Donna, was a founder of Cohen and Watt, a small public relations firm, which was retained to develop a marketing scheme. Donna Cohen and her partner, an energetic young mind named Jaime Watt, pulled out all the stops and came up with ideas that dismayed traditionalists in the law fraternity.

They reviewed the presentation skills of lawyers in the firm, particularly the new arrivals. Strengths and weaknesses in delivery and appearance were highlighted, and suggestions made for improvements and ways to disguise shortcomings.

A newsletter called "Law Talk" was sent to clients, the press and anyone who could be added to a growing mailing list. The glossy publication featured articles about various aspects of the law authored by members of the firm. It introduced new arrivals to Cohen, Melnitzer and occasionally had feature items on members of the support staff. The firm stepped up its special promotions, inviting clients and friends to various social functions, particularly events at the Grand Theatre, to which the firm was a generous financial contributor.

One of the earliest promotions drew some of the greatest response. A central theme of the advertising campaign was the notion that Cohen, Melnitzer provided a service nearly everyone in the community might need and had the best lawyers to come up with solutions to the legal problems facing common folks. "Service, Solutions" was the simple message Cohen, Melnitzer promoted in its advertising. And what better way to advertise than directly to people entering and leaving the courthouse? asked Jaime Watt. The first group might not yet have a lawyer, while the latter might have just realized the seriousness of their problems and be starting the hunt for counsel.

Cohen, Melnitzer rented a billboard promoting the "Service, Solutions" message just outside the front door of the London courthouse. The only other words on the sign were "Cohen, Melnitzer. Lawyers." Depicted in the ad were people from all walks of life — businessmen, construction workers, secretaries, families.

This brash demonstration offended many local practitioners. If this was what was coming from the relaxation on advertising rules, they wanted no part of it. But the public seemed to like it, and the press loved it. Stories and pictures of the sign, along with interviews with Cohen, Melnitzer partners, spread from London across the country.

Locally, the firm got an extra wallop for its promotional dollars when an unexpected controversy cropped up. The man dressed as a construction worker in the billboard ad was, in real life, a police sergeant who moonlighted as a model. The billboard was his first assignment. A furore arose about the propriety of a police officer helping to promote lawyers. Media stories chronicled the officer's travails, and comments from the police chief and others kept the story alive for days. In the end, it was all deemed an innocent episode and the matter was dropped. About a dozen of the billboards were eventually placed at strategic locations across the city.

Melnitzer was gleeful. The Cohen, Melnitzer name was getting recognition and, more importantly, new business was being generated. He could brag even more about the success of his business instincts when a marketing survey revealed that in the course of a year, Cohen, Melnitzer had moved from an unknown entity to the best-known law firm in London.

Criticism of Cohen, Melnitzer's self-promotion continued from many members of the profession. Melnitzer's immediate reaction was anger. Can't they see this is the new reality? he'd hiss. These people don't like it because they weren't smart enough to try it first. They're just jealous and they wouldn't like me whatever I did, he told himself.

He was determined to show the detractors that he and his firm were much more than just flash. He needed another big win to showcase his talents. And he was confident that a case he and other members of the firm had been quietly working away on was just the ticket.

Malcolm Alexander "Archie" Gibbs was a man in his mid-50s, a short, chubby character with a stubborn streak. He lived in the town of Parkhill, a farming community of 1500 about 50 kilometres northwest of London. Gibbs, a general contractor, came from a large, well-respected and hardworking family with deep roots in the area.

Gibbs and his family were embroiled in a longstanding dispute with the tourist village of Grand Bend, 20 kilometres farther northwest on the shore of Lake Huron. Gibbs claimed ownership of the village's major asset — its highly popular main beach. Village council insisted the beach was public property, and any time Gibbs erected signs proclaiming it private, village crews promptly ripped them down. Not satisfied with this sort of response to his land claim, Gibbs corresponded with provincial authorities, but they, too, told him the sandy strip was public.

Grand Bend, a village of about 700 permanent residents, takes its name from the lazy curve of the Ausable River that feeds into Lake Huron near the community. Much of the shoreline along that part of the lake had long ago been pulverized into sand by Lake Huron's unceasing waves, propelled by prevailing northwesterly winds. The perennially shifting sands formed dunes, forcing the river to take a wide detour in its final few kilometres.

Tourism is the lifeblood of the local economy, and the beach is the second-most popular in Ontario. It ranks only behind Wasaga Beach on Georgian Bay, the longest freshwater beach in the world, which has the added advantage of proximity to the millions of residents of Toronto and area. Visitors to Grand Bend can total 50,000 on a good summer weekend, double that on a long weekend. In a season, it draws about 1.5 million sunseekers, many of them from nearby Michigan. It has been estimated that tourism is worth more than $33 million a year to "The Bend."

The focal point of the village is that same main beach, which generations of visitors assumed was public. So did the village. The ownership question picked up steam in August 1979 when Archie Gibbs appeared before council and offered to sell the 305-metre-long main beach to the village. He didn't mention a price. He said he had recently acquired clear title to the land from his uncle, Harold Gibbs, a Parkhill merchant.

It wasn't the first time local politicians had been confronted about the beach. In 1976, Harold Gibbs himself had approached council, offering to sell the land to the village, but council declined. A year later, a London man named F. Donald Ross appeared in the same forum, claiming he had a "vested" interest in the land, even though it was technically owned by Harold Gibbs. Without elaborating, he asked $50,000 for the beach. Council rejected the offer, reasoning it wasn't interested in buying something it already owned.

The situation became far more serious on August 7, 1979, when Archie Gibbs made his brief appearance before village council. He read a terse statement in which he demanded the village come up with an offer to buy the beach from him within nine days, starting tomorrow. "I have in my possession all legal documents making me the owner of part of Lot One, Lake Road West concession, in the village of Grand Bend," he said, using the property's legal description so there would be no mistake about exactly what land he was talking about. "I am open to a reasonable offer to purchase by the council of Grand Bend. This offer is valid until August 17, 1979."

With that brief salvo, Gibbs left council chambers, taking no questions and denying councillors a chance to reply.

Council members that night were agog at the nerve of the man. After a brief discussion, it was decided to send a registered letter to Gibbs warning that legal action would ensue if he continued to place No Trespassing signs on telephone poles in the beach area. The question of ownership was referred yet again to the village solicitor, but a report wasn't expected back until well beyond Gibbs's deadline. The prevailing opinion was that Gibbs was blowing hot air. The village was leasing the land from the province of Ontario for a token amount. It was not collecting taxes on the property — from Gibbs or anyone else.

Their lawyer told council members that a man named Gibbs had obtained some land in the area around the time of the First World War for $265. But the local politicians were advised that even if that deed was legitimate, it was clouded by two issues. First, it was arguable whether the beach-area lands described actually included the portion closest to the water. Second, under the legal principle of adverse possession, or "squatter's rights," the village could claim ownership because of the long history of public use and the fact that the Gibbs family had failed to assert any consistent claim to ownership. The land, it was felt, had become public by default.

Within a year, Gibbs filed a lawsuit against the village, claiming ownership of the beach and damages. Because of a variety of technical problems, the suit had to be discontinued and village leaders breathed easier. But Gibbs refused to let the matter die. He began looking for new lawyers willing to take up his cause. It would prove a difficult task. Gibbs was told the case had little chance of success, that it would be lengthy, complicated and expensive. He was up against a community that was bound to fight like hell to protect its greatest asset, a provincial government that supported Grand Bend's position, and history. Such gloomy assertions didn't dissuade Gibbs. He wasn't about to give up the battle, because he knew in his heart he was right.

After bouncing around several law offices where the advice was discouraging, Gibbs was referred to Cohen, Melnitzer. He'd been told the issue was complex because it might involve fundamental property rights, and Julius Melnitzer had been mentioned as a lawyer who might consider such a challenge. After all, he'd been successful in constitutional cases, fighting long odds and entrenched government interests. The contractor and the lawyer met and each liked what he saw. Melnitzer sympathized with the little guy whose rights were being trampled by governmental indifference. Gibbs was impressed with the aggressive fighter who seemed genuinely interested in his plight and unfazed by the difficulties.

Melnitzer first wanted to do some preliminary research, and he soon discovered a central issue in the case that might have impact far beyond the reaches of tiny Grand Bend. He agreed to take the case. Gibbs, a far from wealthy man, was asked to put some money up front, but Melnitzer was willing to take the balance of his fee from the proceeds of the victory he said was sure to follow. In 1983, the lawsuit was filed again and the laborious job of assembling evidence to prove Gibbs's contention began. It would continue for five years.

Gibbs versus the Corporation of the Village of Grand Bend was finally ready for trial in June 1988, just as throngs of bathers and sunworshippers were returning to the beach for another season. The trial was to be held during the spring assizes of the Ontario Supreme Court in the city of Sarnia, the judicial seat of Lambton County, in which Grand Bend is situated. The crowds at The Bend were separated by about 60 kilometres from those who packed the sunless confines of the courtroom. Presiding was a newly appointed judge, Mr. Justice W. Daniel Chilcott.

The trial would be watched closely, nowhere more so than in Grand Bend, where the head of the village council, Reeve Harold Green, was asked by the press about the possibility of losing the beach. "If we lose it, Grand Bend per se is not going to exist anymore," Green said. "If we lose it, well . . . " He paused to look for words that would adequately under-line the gravity of the situation, but failed. "Grand Bend *is* the beach."

On the eve of the trial, Melnitzer told the press to watch the case, because it would affect the boundaries of many lots along the shores of Lake Huron and elsewhere. That was one way to guarantee an even bigger audience.

Backed by a team of some of Cohen, Melnitzer's sharpest people, Melnitzer had never been as ready for a trial. Paul Vogel, one of the senior partners, and Russell Raikes, a relatively new arrival, had done exhaustive research. They spent hundreds of hours combing government archives for documentation relating to ancient land treaties and surveys. They researched property law and legal theory until they had it memorized. With support staff, they compiled volumes of casebooks, briefs and other documents. The Cohen, Melnitzer brigade, led by Captain Melnitzer, affectionately known to his troops as "The Big Guy," was ready to do battle.

Melnitzer viewed the case as one that would silence his critics once and for all. The publicity would spread his name far and wide, he hoped, and might open a motherlode of similar cases he'd be happy to accept. This was not a case he was even willing to consider the prospect of losing.

On June 6, Melnitzer made some preliminary motions and outlined the case for Justice Chilcott. Gibbs was seeking a declaration of his ownership of the beach and damages of $2 million for trespass and loss of income on the property. In addition, Gibbs wanted $500,000 in punitive damages from the village and the province of Ontario.

The province was represented by Toronto lawyer Tom Wickett, a few years older than Melnitzer and a seasoned litigator. The Ontario government had a major interest in the case because it was the successor to the British Crown, which had originally obtained the land from the Chippewa. Grand Bend's counsel was Dan Murphy, a seasoned, good-natured lawyer specializing in municipal law who lived 50 kilometres north of Grand Bend in the lakeside town of Goderich. In their defence, the province and the village relied heavily on the principle of adverse possession. In documents filed with the court, they contended the public had enjoyed continuous and uninterrupted use of the beach for more than 80 years, and Grand Bend had been spending money on the beach since 1927 to maintain it for public use.

In a civil case, it's up to the plaintiff to introduce his case and then attempt to prove it with evidence. On opening day, Melnitzer quickly conceded the trial would be "complicated and technical." Next, he outlined the evidence he intended to call during the next several weeks to demonstrate that Archie Gibbs was the legitimate owner of the beach.

Melnitzer sounded confident and completely comfortable as he gave the court a history lesson, starting in the early 1800s when the British Crown obtained the lands in the area from the Chippewa. He noted that early descriptions of the land used the shoreline as the western boundary of Bosanquet Township, the municipality from which Brewster, later named Grand Bend, was carved. The Gibbs family became partial owners of Lot One of Bosanquet Township in 1893 and full owners by 1921, he said, and from that time on, demonstrated "a consistent history of assertion of ownership." Melnitzer firmly rejected any suggestion that the Gibbs family, by permitting the public to use the beach, had ever intended to formally dedicate the land for public use.

Archie Gibbs's grandfather, Charles Gibbs, created a subdivision plan to develop lands adjacent to the beach, Melnitzer said. In 1927, the roadway leading to the beach was built because federal officials needed access to their new pier. They expropriated the land for it, paying Gibbs for the right-of-way. Melnitzer said the expropriation clearly showed that the federal government of the day knew the identity of the rightful owner. Later that same year, Charles Gibbs successfully sued a man for taking gravel from the beach, further proof of ownership. And as late as 1979 and 1980, sewer easements across the beach-area lands were obtained from the village and from Archie Gibbs.

Murphy's opening was brief. He said he would demonstrate that long public use established the public's claim to the beach. He said he would argue the beach constituted a park dedication to the community, much like those required in modern subdivision plans. The village, he said, accepted the park dedication in 1927 when it started spending money to maintain the land.

The first witness was one of many experts Melnitzer had found to support Gibbs's claim. Gerald O'Grady, a former senior master of titles for Ontario, testified that Gibbs had "good and marketable title" to the beach, adding the proviso, "subject to the decision of this court."

O'Grady said he had reviewed documents and correspondence dating back to the early 1800s. Grand Bend and much of southwestern Ontario were part of the 404,700-hectare Huron Tract the British Crown granted to the Canada Company. In return for the land, the Canada Company promised to develop it with settlement. Among the documents reviewed by O'Grady were difficult-to-decipher, handwritten minutes of Canada Company board meetings in 1825 and 1826 unearthed by Melnitzer's team. O'Grady said the final agreement in 1836 secured for the Canada Company title to all lands "to the water's edge." The British Crown did not reserve the beach for itself. This is not surprising, he said, since the major interest of both the Crown and the company was farmland with which to lure settlers. Sand had little value to anyone in those days, he noted.

Melnitzer's next witness also had impressive credentials. David Lambden, a professor of survey science at the University of Toronto, had been an examiner of surveys for Ontario and a consultant on surveying matters for several provincial ministries. He was asked to review the field notes of the first surveyor to visit the beach, 153 years earlier. Lambden testified that if the Crown had intended to reserve the beach lands for itself, he would have found some reference to it in the surveyor's notes. There was no such mention in the notes or on a later survey, leading Lambden to conclude the beach was part of the grant to the Canada Company. That land eventually became Gibbs's property.

Melnitzer turned Lambden's attention to the wording in the original land grant, which reserved for the British Crown

·"all navigable streams, waters and water courses, with the beds and banks thereof, running, flowing, or passing in, over, upon, by, through or along any of the said parcels or tracts of land granted to the company."

Lambden deduced that the description of navigable waters and their beds related to moving waterways only. Lake Huron doesn't run, flow or pass through anything, he said.

"Does Lake Huron move?" Melnitzer asked.

"Not as a lake," came the reply. "It is still water."

Melnitzer then pressed him for an explanation of the term "banks," which would prove to be contentious.

"'Banks' I take to mean the land up to the high-water mark of the lake," Lambden replied. "That's where you see the line of gravel, the normal high-water mark."

The professor said he believed the Crown would never reserve the lands above that line of gravel for itself.

Murphy, the village lawyer, took over and grilled Lambden mercilessly, reflecting his fear that the professor had inflicted much damage to the village's position. A skilled cross-examiner with many years' experience, Murphy had only moderate success with Lambden. But Lambden eventually conceded that the Canada Company would have had no particular interest in nonarable land because it would have been unsalable. The professor agreed with Murphy that it was possible the Crown reserved the beach for itself. "That wouldn't have bothered the Canada Company one bit," the survey expert said.

Lambden was in the witness box for five days, and as Murphy and Wickett sought to discredit the academic, clashes between Melnitzer and them were frequent. A pattern was being established. Melnitzer would offer up an expert and the other two lawyers would try to tear him to pieces. Melnitzer defended his witnesses ferociously, sometimes incurring the wrath of the judge.

It was becoming clear that the central issue in the case was the definition of "beds, banks and navigable waters." Chilcott's decision on those words would have an impact on the entire 963,750 hectares in southwestern Ontario that the Crown had granted to the Canada Company (of which the Huron Tract was part) between 1829 and 1859.

It was also apparent the case would last far longer than the several weeks predicted at the outset. Melnitzer was carefully and meticulously building his case. He relentlessly produced experts on surveys and entered as exhibits long-forgotten documents and correspondence relating to the beach. By mid-July, he had tendered more than 200 exhibits.

On July 25, the twenty-first day of the trial, Archie Gibbs was called to the witness box. Melnitzer, fresh from bruising battles with opposing counsel, discarded his abrasive side for a gentle, compassionate approach as he led Gibbs down memory lane for the court. He was determined to show Gibbs was the little guy who'd been wronged and win sympathy for his client.

Gibbs recalled that as a child he had helped an uncle post privacy signs on the beach and in the adjacent Gibbs Park cottage development to the east. He recounted playing on the beach with his 11 brothers and sisters and how he had memorized the locations of various childhood perils: poison ivy, poison oak and chokeberries. He said he and his siblings were not permitted by their relatives to cross Main Street to the northern portion of the beach, which was public. "We would have loved to have gone there as kids because there were swings, teeter-totters, washrooms and people playing music. There were picnic areas and you could play ball," Gibbs recalled. He said that in the late 1930s, there might be as many as 50 people on the Gibbs beach on a summer day. Most were acquaintances of the family.

"Did you see strangers on the beach?" asked Melnitzer.

"Definitely, yes definitely," was the reply.

"What was the family attitude toward these strangers on the beach?" Melnitzer pressed.

"Provided they were not doing any damage and were enjoying themselves on the beach, they [Gibbs family members] tolerated them."

Gibbs said he was disappointed the village didn't seem interested in buying the beach from him in 1979. He testified he had been thinking of selling it for development. Toward the end of his two days of evidence, Melnitzer asked Gibbs if he was still willing to sell the beach to the village, despite the acrimony and the lawsuit. "Yes," he said.

Shortly before the trial took a three-month adjournment, Gibbs conceded his fight was becoming costly. He told the court the trial at that point had cost him nearly $1 million in fees, including more than $100,000 in disbursements for the nine expert witnesses already called. The battle to date had cost Grand Bend an estimated $65,000, the province a similar amount. So far it was a lopsided fight, with Melnitzer proving that he had plenty of ammunition and that he was prepared to buy as much more as was necessary.

Rumors were rife about Gibbs's legal fees and who was underwriting them. The amounts that had been paid to expert witnesses were considered phenomenal by other members of the legal profession. But Gibbs, under instructions from Melnitzer and Raikes, wasn't saying who was footing his tab. The *London Free Press*, which had followed the case closely, reported, "There are rumors that developers are backing him with an eye to building luxury condominiums on the beach."

At one point, Melnitzer engaged in a bit of self-promotion that only heightened interest in the question of his fees. During a recess in the trial, he was joined in the Sarnia courthouse coffee room by another London lawyer who had a case in the city that day. "You know, if I win this case I'm a legend," Melnitzer told the visitor, displaying his usual bragging style designed to impress. "And if I lose, I'm just extremely well-paid."

Just before the lawsuit resumed, Cohen and Watt, the public relations firm, sent out a press release reminding the media about the case and attempting to simplify the issues at stake. Included prominently were the names of Melnitzer and Raikes, as well as the name of the firm.

When evidence was again called, it was October, and Melnitzer was missing. He'd injured his knee playing tennis and had been ordered to rest for two weeks. He had no choice but to stay home and monitor proceedings by telephone. It was difficult to say what hurt him more, his ligaments or the feeling that he had been benched during the biggest game of his career. In the interim, the very able Paul Vogel took over the questioning of several witnesses who talked about the development potential of the beach. On November 3, the plaintiff's case ended after 31 days of testimony from 21 witnesses. More than 320 exhibits had been introduced into evidence.

When the defence was ready to mount its case, Melnitzer wasn't. His knee had improved but his mood hadn't. He complained to Chilcott that Wickett, the Ontario government lawyer, was being unfair with him. He said he had learned on September 6 that the defence was planning to call evidence from a coastal engineer and a historian, both of whom would be filing reports. Being warned of such material three months after the trial began clearly contravened rules of practice that require the production of reports by expert witnesses at least 10 days before a trial begins, Melnitzer argued. An adjournment was necessary, he claimed, because he needed time to review those reports further. He also said his own experts hadn't had time to review them, something which "seriously prejudiced" his case. "This is trial by ambush, my lord," he charged, demanding a two-week adjournment and the right to reopen his case if it proved necessary.

The question of costs was beginning to weigh heavily on Melnitzer. He also demanded that Chilcott immediately assess damages against the province for the delay its lawyer had prompted. Melnitzer sought money to hire and prepare expert witnesses to rebut the province's two new witnesses. Chilcott said he was unhappy at the turn of events, but adjourned the case to late November. He reserved any decision on hitting the province with costs.

"It's now becoming apparent," the weary judge said with some irritation, "that this case will not conclude before the end of the year."

Upon resumption, Chilcott didn't get any happier. Melnitzer promptly popped up and renewed his demand for costs against the province. He claimed the Ontario government had cost the plaintiff an additional $50,000 by its tactics. He said he might have to recall some of his witnesses to court, including Lambden, to rebut the province's experts. The survey professor charged $750 a day, or $105 an hour, and could cost $10,000 before his evidence was completed. Melnitzer said the surprise by the province would also extend the trial by at least eight days. He said fees for himself, Raikes and a law student would be at least $2000 a day.

Wickett told the judge any such motion for costs was premature and shouldn't be made until after all evidence had been called. The lawyer for the province wasn't about to concede anything, and he felt some satisfaction that the other side was starting to squirm about costs in the lawsuit they'd started.

Chilcott reserved his decision again but grew testy with the lawyers for all sides. He said he couldn't be sure who was to blame for the delays, but he didn't like the situation. "My patience is becoming very, very short," he warned.

Although disappointed he hadn't won the skirmish over costs, Melnitzer smiled inwardly at the turn of events. The defence was about to launch its case and the judge was in an ugly mood. Perfect.

The defence called the author of a book about Grand Bend's history to establish that the village had been a popular resort since the late nineteenth century and that the public had freely used the beach since then. A coastal engineer testified the "bank" of a lake is the rise above the shoreline and well above the high-water mark. Engineers and planners were called who warned that development of the beach area could have dire consequences for the village's

sewage-disposal system with possible environmental consequences for the beach.

The strongest witness for the defence was Howard Graham, a former president of the Ontario Land Surveyors'
Association. He said that in the original grant the land from
the water's edge up to the top of the "dry bank," the rise above
the shoreline, was retained for the Crown. He said such a
provision was government policy when the Canada Company was granted the Huron Tract. He testified for five days
for the province, outlining his views. After answering
Wickett's last question, Graham made a move to leave the
witness box, thinking his job was done. He had forgotten
Melnitzer was waiting to cross-examine him.

"You'd better sit down, Mr. Graham," Chilcott said. "You
ain't seen nothin' yet."

The judge was right. Like a pit bull terrier that had slipped
its leash, Melnitzer tore into the star defence witness with a
passion. The grilling took six days. In one exchange,
Melnitzer referred Graham to field notes made by a man who
first surveyed another part of the Huron Tract. The notes
revealed he had clambered down steep riverbanks and surveyed lots right to the edge of the water. This was well below
any "dry bank." "That," Melnitzer suggested tartly to the
witness, "is hardly consistent with the Crown's intentions
[to keep such land] as you claim them to be."

"That is correct," Graham was forced to concede.

The trial continued, and in late January a long-simmering
feud between Melnitzer and provincial lawyer Wickett broke
into the open.

Melnitzer complained Wickett was withholding documents, only to spring them on him at the last moment. He
said he was under the threat of "constant ambush" because
of the "tactical games" Wickett was playing. He accused the
lawyer of "stonewalling" requests for documents. "On every
document he's playing footsie with me," Melnitzer said.
"He's been playing games from day one." At issue was a
compilation of case law Wickett was going to use in his

closing argument. Melnitzer sought help from Chilcott in getting the list.

Wickett fired back that Melnitzer's request was an "unexpected outburst" and not valid. He said Melnitzer already knew what most of the material would be and that Melnitzer, too, had produced unexpected documents during the trial. "It is by no means a one-way street," he complained.

The government lawyer denied he was conducting any sort trial by ambush, but Chilcott interrupted him with, "You might have a hard time convincing me of that." Chilcott then ordered Wickett to turn over his final list of material to Melnitzer.

One of the last witnesses to testify was Grand Bend's newly elected reeve, Bob Sharen, whom Murphy led through council minutes of meetings held in the 1970s when Sharen had served an earlier term as the top elected official in the village. Sharen was recounting the 1977 meeting at which Londoner F. Donald Ross offered to sell the beach for $50,000. Melnitzer, grinning broadly, said to Murphy in a stage whisper, "Ask him if he wishes they had taken it."

The lawyer for the little guy was feeling playful. The evidence had gone well for Gibbs, and Melnitzer felt certain he had neutralized most of the defence evidence. The case was almost over.

When it was his turn to question Sharen, Melnitzer had another go at the "little guy" scenario. Sharen had admitted that he, personally, had removed No Trespassing signs Gibbs family members had posted on the beach throughout the 1970s. "How often did you remove these signs?" Melnitzer asked.

"As often as your clients put them up," Sharen replied.

The evidence ended shortly after. The trial had consumed 59 days over eight months. Dozens of witnesses had been called and 494 documents filed as exhibits. Gibbs's fees had probably topped $3 million, Grand Bend taxpayers were hit for $300,000, and provincial taxpayers another several hundred thousand dollars.

In his closing argument in February 1990, almost seven years after the suit was filed, Melnitzer pressed three points of law: legal title, possessory title and damages. Legal title related to the "beds and banks" issue. He argued that the land to the gravel line was granted to the Canada Company and therefore was now owned by Gibbs. Possessory title was the village's claim that it had acquired the beach by default. Melnitzer dismissed that, pointing to the continued assertion of ownership by the Gibbs family. And he said Gibbs was entitled to the damages he sought because of the unfair and illegal acts of the village and the province.

Chilcott indicated he would need a good deal of time to review the weight of evidence. He predicted his decision might not be available until the fall.

The other partners at Cohen, Melnitzer were glad the case was finally over. Staff had been pressed into overtime to meet the ceaseless demands made by Melnitzer. The billable hours had climbed into the thousands. Law students, clerks, secretaries and several lawyers had been involved. Normally compliant with the wishes of Melnitzer, his partners had become disenchanted with the founding partner's costly obsession. Since his modest initial retainer, Gibbs had paid nothing. As the case dragged on, the partners began to insist Melnitzer either get more money from his client or settle.

By the time the case ended, the partners were unhappy. The experts had been paid and other expenses covered, but revenue was needed. At first, Melnitzer brushed off their concerns. But the pressure continued. He promised that he'd win the case and that the firm would be paid from the damages and court costs Gibbs was sure to be awarded. Gibbs, he said, was soon going to be a very wealthy man. But the topic of payment wouldn't go away. After final arguments had been presented, the partners continued to press Melnitzer to get something from Gibbs.

In May, Melnitzer surprised those attending a partners' meeting with an announcement. "Our friend Mr. Gibbs has just received some good news. And it's good news for us. Archie's just inherited some spare change that he can put toward our fees. We'll be receiving $1.1 million very shortly. The rest we'll settle up when we win this."

Sure enough, the money eventually arrived and the partners were satisfied. But Gibbs was unaware of what was happening behind the scenes. He hadn't lost any wealthy relatives, and Melnitzer wasn't making any requests for money. Gibbs remained under the impression Melnitzer's fee was due only after the case had been won.

The Grand Bend decision proved to be a long wait. Chilcott was thorough and he took the time necessary to sift through the mountain of evidence and pages of testimony.

On December 20, 1990, the 118-page ruling was released. Word of a decision raced like wildfire through Cohen, Melnitzer. Everyone dropped what they were doing and scurried to Melnitzer's office, which is marked by a sign announcing Fierce Lawyer at Work. The Big Guy was hunched over the telephone, obviously intent on the message from the other end.

"Skip to the end," he barked into the mouthpiece at an excited Raikes, who was in Toronto at the Supreme Court office. "Read me the conclusion and fax me the rest."

Chilcott had ruled that the question of the Crown reserving the lands for itself was void because of uncertain wording in the grant to the Canada Company. And he'd decided that the water's edge was marked by the "wet" bank, rather than the "dry" one.

The staff studied Melnitzer's face for a clue. There was silence as he held the receiver tightly to his ear. Melnitzer nodded. Again. Then he broke into a broad smile. "All right!" he whooped. The victory was his. Chilcott had awarded Gibbs $1.2 million for lost revenue from the beach. Staff members cheered, hugged, slapped each other on the back and congratulated Melnitzer.

"Call Archie!" Melnitzer hollered. "Party, my place, tonight," he added as he ran down the hall to find the other partners. The media were alerted.

Melnitzer couldn't remember ever being so happy as he asked staff to order up food and champagne. The best of both, he demanded. Screw the expense. He wanted to share his joy with everyone. The entire firm and outside guests were invited, about 70 in all. They dined that night on Norwegian smoked salmon and chateaubriand. As the tributes flowed, so did the champagne, including four one-hundred-dollar bottles of Crystal Louis Roederer, 1983. The focal point of the celebration was a sour lemon cake decorated with a sand scene, on which was inscribed, "Law is a Beach."

At one point, Vogel climbed on the piano bench to get attention. With glass in hand he proposed a toast: "To Julius, the best courtroom lawyer in the country. I don't know of anyone else who could have won this case."

Melnitzer soaked up the adulation. This was a wonderful night. He had beaten the odds through hard work. As he began to relax he became magnanimous. He thanked Raikes, Vogel and law student Debbie Anders for their efforts and their unflagging belief in Gibbs's case.

"I expect the other side will appeal," he cautioned, "so it's not really over yet. But the judge sided with us on all points of law and fact, so we're in good shape."

Melnitzer proposed a toast to Gibbs who appeared somewhat bewildered by all the fuss. Earlier, Gibbs had told the press he had been advised an appeal was likely, so a cloud remained over the beach. "I've been fighting for it for 10 years now, but I understand it could be another five to seven years before there's a final decision," he said. "But we'll win it. I'm 57 now. I've got a few years yet. I can wait."

Melnitzer told the press Gibbs had been vindicated. "Archie is not a speculator, not an opportunist. He's a guy who wanted his own backyard back. Many people were laughing at him at the start of the case. Nobody's laughing anymore."

The partiers paused briefly at 11 o'clock to gather around

the television for the nightly newscast. The story of the victory and the celebratory party was the lead item.

Within days, Cohen, Melnitzer had placed a substantial advertisement in the *London Free Press.* "Congratulations Archie Gibbs," it read. "It has been and continues to be a privilege to represent you." The ad, an unheard-of gesture of self-promotion, was Melnitzer's idea. He'd picked it up from something he'd seen in the *Wall Street Journal.*

Melnitzer became the darling of the media. The case had drawn national attention and he was the subject of newspaper, radio and television interviews. He stressed the David and Goliath aspects of the case and warned of its implications. He and Gibbs continued to deflect questions about the legal fees. As 1990 ended, Melnitzer was on top of the world. He knew 1991 could only be better.

A few months into the new year, he was featured in a cover story in *Encounter,* the weekend magazine in the *London Free Press.* The four-page spread discussed how the Grand Bend case had catapulted him to the top ranks of his profession. Melnitzer was gracious with the writer, Patricia McGee, permitting her into his home for hours of taped interviews. He read and reread the story after it appeared, satisfied that it gave him the recognition he felt was his due.

McGee ended her penetrating article on London's legal star with the following: "There's a sense that Melnitzer will achieve whatever he sets his mind to and that he will become a greater force. In all likelihood there will be other victories and other victory parties."

In the first week of April, the photographer illustrating the spread, Susan Bradnam, had asked Melnitzer to travel the 70 kilometres with her to Grand Bend and pose on the beach in his black courtroom robe. Melnitzer agreed and brought along marketing man Jaime Watt, who had advised him to comply with Bradnam's requests.

Obligingly, he clambered up and down the sandbanks he'd argued so long and hard about. He even rolled up his trousers and stood in the still-frigid water to please the photographer. He drew the line only once — when Bradnam asked him to pop a cork on a champagne bottle and offer a toast to the beach that had brought him fame.

"Can't do it," Melnitzer protested. "That's having liquor in a place other than a residence. It's against the law."

6

Women and Ego

" . . . higher testosterone men tend to have more unstable marriages . . . "

THE CAMERA WASN'T ORDINARILY a friend to Julius Melnitzer. While not homely, the lawyer can't be described as attractive. He has a fleshy face, characterized by full jowls, a slightly receding hairline and a tendency toward dark-rimmed raccoon eyes that is even more pronounced when he's tired. His face seems most comfortable when it wears a frown or scowl. In photographs where he's smiling, he looks strained and unnatural. With a short neck and the broad shoulders of a fullback, he looks very much like the bulldog he can be. He constantly has to watch his weight, pursuing a vigorous exercise and diet regimen to keep unwanted pounds at bay.

In many ways, Melnitzer was unconcerned about his appearance. In the early years at Cohen, Melnitzer, his preferred attire was jeans, loafers and a sweatshirt. He upgraded his wardrobe with smart tailored suits only when he decided appearances were essential to impress others, primarily the bankers with whom he was spending more and more time. In manner, he could be distinctly boorish. At social gatherings, he had little ability to make small talk. He wanted to talk about what he wanted to talk about, and he would interrupt others to do so. He had a knack of offending people he barely knew.

Nevertheless, some people found his restless energy, his aggressiveness and his winner-take-all approach to life appealing. He worked hard but also played and laughed hard. Mountain climbing, tennis, hiking or scuba diving — he tackled them all with equal zeal. He had more than a few sports injuries from overexertion, including knee-damage that eventually required surgery.

Despite his outward appearance, Melnitzer had a teddy-bear quality not far beneath the surface that was attractive to some women, who found themselves wanting to nurture him. He could be extremely polite, attentive and empathetic. As one woman whom he impressed put it, "When he asked you how you were doing, he really seemed to listen and to really want to know." He could display a little-boy sort of vulnerability, surprising those who didn't know him well. At the same time, he could be overpowering, unquestionably the dominant partner in any relationship.

When Melnitzer turned his attention on a woman, he could be dazzling. There were many who would succumb.

Catherine Szirt was one of Melnitzer's 360 fellow graduates from Northmount High School in 1964. Quiet and serious, Cathy was active in volleyball and gymnastics and she enjoyed Shakespeare. Her high school yearbook entry indicated her ambition was a career in nursing. The inscription read, "And this above all: To thine own self be true."

Cathy and Melnitzer found each other's qualities appealing. She was the quiet introvert with sensible goals; he was the extrovert with grand dreams. In their marriage he was the dominant partner. When her nursing studies were interrupted by pregnancy, Cathy, a bright and pleasant woman, was prepared to devote herself to motherhood and be content with the role of supportive spouse, for the time being. But she hoped one day to finish her university degree and get a job.

When her young husband proposed moving to London less than a year after his call to the bar, Cathy agreed. She would be even farther away from her family, but from what she had learned, London sounded like a pleasant environment in which to raise Melissa. And perhaps she could complete her studies and find a position at one of the city's three hospitals.

In London, because Melnitzer threw himself into work with such frenzy, putting in long hours without vacations in the first few years, Cathy and Melissa usually had dinner without him and Melissa was in bed by the time he got home at night. When occasionally they got together with neighbors, Melnitzer's ineptitude at small talk showed. He would say they wouldn't be staying long on Brentwood Crescent because they would be moving to a better neighborhood as soon as Cohen, Melnitzer was more established. Assertions like that made Cathy cringe.

The couple lived modestly in the $350-a-month house, but Melnitzer never felt he had enough money to engage in any serious investing. He began borrowing funds by having the comfortable Szirt family provide formal loan guarantees. He promised he was building a better life for their daughter and granddaughter.

By 1979, Melnitzer, with his first big victories behind him and his reputation on the rise, felt it was time to move into a home more suitable for London's rising legal star. He and Cathy were attracted to an exclusive new subdivision along the banks of the Thames River in the western section of the city. The development consisted of a single crescent, paved entirely in interlocking bricks running past custom-designed homes. They purchased a lot for $80,000 and began building their dream home. The two-storey brick house featured an impressive entrance with high pillars, a rear deck overlooking the river and a huge master bedroom, complete with a raised whirlpool tub that could accommodate six.

Melnitzer was unwilling to be house rich and cash poor and wanted to keep money on hand in case some new investment opportunity presented itself. He engaged in some creative financing for the home on Clearview Crescent that left him with $280,000 in mortgages on a property worth the same amount. The Canadian Imperial Bank of Commerce was talked into holding a $200,000 mortgage when an $80,000 mortgage was already in place.

The grand new home marked a new beginning. But it also marked an ending of another kind. By the time of the move to Clearview, the couple's marriage was shaky. Melnitzer's obsession with work was hard on his wife, who longed for the attention he'd paid her when their relationship was new. Cathy chafed at being a single mother by default. She began having spells of depression.

Meanwhile, despite the amount of time he was spending on work and investments, Melnitzer's self-confessed "roving eye" was at work. He had always found time for other women and had carried on a number of affairs throughout the late 1970s. He didn't feel the need to be discreet. The liaisons were something else to brag to the boys about, to give him standing in their eyes, and he felt no compunction about sharing them. Inevitably, the stories got back to Cathy, and their marriage grew increasingly turbulent.

At one point, mere weeks after the 1976 Belvedere murder case, Cathy went missing. Melnitzer, in the midst of yet another complex case, alerted police. A week later, police told Melnitzer Cathy had been found, unconscious, in a Toronto motel room; she had taken an overdose of drugs and was in bad shape. Before leaving court to go to her side, Melnitzer said she had tried to commit suicide on earlier occasions.

Cathy had been depressed after hearing talk about her husband and an attractive blond secretary from his office. As usual, Melnitzer had made little attempt to hide the affair, which lasted several months. In fact, he had bragged about it. The woman's husband, a law student, learned of the relationship through the legal grapevine and confronted Melnitzer. When the lawyer refused to break off the affair, the student and his wife left town. Melnitzer moved on to another liaison.

The Melnitzers' new home did nothing to rejuvenate their marriage. Cathy, working as a company nurse at Northern Telecom in London, was active in union affairs and was growing less dependent on her husband and his paycheque. Midway through 1980, she demanded that he start being a real husband again or she would leave him.

Busier than ever at work, Melnitzer was taken aback by the ultimatum. Cathy's family told him they were urging her to leave him if he didn't mend his ways. He felt trapped. Just when it was time to be consolidating the financial and career gains earned after years of sacrifice, Cathy was threatening to ruin it all. By this time, she and her family had guaranteed a total of $400,000 of Melnitzer's personal investments. If they separated, he'd have to find other guarantees, or pay off the loans they'd backed. He didn't know where he could turn for the cash.

One attempt to resolve the conundrum was drastic and dramatic. He told a business associate that he had signed himself in as a voluntary patient for about a week at London Psychiatric Hospital for counselling. The associate was puzzled. Melnitzer seemed to be riding high; what could have been that troubling? Melnitzer explained, "I've been under a lot of pressure. I just went there for a breather, to collect my thoughts." While at the institution, known locally as the Highbury Hilton after the street on which it is located, he reportedly collected more than his thoughts. He picked up several new clients among the other patients.

Back home, he tried to patch things up with Cathy, saying the help he had received at the hospital had been enlightening. But nothing had really changed. Melnitzer was trying to buy some time, hoping that Cathy and her family's hostility would lessen.

Just when things at home were reaching a crisis, Melnitzer's eye settled on a pretty law student at the University of Western Ontario, where he was judging the students' "moot courts." During the 1980-81 school year, Melnitzer had noticed a slender brunette named Deena Baltman, a second-year student. She was 22 and single; he was 33 and unhappily married. He was taken with her attractiveness and fun-loving nature; she was impressed with the attention he paid her and his reputation as one of London's best lawyers. They began dating and the relationship bloomed. At the end of the school year in April, Melnitzer left Cathy and moved into an apartment closer to the university. He had decided he had no future with his wife and would have to find some way to resolve the financial arrangements with her family.

In September, after spending the summer with her parents in Toronto, Baltman moved in with Melnitzer for her third academic year. Melnitzer was one of her teachers. A sessional lecturer, he taught advanced criminal and civil law procedure. Baltman did well in the course.

Melnitzer's position with the faculty didn't continue beyond that year as the pressure on his time from his law practice and his growing interest in landlord-tenant matters increased. His relationship with Baltman, however, continued. As she was finishing school and looking for a law firm in which to article, Melnitzer helped find her a position with the practice of a friend. When she was called to the bar, he promptly added her to the roster of lawyers at Cohen, Melnitzer.

Splitting with Cathy had been difficult. At the time, a recession was hurting all businesses, including the law firm. High interest rates were making borrowing difficult and real estate hard to sell. But Melnitzer wasn't about to downshift for recession or separation. Just when his financial needs were greatest, the financial picture at the law firm was weak. He couldn't justify a big draw from its coffers. And he needed to provide for Cathy and Melissa and still shower Baltman with gifts and attention. He had the cost of maintaining two households and he'd have to scramble to replace the $400,000 in guarantees put up by Cathy's family.

Melnitzer and Cathy devised a separation agreement that was relatively amicable. Although not that familiar with family law, Melnitzer knew separation and divorce agreements are filed in court and made public documents. He was concerned that his financial position would become known if he filed the usual financial statements; to file false statements with the court is professional suicide. But if his finances were laid bare in court, the bankers from whom he was beginning to obtain large sums of money would see his situation was much more limited than they'd been led to believe. Lawyers in the case would also know the truth, and Melnitzer knew how lawyers love to gossip about colleagues. It was important to impress upon his legal confreres that he was a wealthy man, much more successful than they. Confidence had to be maintained at all cost.

A clue to his financial picture could be found in the fact that fully four pages of the 18-page separation agreement dealt with the anticipated proceeds from the sale of the heavily mortgaged house on Clearview Crescent. The inordinate amount of detail suggested it was clearly Melnitzer's main asset at the time. Despite his salary of about $150,000, his total assets weren't likely much more than $200,000.

In exchange for an agreement from Cathy's lawyer that his financial position would be kept quiet, Melnitzer agreed to relatively generous terms. Upon the sale of the house, he promised to pay Cathy $100,000, even though the house wouldn't likely sell for much more than the $280,000 in mortgages it carried. He'd pay $3600 a month in support for Cathy and Melissa until the home was sold, dog support of $250 a month to maintain the couple's two large dogs, and Cathy could have all the contents of the house. Melnitzer also agreed to having the grounds for divorce listed as adultery, even though by the time the divorce action began, the couple had lived apart for three years and could have used that as grounds for divorce. In September 1984, the divorce decree was granted. Cathy, who had left her $24,000-a-year nursing job to return to university, had already moved to Toronto with Melissa. She eventually remarried.

Years later, Melnitzer claimed that he'd agreed to the generous terms because he felt he owed Cathy a lot for what they'd been through. He told a banker after his arrest that his road to financial deceit started with the divorce settlement. "I could not bear to see my wife walk away with very little. I overstated my assets at least three times and overpaid my wife in the divorce settlement."

To another banker attempting to unravel his affairs in the wake of financial collapse, Melnitzer gave a similar story. "I took the position with her lawyer that she and I had gone through 13 years together and she was entitled to half," he said. "When you look through the asset statements I gave at the time, I grossly overstated the assets, because I wanted her to do better, rather than worse. So it's kind of a funny thing. I think most spouses tend to understate their assets in their divorces."

These post-downfall explanations show Melnitzer was trying to put the best possible spin on his view of history. He didn't mention how important it had been to hide his true financial condition.

Life with Baltman rejuvenated Melnitzer. He took a renewed interest in controlling his weight and trying to look good. Baltman had a penchant for expensive clothes and jewelry and Melnitzer did his best please her with gifts of both. She particularly enjoyed shopping trips to New York City, and her lover was more than willing to make his American Express card available to her.

At Baltman's insistence, once Melnitzer's divorce was finalized, the couple began looking for a home. She wanted something substantial, befitting two upwardly mobile lawyers. Melnitzer was agreeable, but concerned about where he'd find the money. After some searching, they found a

California-ranch-style house they both liked on Tallwood Road. It was in an exclusive new subdivision, yet the house was one of the least expensive in the development. The address was prestigious, but the $260,000 price wouldn't be too burdensome. A builder's model, the house wasn't available as soon as the couple wanted it. Melnitzer, seeing how much Baltman was taken by it, paid a premium to obtain it for her immediately. The deal closed in June 1985. A mortgage of $190,000 was arranged from Montreal Trust.

The house featured an impressive foyer leading into a Tudor-style "great room" with atrium beyond, where Melnitzer placed his desk and books. This room looked over an intimate backyard filled with a kidney-shaped swimming pool and whirlpool. A marble fireplace dominated the main living area. Melnitzer and Baltman installed a grand piano as a focal point in the room. One U-shaped wing of the house consisted exclusively of the master bedroom and whirlpool-equipped en suite bathroom. With no objections from Melnitzer, Baltman had the bedroom done in pink, with massive pink balloon curtains.

The home was soon filled with the souvenirs and objets d'art the two collected on their travels. Visitors were taken on tours during which the artwork, carvings, sculptures and other treasures were described. The home became a showplace for their art collection, which knowledgeable visitors would later charitably describe as "eclectic."

Baltman enjoyed Melnitzer's boyish side and she encouraged his interest in stuffed toy animals. The house was filled with them, and friends who assumed they were Baltman's were soon corrected. Quite a revelation to more than a few, who knew Melnitzer only as an aggressive street fighter in court. They were also surprised to learn that the lawyer who could savagely tear into witnesses didn't eat raw meat. In fact, Melnitzer was a vegetarian.

She encouraged his love of real animals, too. The couple obtained two English bull terriers they named Barney and Maude. A rather homely breed with large bony heads and tiny eyes, the animals were showered with love and affection and the finest veterinary care and kennel accommodation when necessary. Melnitzer and Baltman fawned over the animals, talking to them in baby talk as though they were children. A few years later, at the height of his success, Melnitzer and Baltman staged a huge gala, complete with birthday cake, and led startled guests in a rousing rendition of "Happy Birthday." The party was for Barney and Maude.

Baltman, with her artistic bent and dreams of becoming an actress, also stirred him to take an interest in theatre and music. He responded by ensuring Cohen, Melnitzer became substantial supporters of the London arts community.

Not long after moving to Tallwood, Baltman and Melnitzer began planning their wedding. Both agreed it would have to be the social event of the season and no expense was to be spared. Baltman hired professional bridal consultants and began looking about London for a suitable venue.

On July 13, 1986, a fine midsummer day, Julius Melnitzer and Deena Baltman became husband and wife under a canopy of trees on the grounds of the Elsie Perrin Williams estate, which had been formerly owned by a wealthy London biscuit manufacturer. The impressive property, with its well-manicured rolling lawns, had been a gathering place for the city's social and business elite for decades. Bequeathed to the city, it could be rented for special events. The estate exuded old money and set just the tone Melnitzer and Baltman were looking for.

Nearly 200 guests attended the carefully orchestrated nuptials. The wedding ceremony was conducted by a rabbi, and a harpist played as Melnitzer walked his bride down the grassy aisle. Baltman wore a lacy, midcalf-length white dress and the groom was in black tuxedo. The reception was held under a huge pink-and-white marquee, while $10,000 worth of flowers, mainly tiger lilies, decorated the scene. There were so many flowers that they'd had to be put in place the previous evening and security guards were hired to keep watch on them overnight. The same guards kept the uninvited at bay during the wedding and reception. Guests were treated to caviar and champagne. Vodka flowed from a tiny fountain. A unique touch was an hors d'oeuvres table laden with hand-sculpted, deep-fried potatoes in the shapes of elephants, ducks, horses and chickens. The food was kosher, having been brought 150 kilometres from Hamilton, because there were no kosher caterers in London.

When guests sat down for dinner, they were entertained by an ensemble from Orchestra London. For dessert, they were invited to create their own sundaes from a make-it-yourself ice-cream table. While it wasn't the largest wedding ever staged at the estate, it was by far the most elaborate. Baltman and Melnitzer presided over the event with regal grace, quietly satisfied they had succeeded in their bid to impress. Notably absent among the family members was Melnitzer's daughter Melissa, then 16.

Married life did not appreciably change their relationship. Aside from his willingness to let her keep her name and have half his assets, Melnitzer's life with Baltman was rather traditional, yet full of contradictions. He later tried to explain it to bankers and their lawyers.

"My wife's never had her own bank account. I took the position from the moment she moved in that whatever was hers was mine. I don't have a marriage contract. I don't believe in them. I suppose it's somewhat the same attitude I have toward the law firm. It's not particularly healthy.

"But my wife has never had a bank account. She's never applied for credit on her own. She has no liabilities. She has put all, every cent she ever made went into the bank account at the CIBC and anything that I ever purchased, the intention was always — and that's what I promised her when she discussed it — that it was half and half.

"I always made sure that she had no liabilities because she's not sophisticated in that regard. She was a litigation lawyer — a young litigation lawyer. But all the assets, particularly the personal ones, were ours together."

Melnitzer was clearly trying to preserve the interests of his wife after his fall, but his explanation of their financial arrangement also demonstrated the dominant position he held in their relationship. By controlling the banking, Melnitzer had been able to manipulate his funds without having to answer difficult questions from his spouse.

Baltman had always been fascinated with theatre and Melnitzer didn't discourage her interest. She became involved in amateur productions in London through the Players' Guild at the University of Western Ontario, where she played the only female part in *The Rainmaker*. Baltman appeared in a number of productions mounted by the London Community Players, including the role of the maid in *Arms and the Man* and one of three roles in an original one-act production called *A Play on Words*. When she was mentioned in reviews, the comments were always positive. She took acting classes in London under Martha Henry, the great lady of Canadian stage who came to be the artistic director of the Grand Theatre. Henry later described Baltman as "good, honest and remarkably hardworking." She appreciated the young woman's determination to learn the craft. Baltman took time from her law practice for acting classes at the Royal Academy of Dramatic Arts in London, England, and attended acting workshops and seminars in Toronto when possible. Her new husband encouraged her every step of the way.

When Melnitzer's work demanded increasing amounts of time in Toronto, Baltman frequently joined him, making connections in the theatre community there. In 1986, the couple purchased a condominium in the trendy Yorkville area as their Toronto base. Five years later, after forsaking law entirely to pursue a career in acting, Baltman landed a starring role in the Toronto Fringe Festival production of *Two Small Bodies*. The part required her to appear nude in one scene, but Melnitzer didn't seem to object. As always, he was completely supportive, throwing a lavish party at their new Toronto home to celebrate the opening.

On the surface, Melnitzer seemed happy and dedicated to

his young wife. On occasion, he let it slip in conversation that they were thinking of starting a family and that he was excited by the prospect. Baltman also told some of her friends she was considering motherhood.

Melnitzer was a great one for giving expensive gifts to the two women closest to him. In addition to jewelry, he purchased a $28,000 sports car for Melissa in 1990. She was a student at the University of Toronto at the time. A few months later, he presented a $26,000 sports sedan to Baltman. But his new wife and daughter were not the only women in his life. Melnitzer had not lost his roving eye.

Social scientists speculate that many superachievers, those driven to success, have strong libidos. Studies of competitive athletes have uncovered a connection between aggressiveness and hormones. Tests reveal such competitors have significantly higher than average levels of testosterone, the male sex hormone. On a hunch, James M. Dabbs Jr., a psychology professor at Georgia State University, recently tested the testosterone levels of lawyers, based on his theory that they are a particularly competitive breed. He discovered they have elevated testosterone levels. And he found that within the profession, lawyers who do battle in the courtroom have higher levels than those who seldom venture from the office.

Dabbs shared his findings with the *Lawyers Weekly*, a Canadian publication of news of interest to the profession, noting that testosterone "is related to competitiveness and also to success in competition." A male with high testosterone "would be a controlling, dominating, aggressive type of person," he said. "The higher-testosterone men tend to have more unstable marriages, more divorces, separations, trouble with their wives, leave their wives, more affairs."

The professor was describing many lawyers who work in the adversarial pit known as the courtroom. He was certainly describing Julius Melnitzer.

About the time Melnitzer married Baltman, he began working with a number of accountants. He knew that commercial crime was a growth industry, yet many lawyers felt ill-equipped to defend such cases. Forensic accounting was a specialized field that could be of assistance to the defence, he believed. Working with experts in the field, he began designing and presenting training programs relating to the role, responsibility and use of accounting experts in civil and criminal litigation. Some of his work was as a member of the Advocates Society, a group dedicated to the development of continuing legal education and training for lawyers.

His work resulted in requests for him to speak at seminars and groups considering the legal issues relating to accounting. Among the organizations with which he worked was the forensic accounting department of Ernst and Young, the chartered accountants, at their main Toronto office. Late in 1989, he was conducting a seminar there when his eyes landed on clerk-secretary Calla Reid. He managed to obtain an introduction to the strikingly attractive Reid, a woman in in her mid-20s, and asked her to join him for lunch. Within weeks, Melnitzer had begun an affair with Reid that quickly developed into an intense relationship.

The lawyer was at his attentive and generous best. He gave her the usual gifts of flowers and jewelry. But that didn't seem to be enough and he was determined to impress upon this young woman that he was a very wealthy man. On November 30 that year, he wrote Reid the first of what would be a long line of cheques. It was for $2500. Within a week, he gave her $52,799 more to purchase a luxury BMW car. More cheques for several thousand dollars followed, and in February, he purchased a $475,000 condominium for her. The condo, on St. Clair Avenue just west of Yonge Street, was an eighth-floor penthouse. He gave her another $10,000 for furnishings.

Confronted much later about the payments to Reid, Melnitzer explained that the condominium was a gift to "ease the pain" Reid was bound to feel at their impending breakup. He said the relationship had ended by March, when he wrote her another cheque for $27,500. But the string of cheques continued. He sent Reid monthly payments of $2500 and at the end of January 1991, added two cheques totalling $52,500. The monthly allowances ended in July 1991, when Melnitzer wrote Reid a final cheque for $100,000, announcing it would be his last. The payments traced to Reid during the 20-month period totalled $759,415.

During his relationship with the Toronto woman, Melnitzer was unable to hide the fact that he was married, but he was vague as possible about his spouse, telling Reid not to be concerned, that his wife would soon be out of the picture. He was successful in keeping his liaison with Reid from Baltman, probably because his wife was preoccupied with her acting and travelled in a different circle of friends. When his financial empire later collapsed, Melnitzer was aghast when the court-appointed receiver uncovered the payments to Reid. He negotiated an arrangement with the receivers and the Mounties that kept the secret from Baltman for several months. But Melnitzer soon discovered he couldn't keep it quiet indefinitely and told Baltman about Reid shortly before her lawyer was to find out. Despite the revelation, Baltman decided to stand by him.

After Melnitzer's arrest and the publicity that surrounded it, the brass at Ernst and Young were concerned the company's name might get dragged into the Melnitzer morass because they employed his mistress. Reid was asked to reconsider her future and her employment was eventually terminated.

The court-appointed forensic accountants unleashed on Melnitzer's banking records also turned up another form of indiscretion, one that Melnitzer was more successful in keeping out of the press.

They found he had written cheques totalling $138,000 to Interfaces, an escort agency in New York City. Its advertisement in the telephone book claims their service is "available worldwide." The cheques stretched over a period of about 18 months, starting in late 1989. One of them was for more than $12,000, and another, written on a joint account he shared with Baltman, had her name blacked out.

When confronted with the Interfaces payments, he was even angrier than he had been about the discovery of the cheques traced to Reid. Melnitzer insisted he knew nothing about Interfaces, suggesting it was probably a company related to one of the art dealers in New York with whom he had ongoing dealings. He pointed out that on one date in question, he hadn't been in New York at all. Given the complexities of Melnitzer's finances, the investigators didn't feel this explanation advanced matters much one way or another.

Initial inquiries into Melnitzer's dealings with Interfaces were stonewalled by a lack of co-operation, and pursuit of the intriguing link was discontinued. On the criminal side, the Mounties already had enough information on Melnitzer to support a conviction on the forgery, fraud and attempted fraud counts. There was nothing to be gained by looking more deeply into the Interfaces connection. The prosecutor had few resources to expend on international fishing expeditions, no matter how interesting. The receiver and its lawyers wanted to pursue the New York angle, in case the money spent there was derived from fraud and possibly recoverable, but they were abruptly forced to withdraw from the case by unexpected developments in the bankruptcy proceedings.

Melnitzer's pursuit of the good life was total. He had sought prestige, power and money, and he knew some women were attracted to all three, a fact that made his continual pursuit of them all that much easier. And besides, being seen in the company of attractive women reinforced the successful outward appearance he'd worked so hard to cultivate.

7

Money and Ego

"I understood appearances."

By the late 1970s, Melnitzer had elbowed his way into the London legal community, but he was still frustrated by the amount of time it was taking to get where he wanted to go. At the time, the firm was settling into its new Dundas Street offices and his first two Supreme Court of Canada cases were just around the corner. But Melnitzer was constantly measuring himself against the top lawyers in town and wondering how long it would be before he would overtake them in reputation and earning power. He felt it would take another five to seven years to be the undisputed big fish in this pond, the guy at the top of the biggest law firm in town.

To build such a firm in a short time, he needed more than hard work. He needed money. Money would fuel the firm's growth, help it find even larger quarters, permit the purchase of smaller practices and generally make Cohen, Melnitzer appear to be a vibrant, booming organization, which in turn would draw more lawyers to generate more money for the firm. He wondered if his own law practice could produce the kind of funds he would need to reinvest in the firm to speed its growth.

He was disappointed when he heard estimates of salaries earned by London's top lawyers. Few, he discovered, made much more than $125,000. And most of them were in corporate, commercial law and in litigation, not criminal law. Many of the wealthiest lawyers earned a substantial portion of their incomes outside law, in real estate or other investments.

With his drive, intelligence and fierce attachment to the work ethic, Melnitzer was confident that he, too, could make a lot of money. From his childhood days playing Monopoly, Melnitzer had appreciated the sense of power that flows from a fat bank acccount. But you need to have money to make money.

Unwilling to limit his financial horizons by concentrating his energies exclusively on law, Melnitzer had already made a number of minor investments, primarily in real estate. He was spurred on by his father's success in the later years of his life, parlaying modest savings and loans into a private family firm, Melfan Investments. Melnitzer was given a 25 percent share in the company, but that was later reduced to 20 percent when his sister, Roslyn, was added as a shareholder. He used his holding in Melfan as collateral on loans. In addition, to keep money available for investments, he, Cathy and Melissa stayed in their rental home a few years longer than necessary, living well below their means.

At the time, the gold and silver markets looked inviting, and Melnitzer dabbled successfully in both. Profits were rolled over and ploughed back into commodities or real estate. He established several numbered companies as his investment vehicles and began borrowing, his loans guaranteed by his wife's family, to fund his financial forays. Melnitzer had been dealing with the Bank of Montreal since moving to London in 1974. Not long afterward, the bank granted him a $100,000 personal line of credit, taking as security a hodgepodge of pledges relating to his increasingly varied investments, but basing the loan primarily on his earning power as a lawyer.

A personal line of credit is similar to having overdraft privileges. Also known as a revolving demand loan, revolving reducing demand loan or revolving investment loan, it allows the borrower to withdraw funds up to an agreed limit and the bank collects interest only on the money actually taken. The line of credit can be withdrawn on a demand basis if, for instance, the bank feels funds aren't being used for the purposes originally indicated by the customer. The advantage to the bank is that a credit line encourages a customer to use bank money and thereby incur interest, which makes the bank more profitable. The advantage for the customer is that he or she pays interest only on the funds actually advanced. And the money is as available as the customer's chequebook or credit card.

With interest rates only slightly above prime, a personal line of credit can seem like easy money. The borrower can spend on a whim, and the bank doesn't discourage it. The more the customer spends, the more the bank earns. Under such an arrangement, there is little incentive for responsible lending or responsible spending.

As his financial requirements grew ever greater, Melnitzer succumbed more and more to the lure of lines of credit. His investment successes, particularly in precious metals and real estate, led him to believe he had a flair for business. And, of course, every time he did well, he told his partners.

Within his first few years in London, Melnitzer met Allan Richman, a businessman with whom he developed an instant rapport. Richman, owner of Forward Properties, was a financier who dealt in second mortgages and who owned a number of properties in the London area, mainly rental. He was a money-man who had played the real estate market well and was always willing to entertain new investment ideas. Melnitzer, he discovered, had plenty of those.

Richman's investment horizons were somewhat wider

than Melnitzer's at the time. He spoke of opportunities in the western United States, where he had some contacts. Melnitzer agreed to investigate the possibilities with his newfound friend, and in 1978 the pair visited the Grand Canyon. Melnitzer enjoyed travel and had always longed to see the Arizona landmark. As the two walked along the rim of the canyon, at times oblivious to the spectacular scenery, they talked about money.

"Real estate is the only sure thing these days," Richman said at one point when they paused for a rest. "Gold, silver, the stock market, it may look good for a while but it's no way to earn money. Too affected by outside factors. And what's hot one year may not be hot the next. Land, my friend, land is forever."

Melnitzer surveyed nature's handiwork laid out before them. "Well, they're not making it anymore, that's for sure," he said. "Certainly not like this."

"So, do you think we could be partners?" Richman asked. "With my money and contacts and your ideas, I know we can make a pile. What do you say?"

Melnitzer didn't need coaxing. "Deal," he replied without hesitation. The pair cemented their bond with a handshake.

Within a matter of months, Grand Canyon Investments was formed, owned equally by Richman and Melnitzer. Primarily a property development company, it was based in London, where it acquired a number of properties. Its holdings would eventually include choice real estate in the Utah community of Park City, a suburb of Salt Lake City. The pair enjoyed skiing, so Park City was ideal. Located near the Wasatch Mountains, with their 3000-metre peaks, it was Utah's premier winter sports area. Two condominiums and some vacant land were acquired near the ultraexclusive Deer Valley resort. Melnitzer later took winter holidays there, bringing along friends and clients he wanted to impress. Grand Canyon also jointly owned a 100-unit condominium development in Tacoma, Washington, with a firm based in Vancouver, British Columbia.

Even as their dealings increased, Melnitzer and Richman continued to operate on the basis of trust. Few of their arrangements were formalized on documents. Melnitzer began telling his new partner about some of his father's investments and shrewd real estate transactions in Quebec. Richman saw Melnitzer as a budding entrepreneur who lacked nothing but cash. He admired the young lawyer's drive, knowledge of tax laws and innovative ideas. Richman began lending him money for a variety of investments. The loans were secured by Melnitzer's promissory notes, some for a few thousand dollars repayable in a couple of months, others in the tens of thousands for one-year terms. Melnitzer rewarded his partner's assistance by willingly paying the inflated interest rates Richman demanded — 27.5 to 33 percent.

Richman was told that much of the money was being placed with the New York City accounting firm of Price Waterhouse, where Melnitzer had a contact with a nose for good investments. As the Melnitzer-Richman relationship matured, and the amount of money being advanced steadily increased, Richman began asking for more security. Melnitzer responded by producing a document from Melfan Investments that guaranteed his debts. He said he was president of Melfan and so could obligate the family firm in this way. Richman, assured by this arrangement, continued to advance more funds.

Not until much later did Richman learn Melnitzer had deceived him completely: the Price Waterhouse deals never existed; Melnitzer was not president of Melfan; and he wasn't legally able to guarantee anything on the company's behalf. Nor was Melfan worth anything near what Melnitzer had claimed.

As the 1980s began, Melnitzer's personal financial pressures threatened to smother any hopes of financing his own game plan. Not only did the Clearview Crescent home carry an unwieldy mortgage, some of his business investments began to sour, particularly the commodities. In the first months of 1980, silver plunged in value, from a high of nearly $50 U.S. an ounce to $8 an ounce. Gold and stocks also took a beating. High interest rates curbed development, reducing the value of his real estate holdings and ensuring that his carrying costs skyrocketed. Aside from the financial burden of maintaining two households after his marriage break-down, Melnitzer knew he would have to replace the $400,000 in loan guarantees provided by Cathy's family — plus pay the additional expenses of wooing and winning Deena Baltman.

At Cohen, Melnitzer, he was not billing as much as he needed to meet these commitments. To build his reputation, he was pursuing cases with high profile but low return. The most notable was the Boggs case, but there were others on which he was spending time without payment. Meanwhile, Cohen, Melnitzer, like many other businesses, was not being spared the effects of the recession.

Early in 1980, Melnitzer had been elected to the board of directors of Vanguard Trust, a firm with which Cohen, Melnitzer had been dealing for some time. He was allotted 23,810 treasury shares, each worth $2, and had obtained a company seal, which appeared on official Vanguard docu-ments. Three years later, just as he was becoming desperate for funds, a fellow director offered to buy his shares. Melnitzer jumped at the offer and resigned from the board. He surrendered all but a handful of his shares, and proceeds from the sale helped fund his divorce settlement. However, he did not surrender the company seal.

He began creating fake share certificates by merely typing share amounts in the same standard fill-in-the-blank form used by Vanguard and by other small companies that did not have custom-designed share certificates. Vanguard's corpo-rate seal, of course, made them look authentic. His first forgery, dated April 10, 1981, was for 55,000 shares of Van-guard. A second, produced a year later, was for 138,000 shares. Two more, created later in 1982, were for 200,000 shares each. A last, dated 1985, was for 300,000 shares. At

$2 a share, the forged certificates had a face value of nearly
$1.8 million. As his appetite for cash grew, Melnitzer was
soon offering the forged Vanguard certificates and Melfan
documents, including forged financial statements vastly
overstating Melfan's worth, to banks as collateral for personal lines of credit.

Meanwhile, he was constantly bragging about investment
successes to his law partners. Seeing how he'd kept revenue
flowing into the firm during the recession of 1981, the
partners felt Melnitzer must have business smarts equal to
his legal knowledge. He offered them a chance to take part
in various real estate ventures and seemed to have a knack
for producing the returns he promised.

One major exception became evident in 1982, when
Melnitzer and his partners invested in an English-style pub
and nightclub in a working-class section of east London, just
off the Dundas Street strip of muffler shops, car dealers and
burger joints. On opening night, Melnitzer and his fellow
investors were tuxedoed for the invitation-only gala, but the
celebration soon went off the rails when a bunch of neighborhood toughs crashed the party. A rumble erupted, patrons
were roughed up and police had to be called to quell the
disturbance. The following morning, the law offices of
Cohen, Melnitzer were filled with long faces. Among them
was Fletcher Dawson's. He sat with head in hands, saying
over and over, "What have we gotten ourselves into?" The
venture never recovered from its raucous beginning. A bad
reputation was hard to shake and the nightclub slipped
steadily downhill. It was sold many months later at a loss
and became a strip parlor.

Melnitzer was stung by this turn of events. This was not
the sort of investment with which he wanted his name or
those of his friends and associates linked. He vowed there
would be no repeat. From then on, he guaranteed that anyone
who placed funds with him received at least the promised
return. Sometimes more. There would be more bad investments, but he absorbed the losses himself. To pay off his

various business partners, including Allan Richman, he began borrowing money from other investors and financial institutions. He wouldn't betray the trust of his friends again, even if he had to commit fraud to avoid doing so.

In April 1984, just as arrangements were being finalized for his divorce, Melnitzer approached the Canadian Imperial Bank of Commerce about obtaining a personal line of credit. His $100,000 credit line at the Bank of Montreal was no longer sufficient to meet his needs. He couldn't use the phoney Melfan documents with the Bank of Montreal because Melfan did its banking there and the risk of his forgeries being detected was too high.

It was becoming clear to Melnitzer that he was slipping into a financial hole so deep that only a miracle investment, a "killer deal," could extricate him. But the miracle never came, and instead he continued to borrow more money from the eager banks. Melnitzer told the CIBC he was seeking a line of credit of $250,000. As collateral, he pledged one share of Melfan and 455,000 shares of Vanguard. The bank didn't bother to check the authenticity of the shares; it had no reason to doubt the successful lawyer's word. Melnitzer was a founding member of a growing law firm with a solid income, and that was good enough for their lending officers. Besides, the CIBC was anxious to woo Melnitzer away from the Bank of Montreal. Asking too many questions might annoy the new client. Melnitzer was pleasantly surprised at how accommodating the CIBC was. Not long afterward, he obtained yet another line of credit. This one, for $100,000, was arranged at the Toronto Dominion Bank on the basis of a personal financial statement that grossly exaggerated his assets.

Within months, Melnitzer had persuaded the Bank of Montreal to bump his $100,000 line of credit to $250,000. For this, in October 1985, he presented as collateral a share certificate for 138,000 shares of Vanguard Trust, three shares in an Ontario numbered company and a personal guarantee of his debts by his father. The pace was quickening.

Professionally, Melnitzer was increasingly busy, spending more and more of his time representing landlords in their battles with a provincial government they believed was developing sympathies for the newly vocal tenant-advocacy groups. He represented the landlords at the Thom Commission of Inquiry into Residential Tenancies, in its review of rental policies, and on the province's Rent Review Advisory Committee. Then he became counsel to Ontario's largest landlord lobby group, the Fair Rental Policy Organization, denouncing continued rent controls as unfair.

In June 1987, Melnitzer approached the National Bank of Canada, seeking a credit line of $2 million. The bank agreed, taking as security 12 preferred shares of Melfan Investments, a guarantee from Melfan that it would cover Melnitzer's debts up to $2 million, with supporting documents from Melfan authorizing the guarantee. All were forged. The money was used for a string of investments, among them the $2.8-million purchase, with Richman, of a 102-unit London apartment building.

Within two years, the lawyer approached the Royal Bank of Canada, looking for a $3-million line of credit. The banker with whom Melnitzer dealt later conceded he had relied on word of mouth that his potential client was a wealthy man. After several months of negotiations, the Royal granted the credit line, first obtaining a fistful of security. Among the forged documents it accepted were a guarantee of the debt by Melfan, a list of Melfan directors, Melfan financial statements and a statement of Melnitzer's personal financial affairs.

Melnitzer had begun to realize he would never live up to his own expectations. No one knew better than he the extent of his failures as a businessman, and these tormented him. He didn't have the intuition or the business savvy of his father. His determination to succeed had clouded his better judgment. He stuck with investments longer than he should, hoping for the big turnarounds that never came. Fortunately, the banks were like a safety net, standing by with their money, ever ready to bail him out. He covered his mistakes with their money.

He knew that, aside from the requirement that he pay them back, the bankers also expected him to look super-successful. "At a certain point, I realized that the bank wouldn't lend you any money unless you looked like you had it, so I started spending," he later said under oath. To the Mounties he admitted, "I sometimes spent money on things I didn't want to spend [on], you know, because I think, unfortunately, I understood appearances."

And so he played the part. Conspicuous consumption became his way of life. He ditched his compact Gremlin and Duster cars for expensive imports and began buying tailor-made suits despite his personal preference for loafers, jeans and sweatshirts. When a group of friends or business associates dined out, he insisted on picking up the tab. He nearly wore out his American Express and other credit cards, ringing up monthly bills of about $25,000.

Melnitzer had always been impressed by people who collected art, although he was the first to admit his knowledge of the art world was minimal. He began to look to art as an investment that might help him out of his bind. "At a certain point I figured I would have to make a very big killing to get the money out of this [situation]," he said later under oath. "I'd done a fair bit of research about it, and I felt that one of the best ways to do it in the long run was art. I felt that art, properly bought, had enormous capital-appreciation value. It went up and down, but at the right time, you know, there were crazies around who'd pay all kinds of money for it. The other thing about buying art was you didn't have to involve anybody else. There were no mortgages involved. You could control the whole thing yourself."

Melnitzer read everything he could find on art investment. His conclusion was that art seemed virtually immune to the violent dips that plague real estate, commodities and stock markets. He plunged into art like the "crazies" he later described, working through dealers in Toronto and New York City, purchasing paintings he liked and believed held investment potential.

Among his many acquisitions were five original oil paintings by Leroy Neiman — *French Cafe, Bistro Garden, Superplay-Night Football, Down Hill Skiing,* and *French Hunt Scene* — which he insured for $240,000, $234,000, $210,000, $67,000 and $66,000, respectively. Also purchased were two colored, limited-edition lithographs, *Femme au cirque* and *Les Equilibristes,* signed by Marc Chagall, with a total insured value of $70,000.

His new passion for art dovetailed nicely with his long-delayed desire to see the world. With Baltman at his side, he began taking extended vacations, visiting Europe, Russia, Hawaii, Israel, the Far East, North Africa and, of course, Utah. By late in the decade, the two were spending 11 weeks of the year on their globe-trotting forays. Airfares alone totalled about $40,000 a year, and they made it a habit to stay at the very finest hotels. While on these trips, Melnitzer and Baltman continued collecting pieces of art that struck their fancy. Whenever he crossed borders, Melnitzer was absolutely scrupulous in abiding by customs rules. When he returned to Canada, he would hold up other travellers by declaring a purchase as inconsequential as a pair of socks or a *Time* magazine.

The couple's taste in art was diverse. Among the nearly 150 pieces they collected were Venetian glass, wood carvings from Bali, a marble coffee table from India, soapstone carvings from the Northwest Territories, Moroccan daggers and rugs, Thai wood carvings and sculptures, Chinese clocks and candelabra, a Quebec pine cupboard from the mid-1800s, a pure silk hand-knotted Kashmir carpet and a Japanese Meiji-period cloisonné bowl. Partway through their accumulation, Sotheby's appraised the collection at $750,000. To be on the safe side, however, Melnitzer insured everything for $2 million.

Melnitzer found his artwork to be valuable in ways beyond

its intrinsic value. He made sure his investment was displayed prominently. It wasn't tucked away in a bank like investment certificates; it wasn't a vacant parcel of land many miles distant; it wasn't precious metal that few would see. Instead, it was nicely conspicuous and demonstrated that he was a man of culture and taste.

Visitors to his home or office couldn't miss some of the pieces. Several were bizarre enough to provoke comment, the large Thai and Burmese wood carvings in particular. Melnitzer proudly showed off the collection, carefully noting the country of origin. His less than subtle message was that he not only had culture and taste, he also had enough time and money to scour the globe to find it.

With the bank's money at his disposal, Melnitzer could afford to be philanthropic. Besides being a strong supporter of the theatre and orchestra, he gave to the London Foundation, a group that supported a wide variety of community works, and the National Ballet of Canada. He also made substantial contributions to several Jewish organizations and to other theatre groups in London and elsewhere.

By far the most favored recipient of his largesse was the Grand Theatre. At his urging, Cohen, Melnitzer became one of the theatre's most significant sponsors, once a year taking 500 invited guests to a special performance. Melnitzer felt that support for the theatre was good promotion for himself and for the firm. The theatre attracted a well-heeled crowd, and it didn't hurt the firm's profile to have its name listed as a sponsor alongside some of the city's most prestigious companies. An added bonus was that his support for the theatre pleased Baltman.

One bit of Melnitzer's investment-philanthropy made headlines. In 1989, he was approached by an oral surgeon named Harold Gretzinger, who'd heard of the lawyer's wealth and interest in the arts. Gretzinger practised in Sarnia, where Melnitzer was spending time arguing the Grand Bend beach case. Gretzinger brought along with him a dental colleague, Lennie Slipacoff. Gretzinger had a proposition for the high-profile lawyer. Would Melnitzer be interested in obtaining a one-third share in an original Stradivarius violin the two Sarnians had purchased for $450,000 U.S.?

The instrument had been made by Italian violin maker Antonio Stradivari in 1688, at the start of his career, Gretzinger explained. Only about 650 violins made by the famed craftsman still survive, few of them the smaller, more delicate type that characterized his first models. The instrument was in excellent condition and had been played in recent years; it wasn't just a museum piece. Gretzinger, a former member of the National Youth Orchestra, was excited about his find but needed a third partner.

Melnitzer mulled over the prospect. The more he thought about it, the more he liked it. Such a violin, he reasoned, was truly a work of art. It could only escalate in value. And wouldn't the folks at Orchestra London be impressed? Perhaps someone there would like to play it. This was an opportunity he wasn't about to miss. He jumped in with $150,000 U.S.

The violin would become a marketing tool for Cohen, Melnitzer to underline its support for the arts. Orchestra London was interested in a joint promotion when the subject was broached. A press conference was called at the Cohen, Melnitzer law offices to announce that the instrument would be lent to the orchestra for the 1990-91 season for use by concertmaster Joseph Lanza. On hand for the announcement were Lanza and principal conductor Uri Mayer. Melnitzer himself stood back and let his founding partners, Harris Cohen and Ron Delanghe, make the formal presentation to the two men. Lanza then obliged the press by demonstrating his virtuosity on the Stradivarius. "This instrument is so responsive," Lanza gushed. "It suggests to you possibilities and colors. It opens up your imagination to a new range of music ideas."

Lanza's idea was to start performing with the instrument

JULIUS MELNITZER
"Neither a borrower nor a lender be, just help yourself." PROTO: Teachers' Pet. FAV. PAST: Cutting Classes. AMB: Surgeon. DEST: Cutting Classes. ACT: Jr. Chess Club, U.N. Club, Public Speaking Club, Intermural Basketball & Football, Jr. Basketball Team, Class V. P., Class Sports.

At age 16 Julius Melnitzer graduated from high school in Montreal. He was known as a bright student who cut classes to shoot pool. The inscription in his high school yearbook was ironic, given his later abilities to borrow vast sums of money based on forged documents.

The Melnitzer home at 4841 Kent Avenue in Montreal. The family continued to live in the lower right unit of the brick fourplex long after many neighbors had moved on to more fashionable sections of the city. Melnitzer's mother was still living there when he was arrested. (DAVID REICH)

In early 1976, at age 28, the young lawyer had just opened his law practice in London with partner Harris Cohen. He made his name quickly, working extremely hard and taking on high-profile criminal cases.
(LONDON FREE PRESS COLLECTION OF PHOTOGRAPHIC NEGATIVES, D. B. WELDON LIBRARY, UNIVERSITY OF WESTERN ONTARIO)

When restrictions were removed on advertising by lawyers, Melnitzer hired a marketing firm to promote the services of Cohen, Melnitzer. Early in 1987 the firm took the daring step of installing billboards around London, including this one directly across the street from the courthouse. (LONDON FREE PRESS COLLECTION OF PHOTOGRAPHIC NEGATIVES, D. B. WELDON LIBRARY, UNIVERSITY OF WESTERN ONTARIO)

Melnitzer at his custom-made pine desk. The Mounties would later find, in a lower drawer, close to $100 million in forged stock certificates. The photographs on his desk are of Deena Baltman, his second wife (right), and his daughter, Melissa. The stuffed animal was one of many owned by the aggressive lawyer, revealing a softer, boyish side.
(© THE LONDON FREE PRESS. PHOTO BY SUSAN BRADNAM)

Melnitzer became a highly visible spokesperson for an Ontario landlord group, representing their interests against the provincial government's plan to extend rent controls. He started as counsel to the group and was later pressured into becoming its chairperson. (© THE LONDON FREE PRESS. PHOTO BY SUE REEVE)

The sign on his office door tells it all. As a lawyer, Melnitzer was aggressive, hardworking and totally ethical. As an investor who wheeled and dealed with money he obtained from bankers and friends, he demonstrated different moral principles. (© THE LONDON FREE PRESS. PHOTO BY SUSAN BRADNAM)

The home on Tallwood Road in London. Melnitzer and Baltman crammed their home with paintings, objects d'art and mementoes of their globe-trotting lifestyle. They valued the artwork at $2 million, but a receiver later estimated it at a few hundred thousand.

Melnitzer and his wife pose with their English bull terriers Barney and Maude.
(© THE LONDON FREE PRESS. PHOTO BY SUSAN BRADNAM)

And clown at the grand piano during a photo shoot for a magazine article that saluted Melnitzer's legal accomplishments.
(© THE LONDON FREE PRESS. PHOTO BY SUSAN BRADNAM)

Melnitzer demonstrates his musical abilities on the guitar. Although he had little formal music training, Melnitzer jokingly bragged about having written several pop tunes, among them "Hotel California," which was recorded by the Eagles. (© THE LONDON FREE PRESS. PHOTO BY SUSAN BRADNAM)

Some of Melnitzer's activities have been likened to those of Charles Ponzi, the smooth-talking 1920 Boston swindler who devised a pyramid scheme that bilked investors out of close to $15 million. Ponzi's fraud collapsed under its own weight, and he died a pauper.

Melnitzer faces the microphones after his victory late in 1990 in a landmark property rights case on behalf of beach owner Archie Gibbs. It was unquestionably the biggest case of his career, and Melnitzer celebrated with a big party and a self-congratulatory newspaper advertisement. Receivers later found he was paying the fees of Gibbs and others.

(© THE LONDON FREE PRESS. PHOTO BY SUE REEVE)

Melnitzer and partner Russell Raikes upon hearing they had won the Grand Bend beach case. Raikes did most of the legwork and research, while Melnitzer carried the ball in court.

(© THE LONDON FREE PRESS. PHOTO BY SUSAN BRADNAM)

The impressive house in Toronto that Melnitzer acquired early in 1991. He paid $1.85 million and persuaded the Toronto Dominion Bank to grant him a mortgage of $1.5 million, with the promise the bank would not require him to furnish any financial information. (JULIE MATUS)

Considered by some a publicity hound, Melnitzer became distinctly media-shy following his arrest. Here he attempts to race past a CBC cameraman after his court appearance in September 1991. He ripped the viewfinder off another camera the same day. (© THE LONDON FREE PRESS. PHOTO BY GEORGE BLUMSON)

Melnitzer mugs for the photographer at Grand Bend, his marketing man not far away, encouraging him. (© THE LONDON FREE PRESS. PHOTO BY SUSAN BRADNAM)

A sombre-looking Melnitzer arrives at the London courthouse in December 1991 to plead guilty to his crimes. By confessing at an early stage, he was able to obtain the best possible deal at sentencing time. (© The London Free Press. Photo by Morris Lamont)

After pleading guilty, Melnitzer slips out a back door at the London courthouse to his wife's car, a gift from the once high-flying lawyer. (© The London Free Press. Photo by Morris Lamont)

Sergeant Ray Porter of the Royal Canadian Mounted Police was assigned to investigate what turned out to be the biggest bank fraud in North America. In addition to two boxes of documents, Porter collected many more boxes of forged stock certificates, $1.1 billion in total. (© THE LONDON FREE PRESS. PHOTO BY MICHAEL JORDAN)

Beaver Creek institution, the minimum-security prison to which Melnitzer was directed less than two months after receiving his nine-year prison term. Prisoners have keys to their rooms and access to a golf course next door. Melnitzer's plans for early release received a setback when he got into a fight with the only other lawyer in the 120-inmate facility.

immediately. He hoped to get as much mileage out of the violin as possible. The Stradivarius would draw crowds and enhance the orchestra's reputation. Within days, the Stradivarius made its first public appearance, as Lanza played solos during Prokofiev's *Romeo and Juliet.* A week later, Lanza appeared with another violinist who played a 1717 Stradivarius valued at $500,000, which had been lent to him by the Canada Council. The "duelling Strads," as the press billed them, played to a packed house and attracted coverage from CBC television's nightly news program "The Journal." The orchestra was delighted with the attention. So was Melnitzer. Lanza used the violin in countless appearances with the orchestra and with a chamber music ensemble.

Officially, the public was told the Gretzinger-Melnitzer Stradivarius had been provided by an "anonymous group of area collectors." But the secret wasn't well kept and the arts community soon learned of the Cohen, Melnitzer connection. Melnitzer wasn't the least bit upset at the revelation.

Gretzinger had his own reason to be pleased with the arrangement. In exchange, he received free violin lessons from Lanza. Eventually, Gretzinger bought out Slipacoff, while Melnitzer sold one-third of his interest to Allan Richman. Melnitzer was happy to let Gretzinger retain control of the instrument and deal directly with Orchestra London. He was terrified of the possibility of the violin's getting damaged, and lost some of his enthusiasm once he discovered the tax implications of this investment.

By the end of the decade, Melnitzer was borrowing and investing at an ever-increasing pace. He was operating on $5.6 million in lines of credit, plus millions more obtained from Richman and other investors. His schemes relied on the trust placed in him by friends, associates, partners and the banks. He was living the good life on other people's money. To others, he appeared a complete success. But in his heart, Melnitzer knew much of it was bogus, and he feared he might somehow be unmasked. He continued in the hope of soon ending his deceptions with a master stroke, something to demonstrate clearly his business acumen. His restless mind told him bigger risks were required if he was ever to gain big profit. He dedicated himself anew to realizing his financial dreams.

The stage was set for Melnitzer to pull off something truly extraordinary.

8

Never Enough

". . . too good to be true . . . "

B Y 1990, COHEN, MELNITZER was the fourth-largest law firm in London. With 22 lawyers and a support staff of more than 50, it was well placed to continue its drive to become the biggest.

More than ever, the engine powering the growth was Melnitzer, despite the increasing amount of time he was spending in Toronto with the landlord group, the Fair Rental Policy Organization. In November, he was pressured into accepting the unpaid position of the group's chairman. He was flattered at the recognition of his work for the lobby, but there would be less time available for the law practice and the billings it could generate.

Nevertheless, at his behest, Cohen, Melnitzer had arranged to take the top two floors of what would become the city's tallest and most prestigious office tower. One London Place, an $80-million glass and steel structure of 24 storeys, was being built by London Life as its new headquarters.

The building, to be completed in 1992, was designed to

set new standards in office accommodation in the city — and tenants would be charged accordingly. Rent for the Cohen, Melnitzer floors was to be about $600,000 annually, substantial overhead for any business.

The money didn't faze Melnitzer. Not only would the new address give the firm instant prestige, it was a fitting place for a man who wanted the world to put him on a pedestal. Melnitzer looked forward to enjoying the view from the new perch, from which he could look down on the three law firms he sought to overtake.

Melnitzer, who earned at least $360,000 annually from the firm, also sent out its biggest bills, about 20 percent of the total. He constantly reminded the partners of that fact and that he collected nearly all his receivables. When the others didn't pursue their outstanding accounts with vigor, he complained bitterly. "Look," he'd say in exasperation, "this is a business, getting to be a big business. Let's act like business people."

He didn't tell his partners that he was increasingly paying his own accounts to ensure his receivables were in order, or that when necessary he would create fictitious accounts and pay them. A receiver later identified $3.7 million that Melnitzer paid into the firm. His partners thought the money was from clients.

Among those to draw his ire was Harris Cohen, his long-suffering founding partner. Cohen didn't care for open confrontation, so he let Melnitzer have his way in most things. Cohen saw his partner operating in overdrive, with so many irons in the fire it was nearly impossible to persuade him to take the time to sit down and talk things over. The halcyon days of the Embassy Tavern in Toronto were long gone. Melnitzer didn't laugh the way he used to. He was gruff and preoccupied most of the time.

Cohen was conservative and suspicious of anything that seemed too good to be true, so he rarely participated in Melnitzer's investment schemes. He was comfortable with himself and happy to earn a steady, if unspectacular, income.

He continued to let the billings question ride a bit, much to Melnitzer's annoyance, and dismissed his partner's angry tirades as the outbursts of a man who was overworked and overstressed.

Around the law office, Melnitzer seemed distant to many members of the staff. On occasion, however, he could surprise them with his interest. "I've seen him incredibly compassionate," said associate lawyer Russell Raikes. Not long after he joined the firm, Raikes lost a member of his family. Melnitzer became personally involved, offering to do whatever he could and insisting the young associate take the necessary time to recover. Raikes, deeply moved, never forgot that kindness.

But as the 1990s dawned, such instances of compassion were rare. Melnitzer had a lot on his mind, and staff members were inclined to let him initiate any conversation, rather than risk incurring the wrath of The Big Guy. During the Grand Bend trial, the usual routine was for Raikes to drive when he and Melnitzer travelled to Sarnia on Monday mornings. Melnitzer was famous for his black Monday-morning moods, and Raikes kept silent for the one-hour trip. To attempt conversation with his scowling senior colleague was dangerous. "I'd just get my head snapped off," Raikes would recall later.

It's easy to believe that Melnitzer had a lot on his mind. The receiver who later stepped in to try to unravel his affairs complained there was not much of a paper trail. Melnitzer kept poor records because, with his prodigious mental powers, he was able to keep everything organized in his mind.

Melnitzer knew he was calling all the shots at the firm and made no secret about his control. He'd been the dominant partner for years. Without consulting anyone else, he announced one day that Deena Baltman was joining the firm. Then he lectured the staff that she wasn't to get the sorts of files usually reserved for rookie lawyers. She was to be treated as nothing less than "Mrs. Melnitzer."

At gatherings such as staff parties, Melnitzer would be

openly critical of some of his associates, including Cohen. "You're drinking too much, Harris," Melnitzer would say in all seriousness, within earshot of others. In fact, neither Cohen nor Melnitzer drank much. But Melnitzer didn't mind embarrassing Cohen, whose contribution to the firm didn't measure up to his own workaholic standards.

Melnitzer became a fitness nut. He built a mirrored workout room in the basement of his home, complete with the latest in weight-lifting and exercise equipment. He and Deena even hired a personal trainer and became very concerned about their weight. If anyone at the firm put on a few pounds, Melnitzer was the first to say something. If he was making a sacrifice, others could do the same.

He continued to take on new investments. In an attempt to diversify his holdings, to lessen his reliance on land-based deals, he made forays into the stock market. In January 1990, he began investing in a firm known as RMG Entertainment Inc., in Toronto. Before the year was out, he had put $290,000 into the television production company, which specialized in family-entertainment programming for the Canadian market. RMG became involved in several projects, including two comedy series and a family drama, none of which reached the production stage. The company added a touch of glitz to Melnitzer's holdings, and he thought it might help Baltman in her acting career.

In February, Melnitzer sank $2.5 million into a photochemical company, Champion Chemtech Limited, a 10-year-old business in Mississauga, Ontario, that manufactured and distributed photographic chemicals. It also distributed photographic paper and some equipment. It was an upstart competitor for Kodak and Fuji, with subsidiaries in six countries. In exchange for his investment, Melnitzer received 25 percent of Champion's voting shares and a directorship in the private company.

In May, Melnitzer wrote a $1.1-million cheque to his own firm to cover Archie Gibbs's fees on the Grand Bend beach trial. But he immediately found he needed the funds for other purposes and promptly took it back. Many months later, he deposited the same amount into the firm and left it in.

The lending and borrowing with Allan Richman had now reached hundreds of thousands of dollars. The cumulative total over the years was well into the millions. Increasingly, however, the flow of money was now from Richman, Forward Properties or Grand Canyon Properties to Melnitzer, nearly all of it for the nonexistent New York City investments. The loans still carried the high interest rates Richman demanded. From 1989 to 1991, when Melnitzer was through siphoning money from Allan Richman for the fake Price Waterhouse deals, the total stood at $9.15 million.

Meanwhile, Melnitzer was attempting to obtain more funds from the Bank of Montreal. Early in the year, he provided personal financial statements to the bank indicating he had a net worth of $19 million. By September, he was back, trying to persuade the bank to increase his line of credit from $250,000 to $1 million. He presented a signed personal financial statement saying his net worth now stood at $24.4 million. He told the account manager with whom he was dealing that if the bank couldn't accommodate his request, he wanted the banker to return all his financial statements and promise that all information would be kept confidential.

The account manager reviewed the financial statements and made some preliminary inquiries about the Vanguard Trust shares. He discovered that Prenor Trust Company of Canada had acquired 99 percent of the shares in Vanguard. Yet Melnitzer claimed he held 14.6 percent. Rather than concluding he might have detected a case of fraud, the banker decided instead that Melnitzer's affairs were extremely complex and needed further review. He sought and continued to press for more detailed information, including an audited personal financial statement with a specific income and disbursement flow analysis. But the lawyer stalled. In the end, faced with a demand to produce the information, Melnitzer flew into a rage and paid off his existing $250,000 line of credit with a cheque drawn on the

CIBC. He demanded and received back all the documents he'd provided to the Bank of Montreal. Melnitzer was upset that his word had been doubted and vowed never to deal with the bank again. But never, he found, was a long time.

Within months Melnitzer's partner, Ron Delanghe, approached Norman Thompson, a vice-president at the Bank of Montreal, about setting up a meeting between Melnitzer and Thompson at which, Delanghe said, Melnitzer would be seeking a line of credit for $7 or $8 million. Thompson seemed willing to talk, so the meeting was scheduled for August 4, 1991. It never took place. Shortly before the appointed time, Melnitzer was arrested.

Melnitzer continued to live in style throughout 1990. In February, he and Baltman skied in Utah and shopped in New York City. The next month it was a trip to Malaysia. In May, they visited Paris and took a rail tour of France; in June, a trip to Russia and Italy; in August, New York City; in October, London, England. Early in December it was skiing in Utah again and a visit to Las Vegas; a few weeks later another trip to London; finally, at the end of the month, Hawaii.

Melnitzer's spending was far beyond what he could afford, even with his considerable income. He was becoming quite adept at moving money and creating documentation and stories to obtain further funds. But no matter how much he raised, he spent more. He played the banks off each other; if one was reluctant to grant him a line of credit, he would threaten to take his business elsewhere. He asked for and received letters of recommendation from several banks, and he showed these to their competitors to obtain funds. When he provided documents about his financial worth to the banks, he always asked that information about his situation and his plans for the money be kept confidential. The bankers agreed. Melnitzer, a boyhood wizard at chess and Monopoly, had become a man with a passion for the adult game of high finance.

An economic downturn became a slide into recession as

the year progressed. Businesses were failing, stock markets were flat and the real estate market was becoming anemic. After an unprecedented seven or eight years of growth, the economy, it seemed, had spent itself.

As the slowdown spread, businesses began reevaluating their holdings. Corporate fat was trimmed. "Downsizing" was the new business buzzword. Investment and expansion plans were placed on hold, putting a chill in the bankers. They began looking at their own business, checking and rechecking loans in a bid to reduce their exposure levels. Bankruptcies loomed for some of their clients and the banks weren't anxious to get stung. It was time to take stock, particularly of loans that had corporate shares and real estate holdings as collateral. The value of both had tumbled, and many bankers decided to press for more security as protection against the further devaluation of such assets.

Several of Melnitzer's bankers did exactly that. The Melfan and Vanguard shares and the real estate holdings were no longer enough. Melnitzer was asked either to pay down his credit lines or to produce better security to retain the lines he had. Meanwhile, Allan Richman was being pressed by his own banks to reduce his debt load. Nearly all of Richman's holdings were in real estate, so he was vulnerable. Richman was looking for some of his money back from Melnitzer — with the usual healthy interest.

As spring became summer, the pressure on Melnitzer continued. Bankers were on the phone to him, demanding he clear off the lines of credit or come up with better security. Richman, too, was after him, pleading hardship and threatening to invest elsewhere in the future. Meanwhile, Melnitzer's hope was fading for the killer deal, the one that would make him millions and get everyone off his back. He realized he had to do something to satisfy the bankers. And soon. If he didn't, his financial empire would collapse. All the bankers had to do was try to collect on the security they held. A few phone calls to Melfan and Vanguard, and his frauds and forgeries would be revealed.

As the pressure mounted, Melnitzer began losing sleep; all his mental energies were directed toward finding a solution. He'd hoped the Grand Bend decision would have been rendered by now, awarding the beach and many millions of dollars to Gibbs, who could then afford to pay him off. But the months were passing and there wasn't a word from the judge. After much thought, Melnitzer realized he could find no legitimate way out of the maze he'd concocted.

He was caught in a quandary: should he create more forged documents to increase the security or should he pay down the lines of credit? If he created more documents to offer as collateral, he still ran the risk of having the bankers look behind what he was offering. Even though he'd persuaded them to keep his dealings confidential, Melnitzer was worried someone, somewhere, might get suspicious. No, he reasoned, this was not the time to create more phoney paper. Better to pay down the lines for the time being. He could always come back to the banks later for more money, if he could only satisfy them now. Yes, pay down the lines. But that meant he needed to find some cash fairly soon. A little less than $6 million would do it. There had to be a way.

It hit him one night like a thunderbolt. Why not lean on some of the investors who'd made money through him during the past few years? He'd established a positive track record with them. They trusted him. If enough of them could be interested, they might come up with sufficient funds to keep the bankers at bay. When the economy improved, he could pay all the investors back. All he needed was a scheme.

It wasn't long in coming. From Melnitzer's fertile mind sprang the Singapore Deal, an exotic-sounding plan he hoped would be his salvation. The friends, associates and partners he approached about it would never know the deal was total fabrication and what they didn't know wouldn't hurt them. After all, he reasoned, the banks were profiting handsomely from some little white lies he'd told them. And the professional money lenders had either been wilfully blind or too stupid to trip him up; what was the likelihood that his own friends and associates would see through his scheme?

The former British colony of Singapore, now a modern city-state of 2.7 million people, lies at the tip of the Malay Peninsula. Strategically located, it is the largest port in Southeast Asia, fourth largest in the world, with plans to become a major centre in the fast-growing Pacific Rim. Melnitzer was familiar with the city from trips he had made to nearby Malaysia, from which Singapore had seceded in 1965. While in the area trying to help Champion Chemtech establish a factory in the Malaysian capital of Kuala Lumpur, he'd developed a fondness for Singapore and had entertained thoughts of actual, legitimate investments there, but the right deal hadn't materialized. Millions could be made in the bustling seaport, he believed, and he wanted to be part of the action. His firsthand knowledge of Singapore, its government, economy and geography would come in handy.

Melnitzer first mentioned his latest investment opportunity at a meeting of Cohen, Melnitzer partners in late July 1990. He was animated as he spoke, barely containing his excitement. "This is almost too good to be true," he said. "I can't believe it myself. I've got a deal that's safer than Canada Savings Bonds, and I'm going to double my money in two years. Here's your chance to get in on it."

After that dramatic opening, his listeners were all ears.

"I've been involved in this deal in Singapore for about three years. I've got some partners there. We bought some vacant downtown property on Orchard Road. It's the main drag, where all the action is. Shopping, tourism, you name it.

"We paid about $20 million for it through this company we formed that has 'pioneer status' under Singapore law. That gives us a terrific tax break. We were planning to sit on our investment for a while. Last month, the government of Singapore came to us with an offer of $55 million. I'm not sure what they've got in mind. Convention centre, hotel complex or something. They're thinking big these days.

"Problem is, they have this tight-ass constitution that prevents the government from running any kind of deficit. So to get around the problem, they've agreed to pay us some money up front, just over $8 million. But the deal doesn't formally close until the middle of 1993. That's when we collect the balance."

The Cohen, Melnitzer partners were beginning to feel Melnitzer's excitement. Seldom had they seen him so enthusiastic.

"The government of Singapore has accepted title to the land, but it's being held in escrow until the closing date," he continued. "The deal is, the government will pay $2 million a year until closing and that'll be taken off the $55 million. They're paying a premium for the land, but the escrow deal freezes the price and lets them budget for the balance owing.

"The way things are booming in Singapore these days, it's probably a good move for them to want to freeze the price. There's no way of knowing what it might cost in two more years. Man, that place is hopping! It's going to be another Hong Kong, you know.

"So the deal is, I'm in for 49 percent through a company I own. The balance is owned by three businessmen in Singapore. I can't increase my share or the company loses pioneer status, and we all get nailed for some heavy-duty taxes. It's rather complicated.

"A couple of months ago, one of my partners had to bail out. He's got some real money problems from another deal that went bad. He got out just before we made the sale. Worst piece of luck I ever saw. Anyway, we've been looking around for a replacement partner in Singapore. But I said to the guys, 'Wait, just a minute. I've got some people back in Canada who might be interested in a piece of this.'

"The bottom line," Melnitzer said, slowing down to gauge the reaction to his pitch, "is if you can collectively come up with a little over $5 million, you can get in. After two years you're out with up to 50 percent return annually on your money. Basically, you double what you put in."

He paused. A low whistle came from someone in the group. An appreciative hum filled the pause. Glances were exchanged.

"This thing is golden," said Melnitzer slowly, emphasizing every word. "We've got a government guarantee here. It's rock solid. This is the chance of a lifetime — my best deal ever — and I'm offering you a chance to be part of it. If you put enough in, you can afford to kiss the law racket goodbye.

"There's just one thing," he added. "If you have to borrow money to get into this, do us all a favor. Don't mention my name to the banks. I don't want them to know what I'm into here. This thing has got to be on a strictly need-to-know basis. If they get wind of this deal, they might screw it up, tip somebody off. I've been dealing with a lot of bankers lately and, frankly, I don't trust them. So mum's the word. Okay?"

The questioning was intense, but Melnitzer had all the answers. He'd thought through the scenario carefully and the partners couldn't surprise him.

What was the best way to get into this? they wanted to know. Melnitzer suggested creating a numbered company as the investment vehicle. How soon was the money needed? As soon as possible, he said. The Singapore partners would be uncomfortable with any needless delays.

What sort of security would be provided? Melnitzer replied it would be secured by promissory notes from him. There was no way the deal could go off the tracks, he insisted, but if something cropped up he would make good. He reminded them his word had been his bond in the past; this time was no different.

What about windfall profits? What would be the tax impact in Canada? the lawyers asked. Not entirely sure, Melnitzer conceded. But he promised he would bring in a financial consultant to speak to the group to explain the best way to minimize the tax implications.

The answers reassured the partners, and Melnitzer's enthusiasm and confidence had seduced them. Several immediately expressed an interest in participating. A couple wanted to think about it and see what money they could assemble.

Harris Cohen wasn't interested. He was unhappy at the sort of security being offered and he didn't believe anyone could double their money in two years. Another harebrained scheme, he thought. If the others wanted to risk their money, fine. He would have no part of it.

One of the newest partners, Ken McGill, was particularly enthusiastic. With his wife, Margaret, McGill was the first to put money into the Singapore Deal. The couple invested $150,000. Not long afterward, Paul Vogel came up with $50,000. In the next few weeks, Ron Delanghe and his wife, Bonnie, invested $925,000 and Fletcher Dawson put in $100,000. In October, Melnitzer extended his offer to others. He approached Ivana Klouda, administrator of the law firm, who gave him $100,000, mortgaging her condominium to do so. The same month, Melnitzer tapped Jaime Watt, his marketing man, who put in $25,000.

Disappointed more members of the law firm hadn't signed on, Melnitzer began to approach other friends. One was Barry Parker, a vice-president of income-producing properties for Sifton Properties Ltd. The Sifton firm, one of London's most respected builders, was erecting One London Place, the new high-rise in which Cohen, Melnitzer was planning to relocate. Parker, told the same story as the others, came up with $450,000. He joined the others in an investment group and all received quarterly interest payments of 10 percent in February and May 1991.

In October 1990 Melnitzer deposited the $1.8 million raised this way into his accounts to reduce his indebtedness on several fronts. But the banks continued to pressure him and he had to raise more. He approached his reliable old friend, Allan Richman, about the once-in-a-lifetime opportunity in Singapore. He said he was putting together three investment groups — one from the law firm, one of friends and associates and one he'd like Richman to lead. Richman was in. He found some investment money and in November gave Melnitzer $1.8 million. In return, he received a promissory note, plus a guarantee signed by Melnitzer as president of Melfan Investments.

The Richman money helped, but it still wasn't enough to satisfy the bankers.

About the same time, Melnitzer contacted Jules Fleischer, a friend from law school. Fleischer, a wealthy man who spent part of each year in the Turks and Caicos Islands, was told the same story as the others. He issued Melnitzer a cheque for $200,000. In January 1991, Melnitzer approached London dentist Hyman Goldberg. He and Goldberg had been friends for a decade, and Goldberg had invested with Melnitzer on many occasions, always receiving the handsome returns he'd been promised. Goldberg and his wife, Laurie Seaman, socialized with Melnitzer and Baltman on many occasions. Seaman, a talented artist, had sold several of her oil paintings, etchings and other works to the couple. Melnitzer told Goldberg the well-rehearsed story about the Singapore Deal, but although Goldberg trusted his lawyer friend, who seemed to have the Midas touch, he wasn't satisfied. The dentist wanted something the lawyers and business types didn't seem to care about — some sort of documentation.

Melnitzer got back to Goldberg a month later, in February, with a two-page letter dated October 3, 1990, under the letterhead of Allen and Overy, a law firm in London, England. It was addressed to Geoffrey M. Foster, vice-president of the Canadian Imperial Bank of Commerce in London, Ontario, who Melnitzer indicated was his prime banker. The letterhead was impressive; it listed 96 lawyers by name. The document read as follows:

Dear Sir:

We understand that Mr. Julius Melnitzer, in the process of arranging financing with your bank, has outlined to you a transaction regarding vacant property on Orchard Road in Singapore with which he is involved. Mr.

Melnitzer has asked us to review the documentation relating to the transaction, and to provide you with an outline of same for financing purposes.

Our comments are as follows.

(a) In February of 1988, Mr. Melnitzer, through a corporation owned by himself, purchased the subject property with three partners who are citizens of Singapore. Mr. Melnitzer's corporation retains a 49 percent interest in the property;

(b) The property was purchased for $20,000,000. The entirety of the purchase price was paid in cash. The property has never been encumbered since the purchase by Mr. Melnitzer;

(c) In June of 1990, the property was sold to the Government of Singapore for $55,000,000. The date of final closing is June 26th, 1993, but the transaction closed in escrow on September 22nd, 1990;

(d) Under Singapore law, the effect of a closing in escrow is:

(i) The solicitors for the Government of Singapore have accepted the certificate of title;

(ii) The Government of Singapore has provided a deposit in cash for 15 percent of the purchase price and a letter of credit for the balance;

(iii) Mr. Melnitzer and his partners may not encumber the property in any way until the date of closing.

(e) The terms of Agreement of Purchase and Sale also provide that the Government of Singapore will pay interest of $2,000,000 a year from the date of the Agreement to the date of closing. The totality of the interest paid will be deducted from the balance due on closing.

Yours faithfully,

The letter was signed in an illegible backward scrawl.

Goldberg had his documentation and he was satisfied, even though it didn't spell out whether the funds were in U.S., Canadian or Singaporean dollars. He and Seaman invested $250,000 on March 1, accepting promissory notes to secure the funds.

The letter had been forged by their trusted friend. There wasn't a shred of truth in it. Melnitzer had merely taken the letterhead from some correspondence he'd received a few years before and typed in the fiction. The only use he made of the letter was to pry money from Goldberg and Seaman. Foster, the banker to whom it was addressed, knew nothing about it.

Melnitzer had now collected a little more than $4 million for the Singapore Deal. But he still needed more if he was going to pay down the credit lines.

In May 1991, he approached Delanghe again, telling him another Canadian investor had been unable to carry a $1.5-million piece of the Singapore transaction. "This guy's from Toronto and he bought in, but his involvement depended on his selling a nice piece of real estate there," Melnitzer told Delanghe. "The deal fell apart and he's tried to find another buyer. But real estate's in the dumper and he hasn't even had a nibble. So he's had to back out. Ron, do you think you could take over his share?"

Delanghe said he would do his best. The real estate lawyer turned to one of his biggest clients, Glen Sifton, owner of Sifton Properties. Delanghe and Sifton were also friends and had some personal investments together. One of them was with Melnitzer in a popular London dessert shop. Delanghe explained the investment opportunity to Sifton, who liked what he heard. He came up with the $1.5 million, giving it to Delanghe. Melnitzer signed a promissory note to Delanghe to secure the money, and Delanghe assigned that note, and his earlier note securing the $925,000, to two of Sifton's firms, Sifton Holdings Limited and Awata Corporation.

Sifton never dealt with Melnitzer directly on the Singapore Deal. He trusted Delanghe, who had placed his trust in Melnitzer.

The new money brought to $5.55 million the amount Melnitzer had raised from his partners, associates and friends. It hadn't been easy, but he was satisfied that, when he used the funds to pay down his credit lines, he would finally have the bankers off his back. His relief was momentary; he couldn't escape the fact that he was eventually going to have to find money to repay the Singapore crowd. His headaches were just beginning.

When Melnitzer took the time to reflect on what he had created, he knew most of his transactions relied on robbing Peter to pay Paul. He was not investing money where he said he was. He was merely using it to pay out people or banks from whom he had already obtained funds. His was a money-moving scheme that was snowballing faster than he'd anticipated. The deeper he got into it, the less chance there was of finding the miracle investment that would clear the slate.

He'd been able to satisfy the early investors by paying them off with money he obtained from later investors or from his lines of credit. But his desire to ensure his investors received handsome dividends was becoming burdensome. The amounts he was paying out in interest forced him to constantly run faster just to stay ahead of his growing list of creditors. Every dollar he obtained carried with it the obligation to find more dollars with which to make his investors happy. To repay the Singapore investors double their money, he would have to take in twice as much money from other sources under some other pretext.

As a lawyer, Melnitzer was all too aware he had created what is known in legal circles as a "Ponzi" scheme, a pyramid-type investment plan in which there may be a core of legitimate dealings, but more often than not there wasn't. Rather, the person orchestrating it uses funds provided by later investors to pay attractive dividends to earlier investors.

The scheme is named after a colorful character nicknamed the Boston Swindler, with whom Melnitzer had much in common.

Charles Ponzi, a silver-tongued confidence man with little formal education, turned the investment world on its ear in a period of about six months just after the First World War. By the time he was arrested in Boston in August 1920, he had taken the people of New England on a $15-million ride.

A dapper little man who was born in Italy, Ponzi concocted his investment scheme in late 1919, with $200 he had borrowed. He was 37 and yearned for the good life he saw around him in America. A devoted son and attentive husband, Ponzi had a quick mind and a well-developed ability to lie.

After pondering and rejecting several get-rich-quick schemes, Ponzi latched onto the International Reply Coupon as his ticket to easy wealth. In 1907, at a meeting of the International Postal Congress in Rome, the Universal Postal Union was created and the reply coupons came into being. The congress came up with the coupon plan to address a growing concern created by the millions of Europeans who were forsaking their homelands for the brighter prospects of North America. The new Americans and Canadians were sending home a flood of correspondence. Too often, however, those left behind were so impoverished, they sometimes had difficulty finding even the small change needed for stamps to mail a reply.

The International Reply Coupon made it possible for the writer of a letter to prepay the return postage. The coupon, included in the letter, could be redeemed in the old country for stamps. The price of the coupon was fixed in each country that was party to the agreement and didn't change as currency values fluctuated.

Ponzi memorized the intricacies of the system and saw his El Dorado. He realized it would also work in reverse. European currencies were depressed compared with that of the U.S. at the time. Ponzi's plan was to send U.S. currency to contacts in Europe, have them convert it to the local currency, purchase International Reply Coupons, send the coupons to him and he would convert the coupons into U.S. stamps. The value of what he received would be far greater than what he paid. Provided European currencies remained depressed, Ponzi calculated his profits at greater than 200 percent. And it was all legal.

He established the Securities Exchange Company in a tiny office on School Street in Boston and devised an investment scheme with the International Reply Coupon at its core. In a well-rehearsed presentation, he told potential investors about the coupon system and how he could make them rich. Ponzi said he needed their money to take advantage of the coupon system on a large scale. He promised to pay 50-percent interest on their investments in 45 days. This was at a time when banks were paying depositors interest of four percent a year. The first person to invest, a factory foreman, put up $50 just five days before Christmas, 1919. He was promised $75 by February 5. Other workers in the same factory, who looked up to the foreman, also began investing with Ponzi. The returns were paid as promised and it wasn't long before crowds began flocking to the Securities Exchange Company. Ponzi, like every swindler before and since, relied on the greed of his fellow man for success. Many of his investors declined to accept their dividends, preferring to roll them back into the scheme in a bid for even greater profits.

Ponzi became the toast of the town. He was courted by bankers and became an overnight celebrity. When police grew suspicious, he calmly explained to them how the International Reply Coupon worked and how it was the basis of his operation. When the authorities checked into it, everything appeared legal. But they remained suspicious and were frustrated that the cocky entrepreneur couldn't be charged with anything.

Meanwhile, Ponzi was skimming a percentage of his take to buy an impressive mansion, a big car and shares in a

couple of banks with which he was dealing. Always impecca-
bly dressed in the latest fashion, wearing a straw skimmer
planted at a jaunty angle and sporting a gold-headed walking
stick, Ponzi knew the importance of looking successful.

Aside from an initial purchase of reply coupons to prove
the system worked, Ponzi never again bothered to make
postal transactions. It was far simpler to move money from
one investor to another without getting bogged down in the
mechanics of the coupon exchange.

While he was riding high, Ponzi enjoyed the attention of
cheering supporters, who filled the streets outside his modest office. And he enjoyed joking with newspaper reporters
and glibly outsmarting policemen, postal inspectors and
experts in high finance, who were perplexed at his operation.
But as his scheme grew into the millions, he began losing
sleep. How long could he juggle the money and satisfy the
increasing circle of investors? He began to dread every new
investment dollar, because it meant he would, in 45 days, be
obliged to replace it with $1.50.

The scheme collapsed under its own weight amid bad
publicity and an official investigation. Once the "wizard of
finance" couldn't meet his obligations, the police pounced.
Ponzi was relieved of the nightmare he'd created.

In the end, he had collected $15 million from investors,
but he had little to show for it. The vast majority of what he
had collected had been paid out to satisfied investors. Only
those who joined the scheme in its last stages lost their
money. Court-appointed receivers and bankruptcy officials
probed the ashes of his empire, turning up assets of only $1.3
million and a mere $61 worth of postage stamps. His liabil-
ities totalled slightly less than $4 million, including about
$16,000 borrowed from his wife and her relatives. His activ-
ities brought about the collapse of several banks.

Ponzi was sent to prison and later deported to Italy. His
wife never forgave him for deceiving her. Alone and destitute
at 66, he died in the charity ward of a hospital in Rio de
Janeiro in 1949.

There have been other famous Ponzi schemes in recent history. A U.S. promoter in the late 1960s and early 1970s fleeced investors for $100 million, promising to pay healthy returns by importing large amounts of low-grade wine from Europe. In Canada in 1974, more than 500 Montrealers invested $2 million with a promoter who claimed he had devised an infallible system for betting on racehorses.

Perhaps the wildest and most notorious Ponzi scheme was the 1973 Home-Stake Production Company swindle in the U.S. Robert S. Trippet, a Tulsa, Oklahoma, lawyer, ran Home-Stake, claiming it was an oil-drilling company. He sold tax-shelter partnerships to hundreds of wealthy investors looking to reduce their income tax liabilities. The company, of course, was not involved in oil drilling, but Trippet and his associates pulled a variety of scams to cover up that fact. One ruse involved disguising a California vegetable farm to look like an operating oil field by painting its irrigation pipes to resemble oil derricks and pipelines. When Home-Stake was uncovered, investors lost more than $100 million. Among them were such high-profile show business person-alities as Andy Williams, Barbra Streisand, Liza Minelli, Barbara Walters, Candice Bergen and Bob Dylan. Top exec-utives of major American corporations were also stung, as well as two bankers and a financial expert who'd written best-selling books about Wall Street, revealing some of the cons played there by the fast-money crowd.

Some economists suggest that nearly all of us are unwit-tingly involved as investors in giant government-backed Ponzi schemes. The social security system in the U.S. and the Canada Pension Plan might be illegal if they were in the hands of private operators. But because they are run by governments, they are permitted to continue.

Despite impressions to the contrary, the money Canadians are required to pay into the Canada Pension Plan is not saved by the government, invested and then used for their retire-ment. It is paid out almost immediately to workers who have already retired. The money today's workers will draw when they retire will, in fact, be contributed by people working in the future. This has some serious implications for the plan. As members of the baby-boom generation who have contributed to the plan for decades retire, their benefits will be paid by the smaller base of contributors still working. Economists predict the contribution rate will have to rise substantially. If it doesn't, the system will collapse as the baby boomers start to make their claims, and they, as the last contributors, will be victimized. This is essentially what happened when Charles Ponzi finally stumbled.

Melnitzer got through 1990 without being tripped up. In the waning days of the year he received the good news about the Grand Bend victory. But as expected, the decision was appealed, tying up any chance of a quick recovery of the $1.1 million he had paid on behalf of Archie Gibbs.

Still, as 1991 began, Melnitzer was upbeat, certain he'd find a way to please both his investors and the bankers. To outsiders, his reputation was at its highest. He was viewed as not only a top lawyer but also as a smart money-man. In public, Julius Melnitzer seemed comfortable, successful and happy. Inside, he wasn't any of those things, realizing his life had become a giant board game. He determined that to keep winning, he just had to keep on top of things, stay sharp, plan his moves carefully and anticipate the opposition.

The con man was confident he could do it.

9

Forging On

"I don't believe in fraud on banks."

BALTMAN AND MELNITZER WERE gradually becoming Torontonians. Baltman was dedicat-
ing herself to acting, and the bright lights of Toronto were
proving irresistible. Meanwhile, Melnitzer had become
associate counsel at a law firm in the city, Torkin, Manes,
Cohen and Arbus, and his duties with the Fair Rental Policy
Organization were increasing. The couple began to wonder
why they were maintaining homes in two cities.

Their sixteenth-floor condo in Yorkville was nice enough,
but Melnitzer reasoned that if he was going to make a
commitment to Toronto, he needed a truly impressive home.
By late 1990, once Deena was acting full-time, they began
looking for a suitable place. If bankers or investors were to
come calling, they had to see the substantial residence of a
wealthy man and his wife.

Melnitzer and Baltman found just what they were looking
for in the fashionable Rosedale area, home of the city's blue
bloods. The three-storey stone house at 88 Roxborough Street

East was worthy of an ambassador and required the wallet of a sheik. The deal closed in February 1991, at $1.85 million. But again, Melnitzer had no intention of tying up a lot of money in personal real estate, so he made inquiries about assuming the substantial mortgage on the property. The Toronto Dominion bank held the $1.5-million mortgage, and Melnitzer called upon his talents as a con man to take it over.

The TD bank asked Melnitzer to complete an "application for personal credit" on January 22. Six days later, he returned to the bank's commercial banking centre in Don Mills with the completed application, together with financial statements for 808756 Ontario Inc. (the numbered company created for the Singapore Deal) and for Grand Canyon Properties. He also provided a letter of recommendation he had obtained from the CIBC. In his application, Melnitzer claimed $45 million in assets he did not have. Nor was he entitled to commit the numbered company or Grand Canyon for any of his debts. When confronted later with the financial statements for 808756 Ontario Inc. that he had presented to the bank, Melnitzer admitted, "Those are just the forged Melfan statements with the numbered company typed on the front."

Melnitzer, determined to assume the mortgage but anxious to avoid detection, went a step further. The agreement of purchase and sale for the Roxborough property contained an unusual clause, inserted at his insistence: "It is understood that the purchaser will not be obliged to provide any financial information to the bank in order to be permitted to assume the mortgage."

Bank officials puzzled over that provision, and had they harbored the slightest suspicion about this borrower, the clause would have sent them distinct warning signals. But Melnitzer came well documented and well recommended. Satisfied with the situation, they approved the transfer of the mortgage into his name. Because of its size, the mortgage called for monthly payments of $13,691.54.

Melnitzer and Baltman immediately embarked on a

campaign to have the old home rejuvenated, determined to make it a reflection of their good taste. Money was no object. An interior designer was retained and promptly ordered custom furniture totalling more than $90,000. Decorators and landscapers were hired to transform the home and its grounds into a suitably resplendent base of operations. A fitness and weight room was created.

Once they moved in, the condo on Cumberland was put up for sale at $525,000. Melnitzer had the Tallwood house in London appraised by a real estate agent while they debated its future.

The work at Torkin, Manes and at the Fair Rental group was coming along, but as usual, Melnitzer was anxious to move into the big time in legal and governmental circles. One of his contacts was well-regarded Toronto lawyer John Bogart, a Queen's counsel. Bogart had heard of Melnitzer and was willing to introduce him to potential clients — for a price. After some negotiating, Melnitzer and Bogart struck a deal. In return for such introductions, Melnitzer advanced $100,000 to Bogart, one-third of their agreed-upon total of $300,000.

As he was taking steps to consolidate his presence in Toronto, however, Melnitzer's mind was still very much in London. The banks had been tamed, but the Singapore Deal was eating away at him. Even as he was seeking that last $1.5 million from Delanghe and Sifton, Melnitzer was trying to devise a way to repay his friends and associates. Deceiving the banks had been easy. They were fat cats with plenty of money to spare. If they were going to be so trusting and lax in their business dealings, they deserved what they got. If they lost money, they'd just boost their already too high interest rates.

But Melnitzer discovered he was uncomfortable taking some of the people who were closest to him on a ride. The pangs of conscience surprised him. What if something happened to him and he was physically unable to carry on? Or what if the Singapore Deal was revealed for the scam it was?

Melnitzer was irritated at himself. Why had he let the pressure from the bankers get to him, forcing him to lean on his
friends and associates? He had taken more than $10 million
from his good friend Richman, who'd always found money
for him when he needed it. Melnitzer had to figure out a way
to solve the problem of the Singapore people. He didn't want
to keep them on the hook for two years. The answer became
increasingly obvious: it was time to go back to the banks. If
he did make a blunder, better to have the banks lose than the
Singapore investors.

Many months later, after his swindles were uncovered,
Melnitzer was brutally frank when he explained his decision
to revisit the bankers. "If I was going to go down," he
conceded to the court-appointed receiver, "I guess on the
scale of priorities the banks were less important than my
friends." At the same time, he claimed the Singapore Deal
and its aftermath had caused him much worry. "I don't know,
when I did that Singapore Deal, everything just sort of
cracked," he told one of his banker-victims, "Somehow —
and believe me it's hard to say, and my values are totally
different from actions — I don't believe in fraud on banks.

"I don't know why I'm saying this on the record, but if you
ask anybody who has practised law with me, my word was
my bond. I think that the fact that my friends and people who
I've been [with] for 20 years . . . I just . . . I could worry about
the banks, what I've done with the banks, but what I've done
to my friends . . . "

Still, when he opted to return to defrauding bankers,
Melnitzer wasn't about to admit his career as a con man was
doomed; he was merely acknowledging it had its risks.

Melnitzer started the renewed search for bank money with
Stephen Suske, president of Devonshire Financial Group
Limited, in Toronto. The two had been introduced by Richman in 1989. Suske was in the business of acting as a
financial intermediary to help arrange investments, princi-
pally in the real estate field. He had represented both Richman

and Melnitzer in various investment schemes, quickly concluding that the lawyer from London had a wide interest in investments and an apparently fat bank account.

Shortly after Melnitzer and Baltman purchased the Rosedale home, Melnitzer asked Suske to arrange some financing for other investments. He wanted Suske to find a lender to provide him with a $6-million line of credit. In return, Melnitzer promised Suske a $75,000 finder's fee. Suske agreed and made his first contacts with two smaller financial institutions.

The first place he approached was the Hongkong Bank of Canada. After a promising start, negotiations soon bogged down, so he initiated similar talks with the Mutual Trust Company. When he visited both institutions, Suske took documentation, provided by Melnitzer, which be believed to be genuine. The main item of security was a listing of guaranteed investment certificates (GICs) with a total value of about $9.6 million. These certificates would be placed as security by means of a debenture on 808756 Ontario Inc. (the Singapore Deal company). The stated purpose of the line of credit was to provide the numbered company with cash for the purchase of real estate all across North America. Suske gave Mutual Trust a list of the GICs purportedly held by 808756 Ontario, false financial statements for 808756, a personal statement of Melnitzer's affairs, a list Melnitzer had created relating his business experience and investments, and a letter supposedly prepared by an accounting firm about 808756's financial statement.

While he was awaiting word from Mutual Trust, Melnitzer was advised the Hongkong Bank would extend a $6-million line of credit, but on two conditions: it would take a debenture on the GICs if they were assigned to the bank and were registered under the Personal Property Security Act; and it insisted upon an acknowledgment from the bank that issued the guaranteed investment certificates confirming their authenticity.

"No way!" Melnitzer exploded when he learned of the

conditions. "What's their problem?" he demanded of Suske. "Don't those bastards trust me? There's plenty of other banks out there I could be dealing with. Don't they know who I am? I was doing them a favor, and look what they do."

Melnitzer suggested Suske try to make some alternative arrangements that didn't require such onerous conditions. But the bank wouldn't budge and was soon out of Melnitzer's financial picture. The Hongkong Bank, by being careful, applying the rules and demanding nothing unusual, had saved itself a potential loss of $6 million.

Meanwhile, Mutual Trust was still mulling over Melnitzer's documentation. The company's credit committee was impressed with the financial information provided. The firm indicated by letter that it was prepared to offer the $6-million line of credit, but was also seeking a number of conditions relating to the security it expected to receive. After further negotiations and amendments, Melnitzer accepted the terms in April. As arrangements were being completed, Kelly Ehler, manager of real estate lending at Mutual Trust, met with the lawyer to seek some additional financial and personal information.

Melnitzer provided the details, but Ehler thought he seemed somewhat annoyed. It didn't take long for the lawyer to say what was on his mind.

"Look, Kelly, I'm not very happy with some of the conditions you're placing on this," he said. "Back in London and now in Toronto, people respect me. I've built up a good law practice that is based on trust. My word is my bond. People know that and accept it. I've done well in real estate on the same basis, you know. I realize Mutual wants to protect its ass from getting ripped off. But believe me, if I give you a commitment, I stand by it.

"I'm into a lot of deals all over the place, as you know. I have partners and competitors to look out for. A lot of my stuff depends on confidentiality, keeping a lid on certain information. I'm not a secretive kind of guy, but I haven't become a successful investor by yakking about what I'm into with every Tom, Dick and Harry who happens along. People talk, and it's the talk that can kill you."

Ehler nodded his understanding. He wasn't about to antagonize a new customer who could be profitable for Mutual Trust.

"I don't want any of my personal financial affairs known to anybody. Understand?" Melnitzer continued. "I put that statement of business experience together just for you guys. I absolutely insist you keep it in strictest confidence.

"Now, if you have any questions, any questions at all about my affairs, and you're thinking of asking third parties, I insist you direct them to me first. I'll give you the okay, but you've got to work through me. There are some people out there you could tip off just by asking an apparently innocent question, so I've got to know what you're after. I can supply it. Okay?"

Ehler agreed and proved to be as good as his word. Any further checks he made, he worked through Melnitzer.

After all the time he'd spent on the Melnitzer application, Ehler was surprised a few weeks later when the credit committee reconsidered the matter and rejected the proposed credit line. Members of the committee had second thoughts about the wisdom of permitting Melnitzer to use their money when 50 percent of the loan was without any tangible security. As with the Hongkong Bank, Mutual Trust's change of heart saved the firm a potential loss of $6 million.

After his arrest, Melnitzer admitted everything he had offered to Hongkong Bank and to Mutual Trust had been false. One of the documents he'd given Mutual Trust, in particular, was worthy of an award for creative writing. His recital of business and investment dealings skilfully wove true facts into an impressive, but mainly bogus, representation of his affairs. It was designed to titillate the bankers, to persuade them to open their vaults. From his earlier dealings with banks, Melnitzer believed he had a pretty good idea about how to turn them on. One trick was to include a large number of zeroes to the right of dollar figures when he described his assets.

The typed, two-page document was titled, "Julius Melnitzer, sample of business experience and investments." It read, in its entirety, as follows:

a) During the early 1970s and 1980s, I invested heavily in the gold and silver market with a partner, now deceased, who was a senior broker at Merrill Lynch. By 1982, my personal profit in the gold and silver market had exceeded $18,000,000.

b) Former director and substantial shareholder of Vanguard Trust, now amalgamated into Prenor Trust; purchased several hundred thousand shares soon after formation of the company at average price of $1.50, converted shares to Prenor, subsequently sold shares at $7.00.

c) 50 percent shareholder in Grand Canyon Properties, owning several apartment buildings in southwestern Ontario, 100-unit buildings on Barclay Street in Vancouver and a $7,000,000 apartment complex purchased from HomeFed Bank in Tacoma, Washington. This company also purchased a parking lot in downtown London for an effective price of $975,000 and sold same several years later for over $2,400,000. Other partner in the venture is Allan Richman, president and sole shareholder of Forward Properties in London, which company manages approximately 3000 apartment units and owns aproximately 800 units on its own.

d) Purchased 25 percent of Champion Photochemistry in 1990 for $2.5 million. One of the partners in this investment is Fraser Mason, who is presently a member of the national executive of Ernst and Young and was formerly chairman of Ernst and Young's worldwide mergers and acquisitions committee. The purchase of shares in this company came about when Mr. Mason, who had been retained by myself to search for investments, offered me an investment in this firm, in which he was already a substantial shareholder. I went into this business deal not only for the transaction, but also because it was a beginning to what has become a continuing relationship with Mr. Mason and myself who are presently pursuing active business opportunities. On Champion's behalf in the last 18 months I have:

(i) organized the build-to-lease arrangements for Champion's new factory in Kuala Lumpur, Malaysia and made all banking arrangements with local bankers there;

(ii) I have travelled to South Africa to consolidate Champion's investment in Champion's co-venture with Kodak management in buying out Kodak operations in South Africa.

e) I have developed a close relationship with the "special loans" department of the Hongkong Bank, which has alerted me to numerous opportunities in the Far East, including the purchase of a major shopping complex and vacant land in Singapore. Most of this land has now been sold, with one deal still pending. The profits from those transactions largely account for the offshore cash on my personal statement. My partner in the transaction was the broker at Merrill Lynch with whom I purchased the gold and silver, and who later left Merrill Lynch to in fact become the operating partner for our joint enterprise. In recent years, since her death, I have been somewhat limited in being able to pursue transactions until I established the relationship with Mr. Mason, who now finds and checks out the deals, thereby performing the functions of my deceased partner.

f) My former partner and I were involved in numerous real estate deals all over the United States, which was her home. The entire holdings of our joint venture were sold soon after her death in 1986 and formed much of the seed capital of the numbered company and the liquidity of the offshore funds.

g) One of the original investors in Cableshare, a London company which attracted J.C. Penney, the United States retail giant, as a major investor. I invested in this stock at approximately $1.00 per share and sold same over the years as the stocks climbed upwards to a high of almost $50.00 a share. I sold all my stock before J.C. Penney announced that it was not proceeding with the marketing of Cableshare's home shopping system. The profit to me was approximately $14 million on a $500,000 investment.

h) Presently negotiating with the National Basketball Association and owner of the San Antonio Spurs for purchase of team. I have signed a letter of intent and accompanied same with $250,000 deposit. The deal is conditional on securing an assurance from the NBA that I will be able to move the team from San Antonio, but there are competing bidders and the fact that I and my partner are Canadian, rather than American, may be a problem. My partner in the present offer is a major Canadian brewery whose name I cannot disclose because of a confidentiality agreement. Offered price is $68,000,000. Financing with Wells Fargo Bank.

The document was signed by Melnitzer, below an underlined and capitalized warning: ALL MATERIAL IN THIS STATEMENT IS HIGHLY CONFIDENTIAL.

The paragraph about his success in the gold and silver markets was false. So was the part about Far East investments with the Hongkong Bank, the reference to a late partner and their investments all over the United States, and the business about Cableshare and J.C. Penney. Melnitzer retained more than $100,000 in Cableshare stock and had not cashed out at a handsome profit. He was involved as a director of Champion, but his participation in the firm's dealings was exaggerated. His profit on the sale of Vanguard shares bore no resemblance to what he claimed.

The story about the NBA, however, was partly true. Shortly after the Mutual Trust deal fell through, Melnitzer was bragging to Suske about his plan to buy the San Antonio Spurs and move them to Toronto.

"I think we can pull this off for about $100 million," he said. "I have $25 million to invest in it, Wells Fargo Bank will lend us $50 million, and all we need is another $25 million. Steve, if you find me a $25-million partner, I'll give you a $1-million fee."

Suske went looking for money again. He eventually found some interest among representatives of Los Angeles Kings owner Bruce McNall and hockey superstar Wayne Gretzky, who had recently purchased the Toronto Argonauts of the Canadian Football League. Suske arranged a preliminary meeting with the McNall-Gretzky representatives for August 7 in Toronto. Melnitzer was arrested three days before.

Melnitzer was surprised and disappointed Suske had been unable to obtain a line of credit on his behalf. Suske had been dealing with investors and banks for some time, and Melnitzer had placed much faith in his abilities. He had hoped to avoid personal dealings with bankers again. He'd found them to be slow, plodding and unimaginative. They seemed to take forever to make up their minds, and they all wanted to check with their superiors before making a final decision. He figured he had better things to do with his time than get tied up in endless meetings with money lenders. Especially when in the end, they usually gave him what he wanted anyway.

When Suske had encountered the initial delays at Hongkong Bank and Mutual Trust, Melnitzer had already been devising an alternative game plan.

Since it appeared he might have to turn to the banks himself, he began looking back on his dealings of the past several years to see how he could improve his approach.

Obtaining lines of credit hadn't been all that difficult, he concluded. But he came to the realization it was better to obtain credit in much larger amounts. A line of $2 or $3 million, for instance, meant that once he approached the limit, the bank began demanding to know how he was going to pay it down. It had been Melnitzer's experience that the banks were willing to grant the lines but were inclined to panic when the limit was near. And when the bankers became concerned, they began to look more closely at the security they held and began to pester him. On the other hand, if he wasn't using enough of their money, he was urged to use more of it. So, he decided, it was better to ask for substantially larger lines of credit. As long as he paid his overdraft interest, the banks would leave him alone and not begin to ask the questions and make the demands that could lead to problems.

He was struck by how easy it had been to obtain lines of credit based on forged documents, particularly the Melfan and Vanguard Trust shares. Not a single lender had bothered to make a phone call to a broker or transfer agent to determine the validity of the Vanguard shares. There must be something magical about share certificates, he thought. Maybe it was because bankers feel comfortable with their similarity to bank notes. Shares and paper money are hard to duplicate, and bankers can flip through them and feel something tangible in their hands. Stock certificates were the ticket to riches, he concluded.

When his daughter, Melissa, was a child, Melnitzer had purchased single shares in various companies in a bid to interest her in business and the stock market. He had delighted in explaining how the market worked and then watching Melissa scour the stock listings in the newspaper to see how her tiny holdings were doing. Such single-share purchases are a nuisance to brokers and to the corporations that issue stock, and the buyer faces standard brokerage fees sometimes greater than the cost of the share. But the explanation that it's a gift for a child who may grow into an investing adult can mollify an agent, filling his head with dreams of future transactions.

In April, Melnitzer called his stockbroker, ScotiaMcLeod Inc., from which he had purchased most of his legitimate stock portfolio, then worth about $190,000. He ordered single shares of five corporate giants: McDonald's Corporation, trading at $30.37 a share; International Business Machines Corporation (IBM), at $107.38 a share; Exxon Corporation, at $45; BCE Inc. (Bell Canada) at $38; and Canadian Pacific Limited at $20.88. All were in the name of Melissa Melnitzer and dated April 26, 1991. The price of the shares totalled $241.63, exclusive of brokerage fees. Unlike his purchases of many years before, however, Melnitzer had no intention of telling Melissa, then 21, about these shares.

He asked that the share certificates be fowarded to him directly. He was not content to follow the standard practice of having his broker store them. It took a few weeks for the shares to arrive, time he used to devise a plan to alter the share amounts to give them a purported value in the millions of dollars. The altered shares would be his new security when he approached the banks again to obtain millions of *their* dollars.

The base of operations for the plan would be London, he decided. He still felt more comfortable dealing with business people and bankers he knew. They would be more likely to trust him because of his reputation in the city. He felt he was still too small a fish in Toronto to impress the people he had to impress to pull off his greatest con yet.

He needed a printing firm that he could trust and that could alter the certificates the way he wanted. For years, Cohen, Melnitzer had used the services of Sterling Marking Products, a reputable London firm that provided seals, stamps, printing supplies and such items as the fill-in-the-blank incorporation kits lawyers use to help create small corporations. Cohen, Melnitzer had represented the company on a number of legal matters, and the two firms had a good working relationship. In addition, Sterling's manager,

Sam Hassan, had a brother, Hamoody, who was a lawyer at Cohen, Melnitzer. It was to Sam Hassan that Melnitzer went with his unusual proposal.

"Sam, I've got a job for you like you've never seen before," Melnitzer said. "I've got this big client who's charged with using forged stock certificates to get loans at some banks. I can't give you all the details, but I'm putting his defence together, and I'm looking for a printer who can come up with fake copies of stock certificates that are so good only a trained expert can tell the difference from the real thing. I thought of you guys first because you're the best. Do you think you could give it a try?"

Hassan was taken aback. "But we've never done that sort of thing before. Isn't it illegal, like printing money?"

"No, nothing to worry about on that score," Melnitzer said, trying to sound reassuring. "It's not like money at all. The very act of printing money is illegal. The printing of stock certificates isn't. I wouldn't ask you to do anything illegal. What *is* illegal is to take a forged stock certificate and act upon it as if it were genuine, or to intend to act upon it as if it were legit. You know, plan to rip somebody off with it."

"Oh, yeah," Hassan replied, but he wasn't convinced. "You mean as long as they aren't used as if they're the real thing, it's okay?"

"That's right," came the reply. "And in this case, the purpose is to help me defend this guy. The cops have charged him with fraud and forgery. I can't really talk about why, but I need to prove printing technology has improved so much that even a smaller shop like yours can do a credible job of coming up with a fake certificate that could lead guys like my client to be deceived. It's as simple as that. What do you say?"

"I'm not so sure," Hassan said. "I'd like to think about this, check with the boss, you know. How soon do you need an answer?"

"Pretty quick, actually," the lawyer said. "Hate to push you on this, but the trial is only a few months away and I've got to see what you can come up with. It'll affect my entire defence strategy. This client has some bucks, so it could be pretty lucrative for both of us."

Hassan promised to reply as soon as possible. He explained Melnitzer's request to company president Bob Schram, who had some misgivings and thought it best to contact the firm's legal counsel, Michael Lerner, one of the top lawyers in London. On Lerner's advice, Melnitzer was asked to explain the purpose of the job in writing. The printer's lawyer felt it prudent to have the request on a document to protect Sterling's interest in the event of any future misunderstanding. It proved to be a wise move.

On May 15, Melnitzer sent Sterling the requested letter on Cohen, Melnitzer letterhead. He spelled out his requirements, confirming Sterling was being asked to help the law firm. The following are excerpts from that letter:

"Sterling has agreed, to the best of its ability, to maintain the utmost confidentiality and has further agreed that it will destroy, for security reasons, the materials used in the reproduction process once the assigned task has been completed . . .

"We confirm that these certificates will be used for the sole purpose of advancing litigation in respect of which Cohen, Melnitzer has been retained. We warrant that Sterling will not be disclosed as the printer of these certificates unless written permission is given . . .

"Cohen, Melnitzer agrees to assume all liability arising for any reason whatsoever from the printing of these certificates and agrees to indemnify Sterling fully for any costs and liabilities incurred . . .

"Cohen, Melnitzer confirms that we have investigated fully any potential consequences of Sterling having taken on this retainer and we confirm that there is no criminal, quasi-criminal, regulatory, civil or administrative liability or prohibition attached to the carrying out of this retainer."

The assurances satisfied Sterling and its counsel. Hassan agreed to see what the firm could do once Melnitzer delivered the stock certificates with specific instructions about how they were to be altered. Hassan was unable to quote a firm price until he saw how much was involved in tackling this unusual project. Initial estimates were that it could be completed for less than $25,000. As the job expanded in months to come, the total would grow to $100,000.

Once the certificates materialized, Melnitzer asked Sterling to remove Melissa's name and replace it with his own. He explained the certificates were actually owned by his daughter and he'd purchased them as gifts. But he didn't want to involve her name needlessly in the court case, and since the documents were being altered anyway, he thought replacing her name with his was best.

Melnitzer then provided detailed instructions as to how he wanted the certificates changed. He told Hassan the dates and amounts had to reflect dates and amounts that were of significance to the court case in which they'd be used. The certificate numbers, for the most part, could remain unchanged. He also asked for five of each of the certificates.

The McDonald's certificate was to be made out for 95,193 shares and dated November 12, 1987.

The Canadian Pacific certificate was to be made out for 94,622 shares and dated November 25, 1987.

The IBM certificate was to be made into two capital stock certificates, both dated November 11, 1987, one for 98,435 shares, the other for 25,806 shares. A single digit at the end of the certificate number was to be changed to differentiate the two.

The BCE certificate was to be made out for 71,628 common shares and dated November 19, 1987.

The Exxon certificate was to be made into two capital stock

certificates, both dated November 18, 1987, one for 96,998 shares, the other for 50,412 shares. Again, to differentiate between the two, the last digit was to be altered on the second certificate.

If they'd been legitimate, the shares Sterling was to create would have had a total value of about $30 million.

The print order had barely been placed in May when Melnitzer approached the Royal Bank of Canada seeking to replace his $3-million line of credit there with an $8-million line. He was prepared, he said, to offer share certificates with a total value of $12 million as security. At the time, he had used up almost half the $3-million line and said he needed additional funds for significant real estate investments, which he did not divulge. The Royal considered the request, agreed to it and said it would collect the pledged share certificates later.

The Toronto Dominion Bank was Melnitzer's next target. In late March, a number of senior managers at the bank had been invited to a luncheon by Cohen, Melnitzer. Among them was Gary Shore, manager of the bank's commercial banking centre in London. Melnitzer introduced himself to Shore and said he'd like to get together with him sometime to discuss business. On June 5, about two weeks after the lawyer reached the limit on his existing $100,000 line of credit at the TD, Shore was invited to lunch by Melnitzer. The lawyer needed money and asked Shore if the bank would grant him an unsecured line of credit for $500,000. Melnitzer didn't seem surprised when Shore advised him the bank's limit for unsecured lines was $100,000.

"But perhaps there is something else we can do for you," said Shore, thinking Cohen, Melnitzer might be a nice catch as a client. He knew the CIBC was the firm's main banker.

"Yes, Gary there is," Melnitzer said, giving Shore the impression he was taking him into his confidence. "You may be aware I have a lot of investments, in real estate and marketable securities, blue-chip stuff. It was in the millions last time I looked. But my liquidity is poor right now, and I've been trying to come up with some cash. The brokerage houses will only leverage my holdings at 50 percent. I'm looking for 70 percent. That's not unreasonable. Do you think the TD would be interested in helping me out?"

Shore said he'd have to look into it and promised to get back to Melnitzer. In further discussions, Shore asked what the funds would be used for specifically, and the nature of the securities Melnitzer was prepared to offer.

Melnitzer replied that the funds would be used to pay out the $1.5-million mortgage the TD held on the Roxborough home in Toronto, $5 million for "up front" money for his bid to bring the San Antonio Spurs to Toronto, investment in additional blue-chip stocks, and investment in a private company called Grand Canyon Properties.

Shore wanted to know about the securities to be pledged. Melnitzer said they had a market value of about $35 million and included shares in McDonald's, IBM, Exxon, BCE and Canadian Pacific. Shore didn't ask for certificate numbers or other details about the stocks.

Later in June, Shore contacted Melnitzer and said the bank was interested in lending against the shares at a 70 percent ratio. Melnitzer met Shore and Jim Young, the TD's manager of professional banking, on June 24 at the offices of Cohen, Melnitzer. The lawyer provided the bankers with a personal financial statement as of April 30 showing personal assets of $60 million and liabilities of $8.5 million. Shore asked Melnitzer for the number of share certificates and serial numbers of the certificates he was pledging. Melnitzer replied by listing the five companies, giving the number of shares and the total dollar amount that represented, which was $33.6 million. He did not provide serial numbers and Shore did not press him on that point.

Several days later, Shore sought an explanation of how Melnitzer had accumulated his significant net worth. The lawyer replied it had come from personal family holdings purchased at a discount, from substantial investments in

Vanguard Trust, from investing heavily in the stock market shortly after the crash of October 1987, and from his law practice.

Shore and the TD were satisfied with the explanation and the security offered, and officially granted Melnitzer a $21-million line of credit. A meeting to finalize the deal was planned for July 29 at Melnitzer's office, later rescheduled and eventually cancelled because of Melnitzer's arrest. No funds were extended to Melnitzer and the TD bank was saved by a whisker from a potential loss of $21 million.

Meanwhile, no matter how busy Melnitzer was with his work in Toronto, the new home and plans for the new scam, he and Baltman continued to live the high life. In January and February there were trips to Utah for skiing, in early May a trip to Ottawa, back to Utah late that month and in early July, a trip to Israel and Egypt.

At its midway point, 1991 was living up to Melnitzer's expectations. He'd bought a fine new home, he had some valuable new connections in Toronto, and it looked as if he should be able to repay the Singapore investors their $5.5 million fairly soon. Although he'd been turned down twice on requests for credit lines of $6 million, all was not bleak. For an investment of $241.63 in stocks — and $100,000 to the printer — he was about to finalize arrangements on credit lines totalling $29 million. The investor in him smiled.

10

A Question of Trust

"We have no reason to doubt Mr. Melnitzer's word."

A BANK CAN BE AN INTIMIDATING place for the average person. The unblinking eyes of security cameras follow customer movements; high counters and centralized cash stations protect tellers — and the bank's money — from customers with dishonest intent; alarms are tucked out of sight; even regular customers may be instructed to sign withdrawal slips in front of bank staff. Those same "valued" customers can rest assured that if their accounts are overdrawn by even a few cents, a banker somewhere is poised to bounce their cheques — and impose healthy service charges.

But there are reasons trust is in such short supply in banks. They have been burned many times in the past. They've been robbed, defrauded and otherwise deceived by people who want money. In response, they have developed policies and practices to reduce the likelihood of being victimized again. They are professional money handlers, and if they alienate a few customers, well, that's just the cost of doing business.

Most of us are accustomed to turning to a bank when money is needed for a new car, home renovation, boat or vacation. Banks aggressively market consumer loans because the interest on such transactions provides the funds for many of their activities, including making more loans and paying interest to depositors. But verbal assurance of repayment from an honest customer is not enough. The bank wants reams of information and security in case the customer defaults. That means paperwork and credit checks.

A loans officer records the particulars of the borrower, along with a listing of all debts. The officer wants to know the exact amounts owing and to whom, including everything from credit cards to rent or home mortgages. Details of employment and income are sought. Significant assets such as vehicles are recorded. The prospective borrower is advised that his or her financial history will be checked with the local credit bureau and that the bank will make inquiries of its own. The applicant is told he or she shouldn't have more than 40 percent of gross income tied up in "debt servicing" — banker lingo for total loan payments. If a car is offered as security, the bank will likely run a separate computer check to ensure it isn't encumbered by another lender.

The loans officer looks deep into the financial soul of the customer, following time-tested procedures that do not rely on verbal assurances about anything. The scrutiny is intense; the trust minimal. Bankers call their methods prudent, but customers have used other words to describe them.

If everything checks out, a customer can be on his or her way with the borrowed funds in as little as an hour, or the process can drag on for days or even weeks. Some small-time borrowers have grown to resent their treatment at the hands of the country's big banks, especially when they face continually rising service charges for nearly every transaction they make, then read in the financial pages that banks are more profitable than ever.

Hearing about the special treatment afforded a con man like Julius Melnitzer does not improve their mood.

Melnitzer realized at an early stage that bankers play favorites, and he exploited that tendency to a mind-boggling extent.

Since almost every Canadian adult deals with banks, the only ways an institution can get new business are to lure customers from the competition or persuade existing clients to use the bank more often. Ironically, however, even though depositor money is the lifeblood of any bank, the handling of deposits is a loss leader. Bankers make their profits on products such as loans, credit cards, securities and service charges. From 1980 to 1991 Canada's chartered banks increased their net-interest revenue from loans by 49 percent, to $11.6 billion. For service charges in the same period, revenue rose a whopping 300 percent, to $5.47 billion.

So, the banks' most profitable customer is one who makes use of many services and borrows frequently or in large amounts. Doctors, lawyers, business executives and other professionals with substantial incomes are valued customers and, as such, receive the lowest loan rates, usually a fraction above prime. Customers with big balances are encouraged to take advantage of preferred, investor-type savings accounts, which draw the best interest. Aside from their incomes, many have investment needs or business ventures with which they may require help from time to time. And the bankers are always there, willing to lend what's necessary. Sometimes more.

Many of Canada's banks have established private banking centres or professional banking groups where their most valued customers can deal directly with vice-presidents and senior managers. It's estimated that 10 percent of a bank's customers provide 90 percent of its profits. Banks have designated some branches and trained staff to cater almost exclusively to this market.

Meanwhile, banks are closing branches in low-income neighborhoods, reducing farm lending and scrambling to get out of loans to Third World countries. The money is being redirected to consumer loans, where the preferred consumers are those who are affluent. In its 1990 annual report, the Royal Bank, for instance, noted that private and executive banking was growing substantially. In that year, the Royal increased the number of its personal and executive banking centres from 17 to 32.

Within their communities, bankers try to know who is banking where. Since a certain degree of confidentiality is attached, sometimes the intelligence has to be gleaned informally, from fellow country-club members or at the community or service-club functions bankers are expected to attend.

Bankers are impressed with position. They tend to make fewer demands on high-profile customers, because irritating them might cause them to take their profitable business elsewhere. It has been said that if you're having difficulty obtaining a loan in the thousands, ask for more. Mention millions, and suddenly your banker will begin paying attention. Melnitzer proved this again and again.

The cash a bank offers to loan is not its own but money it has received from depositors. It's a bit like a Ponzi scheme except that federal regulations require banks to have enough money on hand to be able to meet their obligations. The banking industry doesn't print the money, clean it or renovate it. It merely keeps the stuff in circulation and profits on every transaction on the difference between what it pays for the money (interest on deposits) and what it charges for it (interest on loans).

The decade ending in 1991 was sandwiched between two recessions. Many businesses in Canada that survived the first one succumbed in the second. Canada's major banks, however, came through the 1980s in reasonably good shape, despite losses from billion-dollar loans to the Third World and ill-timed assistance to such North American industries as real estate, oil and gas. The only casualties in Canada came in 1985, when the small Northland and Canadian Commercial banks failed. Based in Western Canada, these regional institutions had few borrowers and made the mistake of concentrating their loans in the volatile western real estate and energy sectors. When the oil-patch-based economy went flat, the banks died. The failures of those two banks were the first since 1923, and they sent shock waves through the banking industry.

The 1980s were turbulent times, however, for financial institutions in the United States. Deregulation of the savings-and-loan industry at the start of the decade triggered a series of events that led to the collapse of several hundred of those institutions. American taxpayers are being called upon to cough up more than $500 billion over 40 years to repay small investors who lost their life savings. More than the U.S. spent on the Second World War.

The savings-and-loans, similar to trust companies in Canada, were heavily into mortgages and home building. Once deregulated, many became involved in a wide variety of highly speculative ventures. The collapse of real estate and the oil-based economy of the American Southwest produced major problems for many savings-and-loan associations. They were stuck with high interest rates on deposits established to lure investor money from the major banks. At the same time, they held mortgages from which they derived too little interest. Caught in such a squeeze, many of the people who ran the savings-and-loans resorted to cowboy-type entrepreneurship that resulted in not only collapse but also criminal and civil litigation.

In Canada, a land of about 27 million people, the six largest banks have a virtual stranglehold on the country's money. Canadians have more than 39 million personal accounts with the Big Six. The Canadian Bankers' Association reported that in the fiscal year ending in 1991, the six had total assets of about $546 billion, nearly all of that in the form of loans. The remaining two domestic banks and all 56 foreign banks had combined assets of about $67 billion.

The Royal Bank of Canada is the country's largest. With assets of \$132.35 billion in 1991, it had grown by 51.2 percent in a decade. It is followed, in order, by the Canadian Imperial Bank of Commerce, Bank of Montreal, Bank of Nova Scotia and Toronto Dominion Bank. The smallest of the Big Six is the National Bank of Canada, with assets of \$36.46 billion. It grew by 90.3 percent in the same 10-year span. Because of their size and apparent invincibility, the banks have spawned critics who say banking is too much of an old boys' network, into which more competition must be introduced to benefit the consumer. In *Towers of Gold, Feet of Clay*, a colorful diatribe against Canada's banking system, author Walter Stewart observed that the banks swelled by 2033 percent between 1960 and 1981. "Their profits grew from the comfortable to the astonishing and they moved upwards in lock-step . . . Banks make this money in good times and in bad; they are shock-proof, inflation-proof, depression-proof and watertight."

When banks encounter problems with bad loans, they merely nudge up interest rates to all borrowers and increase service charges. The domestic banks had made nearly \$400 billion in loans at the end of 1991 and predicted \$2.7 billion would go bad, a rate of less than 0.7 percent. Credit-card fraud costs the banks \$50 million a year; bank robberies another \$4 million. All are considered costs of doing business and are reflected in what the banks charge the rest of their customers — those who don't default on loans or credit cards and who don't make unauthorized withdrawals at gunpoint.

The other major players in the Canadian financial industry are the trust companies. Royal Trust and Canada Trust, the two largest, are both larger than the smallest of the Big Six, on the basis of assets. Trust companies play by different rules than banks. Banks are tightly controlled by the federal Bank Act, while trust companies operate under either federal or provincial charters. But the distinctions between banks and trust companies have become blurred in recent years.

Traditionally, banks have concentrated their efforts on lending money to individuals, companies and governments. Trust companies offer a wider range of financial services, although some may overlap with chartered banks. They provided mortgages before banks were permitted to enter the field. Trust firms also offer savings accounts, term deposits and personal loans. And they are the only corporations in Canada authorized to act as trustees in charge of corporate or individual assets such as property, stocks and bonds.

Like their savings-and-loan cousins in the United States, Canada's trust companies have had their share of bad publicity. It seems that every few years a trust company fails, producing stories of life savings lost by widows and the elderly at the hands of unscrupulous or incompetent trust-company executives. Millions of tax dollars have been poured into bailout schemes or payouts after such failures.

Collapses in recent years include Standard Trust, Principal Trust, Pioneer Trust, Northwest Trust, Seaway Trust, Greymac Trust, Crown Trust, District Trust, Astra Trust, and British Mortgage and Trust. Stability, the trait the federally chartered banks stress, is not mirrored in the trust industry.

One of the major differences between banks and trust companies is in ownership. Under Canadian banking law, no single shareholder can hold more than 10 percent of a major bank's stock. This is designed to prevent self-dealing, the practice of lending to a related company or individual on unusually good terms.

Trust companies have no limits on ownership. Royal Trust is controlled by Trilon Financial Corp., a member of a string of companies owned by the Bronfman family. Canada Trust is 98-percent owned by Imasco Limited, a conglomerate that also controls Imperial Tobacco and Shoppers Drug Mart.

The ownership question is of no small significance and has been a major factor in the instability of trust companies. Some of the smaller trust firms have run into trouble when they slipped into dealings that were not of an arm's-length nature.

A massive fraud prompted the country's most spectacular trust-firm collapse. In 1982, Seaway, Greymac and Crown Trust all went under because of their dealings with a number of individuals, including a man named William Player. Like Melnitzer, he had big plans and little patience with professional lenders.

Player, then 34, a flamboyant entrepreneur from the small Ontario town of Elmvale, had a weakness for cowboy gear and a penchant for quick-flip real estate deals. He orchestrated a complex series of land transactions through his real estate firm, Kilderkin Investments Ltd., that resulted in the three trust companies being defrauded of $330 million in the largest series of frauds in Canadian history. Player eventually pleaded guilty to 35 charges relating to bogus real estate transactions between 1980 and 1982 and was sentenced in 1987 to 15 years in prison. He was paroled in 1990.

The trust-company affair came to light when the participants purchased and flipped 10,931 apartment units in Toronto — fully five percent of the city's supply — in a one-day transaction intended to net Player more than $200 million. The Ontario government, concerned that 25,000 tenants would face rent increases to help finance the deal, stepped in and the scheme unravelled. The $500-million sale, to 50 numbered Ontario companies purportedly controlled by investors from Saudi Arabia, was discovered to have been a sham.

Player's game plan was to take advantage of the fact that he essentially controlled Seaway Trust and that Greymac and Crown were in the hands of some of his business partners. A typical scenario would see Player's firm purchase a property for $1 million, for example. He would then arrange to have a confederate purport to buy the property at something like $5 million. The money would not actually be paid in this non-arm's-length transaction, but Player would arrange a mortgage from one of the three trust companies for up to 75 percent of the sale price. His confederate would then turn over the $3.75 million thus obtained to Player, who would use the cash to close the actual $1-million deal and pocket the balance. The confederate would be paid a fee for his co-operation and Player would be off on another, larger transaction to cover his new commitments. Known as the "Oklahoma" technique in financial circles, the strategy led Player to his eventual downfall.

The prosecutor in the case noted that no prudent lender would have helped Player finance his transactions with the mortgages.

But banks have no reason to feel smug about the frailties of their lesser counterparts in the trust business. During the years Player was using three trust firms as his cash cows, a bank officer was doing the same with his employer.

Brian Molony, the 27-year-old assistant manager of a downtown Toronto branch of the Canadian Imperial Bank of Commerce, embezzled nearly $17 million to feed his gambling habit. The net loss suffered by the CIBC was $10.2 million.

Molony was not detected by routine inspections of his own bank but by pure fluke. One morning, he was picked up for speeding on his way to work from the Toronto airport after a weekend of gambling in Atlantic City. The previous night, he had lost about $1 million of the bank's money in the baccarat pit at a casino. In his car, police found $30,000 in cash, and securities receipts for about $5 million. He was charged with theft over $200 and soon confessed to the massive fraud. The CIBC didn't have a clue that Molony, an otherwise earnest young man marked for promotion, had been deceiving them for more than 18 months.

Hopelessly addicted to all forms of gambling, especially horse racing and the casinos of Las Vegas and Atlantic City, Molony had set up 10 fictitious loan accounts, some in the names of real customers. One of his responsibilities at the busy Bay Street branch was to approve loans. Fellow employees and his superiors, who'd placed their faith in him because of his dedication to work, never questioned his activities. He authorized 93 fraudulent loans in amounts as high as $1.8 million and deposited the funds into his own accounts for his gambling forays. Molony was particularly clever in his transactions, since he wasn't authorized to lend more than $35,000 and his branch no more than $100,000 without approval from head office.

Molony was a consistent loser in his after-hours habit. The $30,000-a-year banker could blow $60,000 in the roll of a pair of dice. He was so popular in Atlantic City that one casino regularly ferried him between Toronto and New Jersey by private jet and limousine. He kept gambling, always thinking the Big Win, which would square everything with the bank, was just around the corner.

His deceit came as a shock to the CIBC. When a bank spokesperson was asked how Molony had managed to get away with it as long as he did, his response was lame: "How the money went missing without anyone finding out about it is a question a lot of people here are asking."

The key to Molony's success was the esteem in which his fellow workers and supervisors held him. In *Stung: The Incredible Obsession of Brian Molony*, author Gary Ross offers a simple explanation: "As a bank employee, you're trained to be careful and skeptical: never sign anything you don't understand, never initial incomplete documentation, alert your superior to anything dubious. In practice, though, you have no choice but to trust your colleagues. For all the built-in security measures — by-the-book procedures, double signatures, frequent balancing — you rely on mutual trust. When someone hands you a scribbled note and says, 'I need a draft, I'll give you the documentation later,' you assume he's acting with integrity. You must. If you did everything as scrupulously as you were supposed to, you'd never get the day's work done."

In April 1982, when he was arrested, Molony's crime was recognized as the biggest fraud in Canadian banking history. He pleaded guilty to a single count of fraud — the theft charge had been dropped — and was sentenced to six years in prison. He was paroled after serving two and a half years.

One of the factors cited in Molony's ability to carry out his fraud was his bank's inability to cope with rapid expansion and change.

As the century draws to a close, the entire Canadian banking industry is changing. Competition is a growing factor, and banks are fighting to hold on to the business they have by offering more services. Whenever possible, they are trying to pry customers away from competitors, and they are placing more emphasis on their most profitable activities, one of which is currying favor with the 10 percent of the clients who provide 90 percent of those profits. To do so, they are having to exercise a commodity they seldom ever trot out for the small-fry customer. It's called trust.

It was into this environment that Julius Melnitzer strode, armed with a substantial reputation and grandiose plans. With a high public profile, an aggressive and growing law firm, the obvious appearance of wealth and verbal and documentary evidence of it, Melnitzer clearly fell into the 10 percent so eagerly sought by bankers.

When he produced documents relating to his holdings in Melfan Investments and his ability to commit Melfan for his debts, financial statements relating to Melfan or documents relating to his Vanguard shares, bankers trusted him. They had the security they needed and didn't want to offend by questioning its validity. During Melnitzer's earlier transactions, only the Bank of Montreal thought to check the legitimacy of the collateral he had pledged. And even though it found the lawyer couldn't possibly hold the Vanguard shares he reported, the bank continued to trust him, assuming his affairs were complicated rather than fraudulent.

None of the bankers wanted to risk alienating a customer who frequently threatened to take his business elsewhere if he didn't get his way. The Bank of Montreal paid the price for invoking Melnitzer's wrath when its officers were faced with his request to increase his line of credit from $250,000 to $1 million. Their insistence on detailed security and audited personal-income statements prompted Melnitzer to fly into a rage and pay off his existing indebtedness with a cheque drawn on the CIBC. At the National Bank, he had been particularly blunt when he warned he would not only bank with the National's competitors but would also smear the bank's name in the community.

Melnitzer skilfully played the bankers off each other, knowing they would do almost anything for his business. He persuaded them to keep his affairs confidential and they complied, he asked them for letters of reference he could use with other institutions and they co-operated. The officials, many of whom were attached to the personal, private or professional banking sections of their institutions, were more than happy to oblige. They visited Melnitzer at his home or office, wherever he wanted, rather than putting him to the trouble of visiting them.

Large lines of credit or loans meant large interest payments and, therefore, large profits for the banks. Melnitzer's banking records later revealed that toward the end of his scam, the CIBC, his principal banker, was deducting $75,000 to $100,000 a month in overdraft interest.

After Melnitzer's arrest, some bankers ruefully admitted they had been wrong to place so much trust in a man simply on the basis of his reputation. They had been manipulated by an extremely clever con artist, but most of them complied willingly because they had their own agendas. The mind-set of some of the bankers who dealt with Melnitzer is revealed in internal bank memoranda later filed as court exhibits, the largest stack of which related to his transactions with the Royal Bank.

Colin Liptrot, Melnitzer's contact at the Royal, was anxious to please the well-respected and affluent lawyer. Liptrot was manager of the private banking centre in London, and at 7:20 a.m. the last day of banking before the lawyer's arrest, had finalized arrangements for a proposed $8-million line of credit by collecting the forged stock certificates at Melnitzer's office.

Liptrot's dealings with Melnitzer had been extensive, and the banker had been determined from the beginning to win the lawyer's friendship and all his business. In a private and confidential letter to Melnitzer dated February 20, 1990, Liptrot addressed his customer in a very unbankerish way. "Dear Julius," it began. "As usual it was a pleasure to speak with you yesterday. I am glad you are still keeping the airlines in business and working as hard as ever!"

The letter went on to ask for details of Melnitzer's real estate assets and concluded with the notation: "Aside from the borrowings at this office we have no firm information as to mortgage obligations, other bank lines or sundry items such as taxes or credit cards. In order to preserve confidentiality I have not spoken to CIBC concerning your, or your firm's liabilities."

Melnitzer was trying to keep Liptrot in the dark about the extent of his financial dealings, and the banker was apparently agreeable to having Melnitzer act as his source of information about Melnitzer.

The Royal Bank's motives were revealed in an unsigned document dated March 13, 1990, entitled Private Banking Credit Application, outlining the Royal's understanding of Melnitzer. It pegged Melnitzer's surplus annual cash flow at $4.75 million, which it said was more than sufficient to meet payments on extended lines of credit. The document then recounted the Royal's main "goals" in dealing with the lawyer. Among them were "acquiring the legal firm's accounts from CIBC" and "to become Melnitzer's sole personal banker." Also included was the expressed hope that Cohen, Melnitzer would continue referring lawyers to the Royal. The law firm had "become an important referral source, a relationship we intend to continue cultivating. The banking business of five partners has been acquired from CIBC in recent months."

The report expressed satisfaction with "independent verification" from Melnitzer's accountants, which detailed his extensive holdings in Melfan Investments. (Only much later would the Royal, like all other banks, learn this material was forged.) It concluded this way: "Julius Melnitzer maintains a high profile in local, Toronto and international legal circles. He is well placed to assist with the ongoing development of this office with worthwhile referrals. His personal financial statements testify to his business acumen . . . We continue to believe this relationship represents worthwhile business for this office and the identified collateral opportunities will benefit other areas of the bank in due course."

Not everyone at the Royal was impressed with Melnitzer, however. Later that same month, Liptrot addressed a memo to Paul Lonergan, the Royal's senior lending manager in Burlington, who was pressing for better security. Liptrot reminded his superior that the bank was seeking to "capture a wider relationship for ourselves." Liptrot noted Melnitzer could become "a useful bridge to the Jewish community in London where acquiring new relationships is dependent upon qualified introductions." The London manager said he would continue to try to obtain all of Melnitzer's banking business, but cautioned that "acquiring business from the upscale market is time-consuming and rarely are total relationships acquired at the outset."

The Royal Bank documents also show how Melnitzer could alternately bully or tantalize bankers. In an April 25, 1990, memo to file, Liptrot recounted a meeting a few days before involving himself, another bank official and Melnitzer. The bankers had asked their customer for additional security in order to further extend his $3-million line of credit.

"Melnitzer was less than amiable on this occasion and chose to berate myself for not fulfilling the vision of private banking as described in our advertising material," Liptrot wrote. "It would appear that our efforts to gain substantial business from Julius and his law firm are likely to come to nought and that our loans will be progressively repaid from their present level of $2.9 million to zero within the next two months and supporting deposits of $1.5 million withdrawn."

Melnitzer didn't live up to his threat, however, and he and Liptrot continued their negotiations for months. In another memo to file, Liptrot recounted one such meeting and noted Melnitzer promised he was "moving his business from the CIBC providing he can find an accommodating banker."

At the National Bank, an internal consideration of Melnitzer's application for a $20-million line of credit noted he dealt with both the Royal and CIBC. The review pegged Melnitzer's net worth at $77 million, a figure originating with Melnitzer himself. "Mr. Melnitzer's significant net worth has been derived from family wealth inheritance, sound investments and legal practice," senior manager David Renwick wrote. "We are able to confirm all sources of income other than the offshore term deposit (listed at $3.1 million), however, we have no reason to doubt Mr. Melnitzer's word."

Renwick's memo concluded, "Based on our good relationship with Mr. Melnitzer, excellent security package, interest coverage and projected profit to the bank, we recommend [this loan]." But just to show they weren't pushovers, the bank officials authorized a credit line of only $15 million, $5 million shy of what Melnitzer sought.

Melnitzer's partners, business associates and friends also paid a heavy penalty for their trust in him. In actual dollars, the losses incurred by these people easily surpassed those of the banks. Unlike big institutions able to absorb big losses, the investors were hard hit. Some may never recover from Melnitzer's betrayal, either financially or emotionally.

Lawyers within a law firm have to trust each other, and members of the public rely on the honesty of the lawyers to whom they entrust their funds. Perhaps the most common breach of trust occurs when lawyers dip into client trust funds to finance personal investments, high-flying lifestyles or such weaknesses as gambling. Most insist later that they intended to replace the funds they had merely "borrowed."

Few do. When tripped up, they are disbarred, and professional compensation funds repay the victims. No such repayment was available for Melnitzer's Singapore investors and Allan Richman, because his frauds were conducted outside his practice of law.

When it came to defrauding other lawyers, associates and friends, Melnitzer had a mirror image in New York City. Divorce lawyer Alvin Ashley took the same sorts of people surrounding him for $10 million. From 1979 until late 1990, when he confessed to his crimes, Ashley operated a Ponzi scheme in which $6 of every $10 invested went to pay off earlier investors in his mostly nonexistent ventures. The balance was used to support a fabulous lifestyle. And like Melnitzer, Ashley did it all simply because he wanted to be a somebody.

Born poor in the Bronx in 1934, Ashley (then Altschiller) practised law inconspicuously for a few years before opting to specialize in divorce work. He was befriended by an older matrimonial lawyer who brought him into a prestigious firm and helped propel the charismatic Ashley to the presidency of the New York chapter of the American Academy of Matrimonial Lawyers. There, Ashley attracted a wide circle of friends, because he was outgoing, generous, entertaining and fun to be with. He frequented expensive restaurants, always picking up the tab, no matter how large the group. He spoke of having a personal fortune of $20 million but was vague about its source.

Always playing the successful magnate, Ashley told his friends he controlled the Detroit-based Little Caesars pizza chain. He gave them guided tours of franchise outlets, and on one occasion in Florida, he became irate when he discovered nonregulation drinking cups, threatening to report the discovery to the chain's regional manager. He even interviewed the son of a man he was trying to impress for what he described as a $125,000-a-year job as controller of the corporation. The truth was that Ashley had no involvement with Little Caesars at all. He had merely adopted the company for his own purposes.

Ashley believed in conspicuous consumption. He spent $150,000 on his daughter's wedding at an exclusive country club. At legal conventions, he engaged in wild spending and gambling sprees. He took friends on tours of the French Riviera and maintained two homes in New York and a summer home on Long Island.

To further impress his associates, Ashley claimed to be friends with Monaco's Prince Rainier and with Queen Elizabeth, who he said was about to knight him. He said that he had played football with the New York Giants and that he had ties with both American and Israeli intelligence. He claimed to be one of the Central Intelligence Agency's experts on bomb detonation. To some close friends, he said he had been reactivated by the CIA to assassinate Iraq's President Saddam Hussein. He told them later that a bad back forced him to decline the assignment.

Most of Ashley's stories were believed by fellow lawyers and friends, and they had no hesitation trusting their funds to such an impressive man. With little more than his personal word as collateral, they gave him money expecting healthy returns from purported investments in golf courses and Little Caesars. A typical deal would call for an investment of $30,000 for a payout of $45,000 within two years.

Ashley was a charmer. And on early investments, he delivered his returns as promised, frequently persuading his investors to roll the proceeds over into other deals.

He started small, at first cajoling money from his neighbors and eventually taking sums as high as $500,000 from members of the legal community, including his legal mentor and many of the top divorce lawyers in New York, Atlanta, Miami, Rochester and Buffalo. He also tapped close friends, his wife's former psychiatrist, his dentist, two brothers-in-law, a godson and his physical therapist. One lawyer was talked into investing $38,000 that had been set aside for his handicapped daughter. Nearly all the money was lost. "This man played on friendships to the most vicious degree imaginable," one of his bitter victims told *New York Times* reporter David Margolick. "The closer you were to him the harder you got hit."

When asked later why he had conned so many people, including his closest friends, Ashley replied, "Because it was so fucking easy."

One of Ashley's lesser victims explained the actions of his former high-rolling friend this way: "He just had a compulsion to be someone else and was actually able to convince himself he was."

But the pressures of living a lie for so long and his eventual and inevitable failure to satisfy an overwhelming list of investors caught up with Ashley. When confronted by his senior partner about the dealings, he broke down and confessed everything. After pleading guilty to five counts of grand larceny in September 1991, he was sentenced to a term of three to nine years. Under New York law, that means he's eligible for parole after serving three. He has also been disbarred and lost his home, his money and most of his friends.

He claims his schemes left him destitute, but for obvious reasons, lawyers no longer trust him. A large number of civil actions have been launched against him on behalf of his victims. Several of his lawyer-victims are convinced Ashley has a fortune stashed away in overseas bank accounts. As one put it, "This guy didn't practise matrimonial law for 30 years without learning how to hide money."

Similar allegations have been made about Julius Melnitzer.

11

Hot July

". . . a significant risk that I would be caught."

AS JULY 1991 BEGAN, Melnitzer was feeling optimistic about his state of affairs. It was the beginning of the summer doldrums for many lawyers and bankers but not for him. The month promised to be busy, because he planned to significantly expand his lines of credit and have them in place before leaving for the Far East and Europe the second week of August.

In May and June, Melnitzer had mentioned the availability of blue-chip stocks to the Royal and Toronto Dominion banks. He said he'd like to obtain lines of credit equalling 70 percent of the value of the stock and had received encouraging responses. As he was lining up those banks for credit lines of $8 million and $21 million, respectively, Sterling Marking Products was continuing to improve its work on the certificates.

Sam Hassan and his technical staff had worked hard to meet the deadlines imposed by Melnitzer, but Hassan reported they were unable to reach the level of quality they expected within the lawyer's time restraints. They showed him their progress but asked for an extension. A deadline for completion of the job had been set initially for June 28, but that was pushed back to July 30 and eventually to October 7.

Melnitzer, disappointed that the task was proving to be so time-consuming, was impatient with the delays. Now that he'd told the bankers about the certificates, he needed something to show them. He was anxious to begin repaying the Singapore investors with bank money and needed the certificates to get it. He had asked Hassan to create five copies of each of the seven shares, stipulating exact share amounts and dates for each. On July 2, he obtained single copies of each of the shares on the understanding Sterling would continue trying to improve its work. He asked the printing staff to keep up their efforts, but said he needed the early copies "to do some kind of testing, like focus-group testing," as part of his preparations for the stock-fraud case he had told them about.

With the shares in hand, Melnitzer inspected each carefully. He was pleased with the workmanship and knew his faith in Sterling was well-founded. Only an expert would be able to tell the difference, he was sure. They were good enough to take to the banks.

He didn't waste any time, contacting the Canadian Imperial Bank of Commerce the same day, just before leaving for Toronto.

For many years, Melnitzer's favorite bank had been the CIBC. He conducted most of his personal banking there, as did many of his partners and the Cohen, Melnitzer firm.

He had begun dealing with the downtown branch of the bank in 1984 and immediately liked the way it did business. Bank officers were receptive to his need for credit lines, and while his account manager was a man named Tom Kahnert, the bank also assigned him Geoffrey Foster, vice-president for Ontario. Foster, a career banker in his mid-50s, was moved by the bank to London the same year Melnitzer became a customer. He would be the lawyer's prime contact with the CIBC.

Melnitzer and Foster were soon on first-name terms, and each respected the other's position. Foster was trying to do his part to help the CIBC catch the Royal Bank, the perennial front-runner in the country's banking race. The CIBC had been gradually gaining ground on the Royal throughout the 1980s with service and marketing innovations, and it was determined to take the top spot. It had been among the first to realize a bank's greatest profits are derived from its most affluent customers. Melnitzer, aggressive and equally innovative, was determined to ensure Cohen, Melnitzer became the largest, most successful law firm in the city. He was willing to borrow to do it, and the CIBC was anxious to lend. The lawyer was exactly the sort of client the bank was trying to encourage, and it was only natural the two developed a symbiotic relationship.

Melnitzer's lines of credit had grown from the hundreds of thousands into the millions as the decade wore on. Foster was well acquainted with the lawyer's expanding reputation in the London area and had an abiding trust in him. He relied on the financial information, security instruments and other documentation Melnitzer had provided over the years in support of his request for various loans. Foster had no reason to believe they were anything but authentic. The CIBC had accepted them — and the apparently wealthy customer — at face value.

Melnitzer made extensive use of his line of credit at the CIBC and was continually asking for an increase in his limit. After asking for more documentation, the bank invariably complied.

An indication of the CIBC's willingness to help came in February 1990, when the bank made a cash advance to Melnitzer of $2.5 million. The money was to purchase shares in Champion Chemtech Limited. After reviewing the Champion operation and the lawyer's plan to acquire 25 percent of the photochemical firm's voting shares, the bank gave him the full amount. Melnitzer was surprised the bank was so forthcoming.

By April 1991, his credit limit had swollen to $8,350,000. When he asked for more late in the month, the bank didn't hesitate to bump it up another $500,000. CIBC records reveal that, at the time, his account was overdrawn by $7.9 million.

During the early months of 1991, Melnitzer had also obtained a $2.5-million revolving demand loan from the CIBC for Grand Canyon Properties, the company he and Allan Richman had set up. A Melfan guarantee backed that loan as well. And when he was attempting to take over the mortgage on the Roxborough Street home in Toronto, he asked his obliging banker to provide a letter of recommendation to the Toronto Dominion Bank. The CIBC complied.

Melnitzer's pattern of spending continued, and as he reached his credit limits, he again turned to the CIBC for more money. In June, about the same time he mentioned his blue-chip shares to the Toronto Dominion, Melnitzer told Foster about them. He wanted to know if he could use them to boost substantially his credit limit with the CIBC. Foster was interested. He and the lawyer worked out the terms of a new large revolving investment loan, while Kahnert handled the details. As with his other bankers, Melnitzer sought assurances that the certificates would not be registered under the Personal Property Security Act.

It was agreed his credit limit would be raised to $20 million effective July 19. The blue-chip shares were to be assigned to the bank, and the earlier security — shares of Vanguard Trust and Champion Chemtech Limited — would be returned to him.

On July 3, Kahnert retrieved the Vanguard and Champion shares from the bank's vault and travelled to Toronto to meet Melnitzer at the Roxborough home. Kahnert turned over the shares and received five new certificates in exchange. They were for 95,193 shares in McDonald's Corporation, 94,622 shares in Canadian Pacific, 98,435 shares in IBM, 71,628 shares in BCE and 96,998 shares in Exxon Corporation.

Kahnert returned to London where the bank finalized details for the new credit limit. Melnitzer held his breath, hoping the bank wouldn't look behind the face of the forged certificates and discover they were fakes. He heard nothing from the bank, and after a couple of days he realized his latest and most daring forgery had been accepted without challenge. Foster, who had relied heavily on the financial statements for Melfan on the earlier lines of credit, saw no reason to doubt the authenticity of the latest security.

In his heart, Melnitzer knew his most recent forgery was fraught with danger. One banker's telephone call to the transfer agent listed on any of the stock certificates and his fraud would be revealed. The CIBC chose not to make any such call.

When asked later by police about the risk he ran from July 3 on, Melnitzer freely admitted he had exposed himself to easy detection when he began offering the fake stock certificates to the banks. "I knew that for a transaction of this magnitude there was a significant risk that I would be caught," he conceded. "I knew that when I did it. I intended to use them . . . to get pressure off myself. I never really intended to go much beyond the original line of credit. What I intended to do was simply to replace the security with something . . . where the banks wouldn't get on your back every time there was a recession. There was a lot of pressure, that was the main reason for it . . . I intended to pay out some private people who I thought would suffer losses and I wanted to take care of them."

He was pressed further by police about the chances he had taken. Didn't he know it was almost inevitable that someone, somewhere, would check out his security? Didn't he know his scheme was virtually doomed?

"I don't think when you do this, you think that far ahead," he replied. "I think if I'd thought that far ahead I wouldn't be in this boat."

Emboldened by his success with the CIBC, Melnitzer began wondering if he could find even more bankers willing to accept fake share certificates, once he obtained more from Sterling. If the banks were willing to forgo PPSA registrations, he might as well offer the same certificates elsewhere to obtain further funds. He'd already committed fraud with the CIBC and hadn't been caught. And if he was ever tripped up, was there really any difference between a fraud of $20 million and one of $40 million?

On July 8, he turned to the National Bank of Canada. His account manager, John Graham, was on vacation, so Melnitzer dealt with senior manager David Renwick. He told Renwick he was looking for a new line of credit of $20 million to replace his existing $2-million one, which had an outstanding balance of $1.6 million. Melnitzer said he needed the money for real estate and other investment purposes, and was prepared to pledge as security blue-chip stock certificates valued at about $32 million. He didn't feel they had to be registered under PPSA, he stressed yet again. Renwick agreed.

Renwick reviewed the bank's files on Melnitzer and was impressed. The lawyer had been a solid customer and his credit line had been operating satisfactorily. The shares he had mentioned seemed like excellent security, given their high liquidity, trading volumes, asset base and earning levels — far better security, in fact, than the shares in Melfan, a private company whose shares would be hard to liquidate. The banker said he needed some further information, but it appeared a substantial new line of credit would be available.

At the bank's request, Melnitzer provided a signed personal statement of affairs dated April 1, 1991, listing annual income of $4,975,000. It showed assets of nearly $56 million and liabilities of $7.6 million.

The statement read as follows:

Assets

19 Tallwood, London	$ 550,000
175 Cumberland, Toronto	500,000
88 Roxborough, Toronto	2,000,000
Equity in law firm	300,000
RRSP	50,000
Melfan	15,000,000
Champion Photo (25 percent)	2,500,000
Grand Canyon	1,250,000
Art Collection (evaluated by Sotheby's)	2,000,000+
Offshore liquid financial instruments	30,000,000

Land in Quebec	125,000
7 units, Hunt Ridge MURB*, Ottawa	100,000
Stradivarius violin (1/3 int.)	300,000
RMG Investments	300,000
Partnership interest in law firm	750,000

Liabilities

National Bank	1,600,000
CIBC	3,000,000
other institutions	1,000,000
various mortgages	2,000,000

*multiple-unit residential building, a tax shelter plan for high-income earners designed to encourage rental housing construction

Melnitzer also provided Melfan financial statements as of April 30, 1990, showing net income for the year of $4 million and retained earnings of $14.1 million. The statements were purportedly prepared and signed by London accountants Marcus and Associates.

The true net worth of Melfan in 1990 was $243,435. No mention that he owed nearly $3 million to the Royal Bank, that he actually owed $8.35 million to the CIBC, that $5.5 million was owed to the Singapore investors, or that roughly $10 million more was owed to Allan Richman, Grand Canyon Properties and Richman's Forward Properties. Melnitzer also neglected to mention that he was insolvent and had been for several months.

Based on the figures provided, the National Bank calculated Melnitzer's net worth at $77.7 million. It was after this review of his request for funds that Renwick concluded, "We have no reason to doubt Mr. Melnitzer's word."

The same day that Melnitzer approached the National Bank about the latest credit line, he and Baltman left for a two-week tour of Israel and Egypt. The cost of the trip by air, road and boat totalled nearly $23,000. Knowing he was coming into substantial funds, the lawyer felt comfortable with the extravagance.

Melnitzer was increasingly busy on several fronts. He learned there was a possibility he might be able to obtain some money from the Bank of Montreal. He had asked his partner, Ron Delanghe, to make some approaches to that bank to restore the relationship Melnitzer had furiously severed when bank officials had pressed him for better security to increase his line of credit from $250,000 to $1 million. Delanghe had talked to a vice-president of the bank and suggested Melnitzer should be granted a loan of $7 or $8 million. He reported upon Melnitzer's return that things looked promising. He said the banking executive had delegated another bank employee to hold preliminary discussions with Melnitzer on August 4.

As it became apparent he might be dealing with even more bankers, Melnitzer realized he would need more share certificates. He wrote to Sam Hassan at Sterling Marking Products to place his order. "Dear Sam: Please be advised that I will require ten copies of each of the certificates that you are producing, rather than five, as originally requested."

On July 22, Renwick and Graham issued the letter of commitment for a $15-million line of credit at the National Bank. It was agreed the shares pledged in support of the line would be collected later.

In a matter of weeks, the bank would learn to its chagrin that Melnitzer had vastly exaggerated his assets, lied about the existence of offshore funds, minimized his liabilities and had forged the accounting material. The National would also learn that everything it had held since 1987 relating to Melfan Investments was forged.

After his Middle East holiday with Baltman, Melnitzer turned his thoughts to resolving the nagging problem of the Singapore investors.

He'd been busily rounding up cash and his personal financial picture was looking much brighter. He felt he could now plan to pay off his friends with the new money from the banks. He took out a scratch pad and began adding up the money he would have at his disposal.

He was getting a $20-million credit line from the CIBC, which, after subtracting the $8 million he already owed them, would leave him with nearly $12 million. He was getting a $15-million credit line from the National Bank, which would mean he'd have $13.4 million left to play with, since his indebtedness to them already stood at $1.6 million. The Royal Bank had promised another $8-million credit line, leaving $6.7 million after the $1.3 million he'd already taken. And the TD Bank had promised $21 million. All of that would be newfound money.

Melnitzer smiled as he added up the figures. By the end of July or the first week in August, he would have lines of credit totalling $64 million, of which he'd be able to use $52.7 million, if needed. He circled the latter figure and smiled. His $241.63 investment in single shares was looking better all the time.

He didn't want to count his credit lines before they hatched, but he was determined to let the Singapore people know he would be repaying them sooner than they expected, and in greater amounts. He approached several, including Delanghe, and explained that the Singapore government had experienced greater revenues than it had predicted and wanted to complete the transaction on the Orchard Road property sooner than anticipated. It was prepared to pay a substantial penalty for revoking its agreement with Melnitzer and his partners, he said. He added that while details were still being hammered out, it appeared the transaction would close within a month. He calculated effective interest for the Singapore investors in London would be about 100 percent.

Delanghe and the others were delighted — interest of 100 percent for investments of a few months! Their friend Julius had been right; this had been the opportunity of a lifetime. Some kicked themselves for not putting up more money. All let him know how happy they were with the situation.

Melnitzer told the investors that, in a few days, he would be issuing them cheques totalling $6.6 million, but he would have to postdate them to the end of August.

After his arrest, Melnitzer told police he felt he had to honor his promises to the Singapore investors by ripping off the banks. He had to be immoral with bankers to be moral with friends.

"My game plan," he said, "was to increase the bank lines, pay everybody off that I had made promises to. Now, you know, if I had been sensible, what I should have said was, I should have gone to these people after the bank lines and said to them, 'Look, the deal hasn't worked out, here's your money back with interest and all your expenses and a little bit.' But I didn't do that, I couldn't do that. I had promised them they'd double their investment and that's what I was going to do."

With vast new sums now or soon to be at his disposal, Melnitzer believed he could juggle his affairs and keep them sufficiently confusing to his various bankers that he could satisfy any one of them with funds taken from another. Less than a month later, after being caught red-handed, he explained his plan to lawyers for the National Bank this way: "I guess I depended on the confusion that trust creates."

He knew from experience that bankers squawked if he didn't use his lines enough or if he was getting close to his credit limits. He planned to keep money moving in and out of his accounts to keep the bankers in the dark about his true state of affairs.

Like Charles Ponzi toward the end of his scam, Melnitzer was now operating at a feverish pitch, juggling astronomical amounts of money. But he had little committed to paper. For the most part, his scheme remained in his head, and as his borrowing activity increased, he felt as though he was on a financial treadmill. Things were happening fast now, and like a chess player operating within stringent time limits, he had to make moves quickly and still try to think several moves beyond. So far, the pliant bankers had made that easy.

Outsiders would later say he was carrying on like a man who wanted to get caught, but they didn't know how easily the bankers had been seduced and how confident Melnitzer was that he could keep them happy.

Late in July, the Toronto Dominion Bank asked to reschedule the meeting to finalize the $21-million line of credit. It had been set for the twenty-ninth. Melnitzer was slightly annoyed, because he wanted to have the deal concluded in advance of his trip to Singapore and Europe. A new date of August 6 was agreed upon, his last day in London before the trip.

On the twenty-ninth, Melnitzer met with Hassan at Sterling Marking Products and reviewed the printing firm's work. He was impressed and asked Hassan to continue the efforts. In the meantime, he collected more of the certificates he had ordered. Melnitzer believed they were of such high quality he could proceed with meetings he had planned with several of his bankers.

That same day, he contacted Tom Kahnert, his account manager at the CIBC. The bank had been asking him to replace some of the security he'd provided for earlier lines of credit. It had agreed to take another stock certificate. Kahnert came to the Cohen, Melnitzer offices where Melnitzer provided him with a sixth certificate.

Melnitzer was gambling and winning, and he decided to have a bit of fun with some of his new money. Always a minor student of the stock market, he had dabbled in a number of stocks, many of them penny mining shares. His holdings had a total worth of about $180,000, the most valuable being his shares in a cable television company called Cableshare. But mining intrigued him. The possibility of a major discovery was always just around the corner with mining exploration firms, and he enjoyed the sport of buying and selling such stocks. He had just disposed of about $80,000 worth of shares in Aur Resources Inc., a Quebec-based company that operated four gold mines and was spending $6 million in 1991 to find more. The stock had dipped to $3.50 a share from a high of about $7, and Melnitzer decided it was time to get back in. He contacted his broker at ScotiaMcLeod and ordered $1 million worth of Aur shares.

On July 30, Melnitzer began to make use of some of his Royal Bank money by depositing it with the law firm. He had arranged to finalize details on the credit-line increase to $8 million the following day. Three separate drafts, in the amounts of $673,357.44, $470,000 and $37,626 were deposited into Cohen, Melnitzer's general account. He later told the official receiver in bankruptcy that the first two amounts, totalling $1.14 million, were payments made on behalf of an existing client. The smaller amount was for a fictitious account. The forensic accountants later concluded the first two payments were to the account of Archie Gibbs from the Grand Bend beach case. The law firm refused to confirm that, however, citing lawyer-client confidentiality. But Melnitzer insisted he had made $2 million in payments for real and fictitious clients in his last two years of practice, including $1.1 million for Gibbs.

The same day, he wrote two cheques on his CIBC account, representing payouts for the Singapore investors, and gave them to Delanghe. One was for $5 million, the other for $1.6 million. The cheques were postdated August 31. They were to be distributed to members of the law firm-based investment group, which didn't include Allan Richman and Jules Fleischer. Melnitzer planned to make separate arrangements with them.

July 31 started early with a visit from his friend, Colin Liptrot, the private banking manager for the Royal Bank. At 7:20 a.m., Liptrot met Melnitzer at the law offices. The lawyer was alone, surprisingly bright-eyed and alert for the hour, the banker noted.

Liptrot had agreed to come at this time to collect the five share certificates as part of the arrangements connected to raising Melnitzer's line of credit from $3 million to $8 million.

The lawyer turned over certificates for 95,193 shares in McDonald's, 94,622 shares in Canadian Pacific, 25,806 shares in IBM, 71,628 shares in BCE and 50,412 shares in Exxon. He also provided financial statements for Melfan and a personal statement of affairs. Liptrot had Melnitzer sign several forms, including his acceptance of the Royal's terms.

"You know, Colin," the lawyer said as he put down his pen, "I'm not sure if this is the right time to mention it, but some other banks have suggested that, based on my holdings, they'd be prepared to extend me a line of credit of $20 or $21 million. Since I'm dealing with you, do you think you'd be interested?"

With that, Melnitzer produced two more certificates, one for a further 98,435 shares of IBM, the other for 96,998 shares of Exxon. "I figure these must be worth another $16 million, anyway," the lawyer said.

Liptrot looked over the certificates and passed them back.

"Yes, I think there's something there to talk about," he conceded. "I'll have to talk to my superiors and get back to you later, if that's okay, Julius. Perhaps after you get back from this trip of yours."

"Fine, fine, no great rush," Melnitzer replied. "Just thought you'd like to know what I have available. Let me know in September."

The two discussed Melnitzer's upcoming trip to Malaysia, Europe and the Mideast. When Liptrot left, the support staff was just reporting for work.

Melnitzer returned to his paperwork, pleased Liptrot seemed agreeable to extending the just-negotiated credit line even further.

At 10:20, he entertained his second banker, John Graham from the National Bank. Graham arrived to collect five certificates for the $15-million credit line the National had approved.

The meeting was cordial, Melnitzer thought. After Graham left, Melnitzer was buoyant. Not even noon yet and he'd already signed on for $23 million in credit. Marvellous!

But there was too little time to waste it congratulating himself. More arrangements and transactions were necessary. He called his old friend Jules Fleischer to tell him that the Singapore Deal was closing early and that he'd be earning interest of 100 percent for his 10-month investment. Melnitzer invited him to come to the Roxborough house in Toronto on August 7 to pick up a cheque that would be postdated August 30, in the amount of $400,000.

It was also time to conclude another matter that had been bothering him for a while — Calla Reid. Aside from his purchase of the condominium and the BMW for his former mistress, Melnitzer had been sending her cheques of $2500 every month since their affair had begun in November 1989. Although the relationship had ended, his sense of duty required him to continue helping her. But he had spent more than $650,000 on her and felt it was time to terminate his financial involvement. The only way he could think of doing so was with a final gift. In one of his last pieces of banking this incredible day, he transferred $100,000 from his account at the CIBC to hers at the Bank of Montreal in Toronto.

Satisfied, finally, that his business affairs were in order, Melnitzer turned his mind to a pressing family obligation. He and Baltman were expected in Montreal to attend the formal unveiling for his father. Alexander Melnitzer had died the previous November and, in Jewish tradition, was buried within a day. During the next year, the loved ones of the deceased are called together again for a memorial ceremony and the formal unveiling of the headstone at the cemetery. The unveiling was Friday, August 2. Melnitzer and Baltman planned to fly to Montreal the day before the service and return to London about 4 p.m. on Sunday, August 4.

When his plane lifted off the runway at London airport, Melnitzer was satisfied with his efforts and confident more than ever that he was on a roll. Even with two weeks of holiday, his banking activities in July had been extraordinary. During the month, he had obtained credit lines totalling $43 million. Within a few more days, he expected to finalize the $21 million from the Toronto Dominion Bank. Liptrot of the Royal had given him the impression that a further $12 million was available there. And there was a meeting scheduled with the Bank of Montreal that he hoped might produce another $7 or $8 million. If the Royal and Bank of Montreal came through, that would bring his credit lines, based on fake stock certificates, to a total of almost $84 million.

12

Collapse

"It looks like I'll be going away to jail . . ."

Chris Osborne was looking forward to his first glass of white wine at a late Thursday-afternoon institution known as "litigation drinks." It was 5:30 p.m., Thursday, August 1 and Osborne was about to convene the weekly gathering in his office on the thirty-seventh floor of the gold-sided Royal Bank Plaza in downtown Toronto.

Osborne, a senior member of the prestigious law firm of McMillan Binch, enjoyed these weekly bull sessions. They let staff get to know each other and provided a welcome respite from the pressures of representing the interests of some of Canada's major corporations. Besides, Osborne, a gravel-voiced man of 45 with an off-the-wall sense of humor, loved swapping tall tales. He enjoyed meeting newcomers to the firm and doing his bit to develop camaraderie in the litigation section of the large law office, which occupied four floors. One of 55 partners in the 120-lawyer operation, he was popular with fellow practitioners and commanded their respect. His Thursday afternoon get-togethers usually drew 15 to 20 participants. He had no reason to think this day would be any different and was expecting the first arrival any moment.

Osborne had just cleared up the last of his paperwork

when Andy Kent, a corporate-commercial solicitor from McMillan Binch's banking group, strode in. He looked all business.

"I'm looking for a litigator," Kent announced abruptly. Osborne looked around. No one else to finger. It appeared he'd been volunteered.

"What can I do for you?" Osborne asked, inwardly cursing his luck.

Kent explained that some brass from the National Bank of Canada would soon be in his office on an emergency matter and he wanted a courtroom lawyer on hand.

The two lawyers went to Kent's office where, in a few minutes, a small delegation of bankers arrived. They included Ian Crook, credit manager for the National Bank, Brad Sutcliffe, manager of business development, and two staff members from the London branch, senior manager Dave Renwick and account manager John Graham.

Crook said it appeared that a customer of the bank in London had committed a massive fraud using forged stock certificates. And it appeared he was about to leave the country. The client was Julius Melnitzer, a prominent lawyer who had already obtained nearly $2 million of the bank's money and had just been approved for another $15 million.

Osborne couldn't help but notice the concern in the banker's rapid-fire recitation. He and Kent peppered Crook with questions. Where are the certificates now? What proof is there that they're forged? Are the experts still around? Can we get them to swear affidavits? Where is your customer at this moment?

Osborne realized fast action was required. An injunction would be required to freeze Melnitzer's assets to ensure he didn't flee the country with the bank's money. He said he would need affidavits from National Bank staff and from the experts who had pronounced the Melnitzer certificates fake. Jennifer Badley, a bright young woman who had juniored for Osborne on many cases, was seconded to help Osborne prepare the paperwork.

When they were finished with Crook and Sutcliffe, Osborne and Badley questioned the two bankers from London. The lawyers decided the bank had enough evidence to ask for an injunction freezing Melnitzer's assets and forcing him to provide the bank with a complete listing of those assets and accounts. A receiver would then have to be appointed to take over his financial affairs. Finally, a lawsuit would be filed in a bid to recover the $1.6 million outstanding from the first line of credit.

Because the bankers were concerned Melnitzer was about to leave the country, but didn't know his whereabouts, Osborne suggested they try for a "Mareva" injunction. Named after the *Mareva*, a ship involved in a 1975 English court decision that was restrained from leaving port until the resolution of a legal dispute over monies owed to its owners by the company chartering it, such an injunction can be applied for without notice to the affected party. But a judge must be convinced there is an imminent threat that the defendant may flee the jurisdiction and his or her obligations. The National Bank officials pointed out that Melnitzer had said he was going to begin drawing funds almost immediately and would be leaving for Singapore in a matter of days. That was the leverage they would use to get the Mareva injunction, thus allowing Melnitzer's assets to be frozen.

Osborne and Badley began preparing affidavits from the bankers that night; the trust-company experts who had determined the share certificates were fake would be interviewed the following day. The work was tedious but the bankers and the lawyers stuck with it. There was much at stake. Finally, at 2:30 a.m., it was decided to pack it in for the night. The RCMP would be called first thing in the morning. Rooms were taken at a nearby hotel, where talk continued until 4 a.m.

The bankers and lawyers were back at Osborne's office within five hours. Crook contacted the Mounties' commercial-crime section to report a stock fraud. Within an hour, Sergeant George Gunn and Corporal Mike Hubley arrived at the

McMillan Binch offices, where Osborne explained the situation.

After the lawyer's recitation, Gunn, a man in his early 40s, was phlegmatic. "Seen it before, don't know how many times," he said. "Same trick, just bigger amounts on this one." His audience was wide-eyed. They couldn't get over the veteran officer's cool reaction at what was to them a shocking crime. A major breach of trust. "So where are the certificates?" Gunn asked. "We better get some fingerprints."

The bankers and lawyers were aghast, then looked at each other in dismay. All of them, including the experts, had been handling the evidence for hours. No one had thought about fingerprints. They broke the news to Gunn.

It was his turn to be amazed.

After he got over his surprise, the officer opted to wait for the completion of the affidavits. The material to be used as the basis for the freezing order would also help the Mounties obtain search warrants to formally seize the stock certificates now in the hands of the National Bank. A separate application, however, would have to be made to search the Cohen, Melnitzer offices in London. In the meantime, Gunn interviewed Renwick, Graham, Sutcliffe and the trust-company officials who came to the McMillan Binch office that day to swear affidavits.

The process was time-consuming, but the bankers, lawyers and police officers knew every detail had to be absolutely correct. This appeared to be a fraud of huge proportions, and an extremely intelligent lawyer was the alleged perpetrator. One mistake now could allow him to wriggle away.

At one point, Corporal Hubley expressed impatience at the pace of the investigation and his concern that Melnitzer might escape. "Let's pop him right now, George," he suggested to Gunn. But the senior officer was content to wait. Haste could undermine the case.

From the middle of the afternoon on, Gunn was in touch with his counterpart in London, Sergeant Ray Porter. He told

Porter to be on standby because he might be called upon to arrest Melnitzer. Gunn began preparing a search warrant for the London law office.

Meanwhile, without support staff, Badley was forced to make copies of the extensive documentation herself. Seven of the eight photocopiers in the office broke down before her work was done.

As the paperwork was nearing completion, a justice of the peace was found who was willing to come to McMillan Binch to authorize the search warrant needed to seize the forged certificates from the bank. He arrived at midnight but had to wait more than two hours until everything was in order. He approved the warrant, and Gunn immediately appropriated the five certificates.

Arrangements had been made to take the application for an injunction before a civil-court judge. It hadn't been easy finding a justice of the Ontario Court, general division, willing to interrupt his holiday weekend. But Justice Harry Keenan had agreed to hear the application at 9:30 a.m. at the venerable Osgoode Hall courthouse.

Osborne, Badley, Crook and others from the bank, as well as representatives of the accounting firm of Coopers and Lybrand, who were to act as receivers, reported to the courthouse at the appointed time. The small delegation found it difficult to persuade security guards to let them into the deserted building on the sultry Saturday morning, but once inside, Keenan was gracious and accommodating. The judge carefully read the thick tome that had been so painstakingly crafted over many long hours. He pronounced himself satisfied with the material and said he believed the National Bank had grounds for concern.

"That looks like fraud to me," he announced as he signed the draft order imposing the injunction freezing Melnitzer's assets and appointing the receiver. The injunction was for seven days. The lawyers and Melnitzer would have to come back to court the following Friday, August 9. With no support staff available, Keenan further obliged his visitors by finding a photocopier and making enough copies of the order to serve on the various banks, as well as on Cohen, Melnitzer and other affected parties, including Melfan Investments.

With Keenan's order in hand, Coopers and Lybrand immediately dispatched staff to London to serve the few banks that might be open on a Saturday. The rest would have to wait until business resumed on Tuesday morning, August 6.

Throughout the day, Alan Driver, a senior vice-president of Coopers and Lybrand, paid repeated visits to Melnitzer's Toronto home on Roxborough Street East. He wanted to advise the lawyer his financial affairs had been taken over by the receiver. There was no sign of life, so Driver left messages on the answering machine at the front door of the massive house. He identified himself and asked Melnitzer to call. He didn't say why.

About 5:30 p.m., Melnitzer telephoned Driver, expressing delight at the contact.

"I was wondering when I'd be getting some business from Coopers and Lybrand," Melnitzer said, his mood clearly upbeat. "What can I do for you?"

Driver quickly explained that his firm had been appointed receiver to Melnitzer's estate and that his assets had been frozen solid by Keenan. He said the lawyer shouldn't try to leave the country or to transact any business. Melnitzer was suspected of having committed a major fraud against the National Bank, Driver said. He wanted to interview the lawyer in the near future to sort out his affairs.

Melnitzer was stunned. After a moment's silence, he admitted it was true, that he had defrauded the bank. The suddenly sombre lawyer said he was in Montreal on family matters but would be returning to London the next day about four o'clock. He promised to be in touch.

Meanwhile, Mounties Gunn and Hubley continued their investigation into the criminal aspects of the case. They were putting the final touches on the application for a search warrant for the offices of Cohen, Melnitzer.

They realized the focus of the investigation would have to shift to London where the alleged crime had transpired. There wasn't much else to do in Toronto. That meant Porter would be inheriting the case, but Gunn wanted to make the transition orderly. He and Hubley drove to London to have Porter review the search warrant for Cohen, Melnitzer. And they began looking for a judge there before whom the warrant could be sworn. The warrant was perfected and the judge was located shortly before 9 p.m. Saturday.

Porter contacted members of Cohen, Melnitzer about 10 p.m. and the lawyers and Mounties met at the law office an hour later. After finding the 19 certificates with their fake worth of $100 million in Melnitzer's desk and talking to Melnitzer by phone at 2 a.m., the Mounties concluded this phase of the investigation at nearly 3:30 a.m. on Sunday.

There wasn't much the Mounties could do on Sunday, August 4, until Melnitzer arrived in town. After Porter and the others caught up on some sleep, he and Gunn discussed the next steps. It would be necessary to alert local banking institutions about the situation and ask them to review their files to see if Melnitzer had provided them with similarly forged documents to obtain funds. But this was a long weekend, and even if bankers could be contacted, things like timed-release safes and other logistical problems meant nothing significant could be accomplished until everyone went back to work Tuesday morning.

It was becoming clear that once Melnitzer was arrested, the media would have to be alerted. That was bound to spread the word.

Porter decided his team should be trying to find out where Melnitzer had printed the certificates. It sounded as if the lawyer was going to be co-operative. He'd been caught virtually red-handed and was willing to return to London for arrest. Perhaps he would realize the jig was up and confess. This looked like a major case with lots of paperwork, and fraud was never easy to prove. If the aggressive Melnitzer was going to fight it, the cost to prosecute would be enormous and months of court time would be required. Let's just see what, if anything, he has to say after we arrest him, Porter thought.

Shortly after nine Sunday night, Melnitzer, Baltman and Michael Epstein, a friend and fellow lawyer, presented themselves at the London RCMP detachment. Melnitzer was told he was being charged with uttering $25 million in forged stock certificates in order to obtain a $15-million line of credit from the National Bank of Canada.

After a formal caution in the presence of Epstein, Melnitzer admitted he had purchased single shares in each of the five companies in the name of his daughter, Melissa, and had hired Sterling Marking Products to alter her name to his, to increase the share amounts and to change the dates — all at his direction. He said he had duped Sterling into printing the certificates by saying they were for a court case he was working on. He said the five original certificates were still in Sterling's possession.

Melnitzer admitted he had provided copies of the doctored blue-chip certificates to the Canadian Imperial Bank of Commerce, the Royal Bank of Canada and the National Bank. All were given as collateral to obtain millions of dollars in lines of credit. He'd been planning to offer some to the Toronto Dominion Bank for a similar purpose.

He said he was using the certificates to replace other documents, also forged, held by the banks in support of earlier lines of credit. Melnitzer told the Mounties he had been feeling under the gun because the banks had been pressing him for better security. That's what prompted his plan to create forged certificates.

Porter asked the criminal lawyer if he clearly understood that what he had done was criminal.

"I sure did," came the reply. "And I don't mean that facetiously. I mean, there was no doubt in my mind that it was." The words were tumbling out. Melnitzer seemed relieved to unburden himself. "I was trying, I guess in the end

I couldn't face, you know, having built . . . through very hard work a successful practice. I guess I couldn't face the shame of having financial problems. I think that's what it boils down to."

Melnitzer admitted he had forged the earlier documentation relating to Melfan Investments, as well as the later share certificates.

"Look, we can make this easy," he said at one point. "Any document that I gave to any bank in relation to a personal line of credit . . . [was] forged. And insofar as I purported to have the authority to deal with those documents, I did not."

He said he'd created the Singapore venture out of thin air in order to satisfy his bankers who were pressing him to pay down his existing lines of credit. Then he felt he had to pay off the Singapore investors, so he returned to the banks with the forged share certificates to get more money. Whenever Porter asked for details, Melnitzer brushed them off, repeating that virtually everything he'd done was fraudulent.

The statement was finished just before 11 p.m., and Melnitzer was taken to London police headquarters for processing and fingerprinting. In the back seat of the police vehicle, the defender-turned-defendant was engrossed in thought.

Being arrested had been one of his ongoing nightmares. Inwardly, he cursed himself for his stupidity. He realized that as a lawyer his career was over. He rationalized that he could live with that. He'd never really wanted to be a lawyer anyway. Should have gone into medicine. He could have been a great doctor and made enough money to stay out of trouble. Earlier, in Montreal, after he learned from Driver that his scam had been uncovered, Melnitzer had contemplated three options. He thought of suicide but rejected it as too painful for family members. He considered fleeing the country but decided that would only delay his inevitable arrest, and he couldn't live like a fugitive. He had opted to return and face the music. Was his decision the right one? he now asked himself.

In the front seat, Porter was wrapped up in his own thoughts. He'd wanted to be a Mountie all his life, and this was clearly the biggest case of his 19-year career. Best of all, it was looking like a guilty plea. Strange, he thought; Melnitzer is crashing and I'm taking off. He could hardly wait to tell the drug boys there was a "fraud going down" tonight.

Melnitzer was fingerprinted and photographed at London city-police cells and released several hours later when Baltman posted bail of $10,000. She didn't have to come up with the cash. She merely promised that if her husband failed to comply with the terms of his release, she would forfeit that amount. It was a relatively small sum to post for a man charged with such a large fraud, but the police and prosecutor felt that Melnitzer was unlikely to violate the terms of his release. Melnitzer was ordered to appear in London court Tuesday morning.

The following day, civic holiday Monday, just as he was preparing a warrant to search Sterling Marking Products, Porter received a telephone call in his deserted office. On the other end of the line was Sam Hassan. The Sterling manager had heard the news of Melnitzer's arrest on the radio and thought he had something Porter might be interested in — originals and copies of stock certificates his firm had been creating for the lawyer. Hassan had called in his staff and was prepared to help the Mounties.

As soon as the warrant was approved, Porter and several officers went to Sterling, where Hassan and his staff were assembled. The Mounties seized 200 share certificates, which, if authentic, would have been worth about $1 billion. They found the original five certificates in the name of Melissa Melnitzer, as well as engraving plates, corporate seals, serial number stamps, printing proofs and screen negatives. A significant part of the haul consisted of finished share certificates ready for delivery to Melnitzer. Several boxes also contained partly completed copies.

Hassan and Peter Khan, Sterling's director of marketing, gave statements to the investigators outlining how Melnitzer had said he needed the work done to help him in a court case. Hassan produced the letter from the lawyer outlining the terms under which Sterling had been operating. He and Khan said they were still refining their efforts at Melnitzer's request and had hoped to have the best possible product available by the fall. Porter found the printers to be extremely forthcoming and was impressed with their honesty. It sounded as if they had been completely deceived by Melnitzer and were still in shock.

Throughout the search and taped interviews, the Sterling officials kept asking Porter and his men for identification and assurances that they were, in fact, legitimate members of the RCMP. At the end of the lengthy session, Porter and his partners were asked to produce their firearms as further proof that their paper identification wasn't fake. Porter left the printing firm with boxloads of evidence and the unshakable belief that the Sterling staff had been so completely fooled they thought Melnitzer might have arranged the search and interviews, even though it was Hassan who called the Mounties. Porter wouldn't be laying any charges against such an innocent, if naive, party.

Also on Monday, Melnitzer called his longtime friend in Toronto, Jules Fleischer, who just four days before had been invited to the lawyer's Roxborough home on August 7 to pick up his $400,000 payout on the Singapore Deal. Melnitzer said he had been arrested on charges of fraud and forgery, that the accusations were true and that he would be going to jail. He told the disbelieving Fleischer his original $200,000 was not recoverable.

"But Julius," sputtered Fleischer, a wealthy man more upset at the betrayal than the money loss, "what about this Singapore business? Was there ever such a deal?"

"No, not really," Melnitzer replied.

The same day, eight shocked partners of Cohen, Melnitzer met to consider what to do. Melnitzer was not invited to attend. They couldn't fathom the deceit of their founding partner and the extent of his fraud. Some had learned that the National Bank was only one of many banks Melnitzer had defrauded and that the police expected to lay many more charges. Concern was expressed about more than just the welfare of the law firm, however, since several of the partners had invested heavily in the nonexistent Singapore Deal.

The shock was mixed with hurt and anger but the partners agreed their prime concern had to be the future of the law firm. They debated whether to extend Melnitzer the presumption of innocence until he was found guilty. It was, of course, the basis of all law relating to crime. To treat Melnitzer, a man facing a charge of uttering forged certificates, as a person who had actually committed the crime was contrary to everything they stood for. He was entitled to due process.

On the other hand, if the firm stood by its founding partner and waited for the legal process to unfold, clients were bound to flee. They might conclude, wrongly, that the firm was attempting to hide something. Cohen, Melnitzer, with its good reputation and high overhead, needed to reassure its clients.

After much debate, it was decided Melnitzer had to be expelled and his name taken off the door. An audit of the trust accounts would be required to prove to clients that nothing was amiss. The Law Society of Upper Canada would be notified immediately.

In the back of the lawyers' minds was the lesson of the "Lang Michener affair." A prestigious Toronto law firm of that name had been widely criticized for failing to expel partner Martin Pilzmaker, who became involved in unethical and illegal practices. Pilzmaker, a high-flying character who bragged about his billings and maintained a spectacular home and a chauffeur-driven Rolls-Royce, was eventually charged with multiple counts of fraud and conspiracy to commit fraud relating to his immigration practice, in which he helped well-to-do Hong Kong businessmen relocate to Canada. Senior partners had become concerned about his activities in June or July 1986 but didn't expel him until September. In November, they reported Pilzmaker to the Law

Society of Upper Canada, which eventually disbarred him. The partners' delay in reporting Pilzmaker — even by a few months — was criticized as an attempt to cover up the affair. Five senior partners were reprimanded for their delay, producing considerable embarrassment for Lang Michener. Following that sorry episode, law firms were warned to be open and forthright when enountering anything similar. Otherwise, they would face sanctions and run the risk of further eroding public confidence in the profession.

The London lawyers decided their best course was to air the dirty linen in public, avoid any suggestion of coverup and move on. The firm was renamed Cohen, Delanghe, Highley, Vogel and Dawson to reflect the main partners, who now included insolvency expert Frank Highley. They agreed Fletcher Dawson would speak for the group. He was most experienced in dealing with the media from his work on high-profile criminal trials. A press release was prepared outlining the situation.

Dawson was talking to the media within hours, saying the firm had "fully co-operated" with the RCMP and had expelled Melnitzer. "It came as a total shock to us," Dawson told reporters. "We are 21 hardworking lawyers here. It's business as usual for us." He said the firm had sent a letter outlining the known facts to the Law Society of Upper Canada and was "welcoming them to come here to conduct an investigation." In the days that were to follow, Dawson would announce that accountants Peat Marwick Thorne had been retained to audit the law firm's trust accounts to ensure nothing was amiss and say that Melnitzer was expelled quickly for business reasons. "We are running a business here and we run our business on integrity." The partnership agreement provided for expulsion under just such a situation.

Meanwhile, Melnitzer resigned as chairperson of the Ontario Fair Rental Policy Organization. "It's a blow to all of us," said the group's president on Monday afternoon. Melnitzer had been scheduled to present a brief two days later on the province's latest proposed rent-control legislation.

Also in Toronto, Torkin, Manes, Cohen and Arbus quickly issued a press release to announce the immediate removal of Melnitzer as associate counsel. Conscious of the lessons from the Lang Michener debacle, the firm echoed the reasoning of the London law firm.

"These charges, which are extremely serious, stem from Mr. Melnitzer's personal business dealings," said partner Ian Tod. "He did not have signing authority on any of the firm's general or trust bank accounts. We have no evidence of any impropriety with respect to our firm or clients, but out of an abundance of caution we have instructed our accountants to conduct a financial review of any matters with which Mr. Melnitzer was involved."

On Tuesday morning, under the scrutiny of a horde of reporters, a tired-looking Melnitzer arrived at court. Obviously ill at ease, he took his seat in courtroom number two, but not on one of the padded chairs around the table reserved for defence counsel. As an accused, he had to sit in the public gallery on a hard wooden bench. He slumped at times as he waited for his name to be called.

His case was adjourned to September 3, the Tuesday following Labor Day weekend. He agreed to report twice a week to Toronto police and bail was continued.

The press was all over the story by now. Melnitzer was good copy: prominent lawyer charged with forging $25 million worth of stock certificates to get multimillion-dollar credit line from bank; Mounties find more than $100 million worth of forged shares; more charges expected.

Reporters contacted Brian Allard, vice-president of commercial banking for the National Bank. From his Toronto office, Allard said there was nothing unusual in a bank employee's uncovering the fraud by checking the validity of the share certificates. "It is a normal course of business with a loan of this size . . . any authorization of a credit limit, it comes to Toronto headquarters. I don't think it matters who you're dealing with, investigations are going to be undertaken."

A spokesperson for the Mounties said he expected further charges would be laid and the police investigation was proceeding at "full speed."

The Law Society of Upper Canada began its own inquiries. "The law firm has been very forthcoming," said Gavin Mac-Kenzie, senior counsel for professional discipline, adding he wasn't yet sure if the society would lay charges.

In the old days, Melnitzer would have been revelling in the press coverage. But the man who had curried media attention for so long was now shrinking from it. That he was coping poorly was revealed on Thursday, August 8, when Greg Van Moorsel, a reporter from the *London Free Press*, tried to speak to him at his Roxborough home. In response to Van Moorsel's first request, made into the front-door intercom, a male voice barked "Julius Melnitzer has no comment" and ordered the reporter off the property. A few hours later, Van Moorsel was back at the door. This time he was greeted by a flushed and enraged Melnitzer.

"Get the hell out of here," the lawyer bellowed, lunging at the startled reporter and ripping the camera from his shoulder. The lawyer turned on his heel and, prize in hand, retreated into the house. Minutes later, dressed in shorts and a casual shirt, Melnitzer crossed the street and left the camera, with its torn strap dangling, on a neighbor's porch. The film was still inside.

Van Moorsel looked around for witnesses and found one in a brown van parked on the street. Inside, private investigator Maurice Ranger, whom the court-appointed receiver had hired to monitor the Roxborough home, had been taking notes.

"It's all here," Ranger assured Van Moorsel, waving a handwritten report of the scuffle.

In London, meanwhile, Fletcher Dawson and some of Melnitzer's other former partners were trying to come to grips with the fact that they had been swindled in the Singapore Deal. They didn't want to give details to the press for fear of jeopardizing efforts to recover their money. One London politician, however, told the press he had lost his life savings of $200,000. He said he had given the money to Allan Richman who, he had just learned, had invested it with Melnitzer. A reporter contacted Richman, who conceded he had invested the politician's funds with Melnitzer. Richman was reluctant to discuss the matter and wasn't about to disclose the fact that he was the biggest single loser of all.

The day after his front-yard altercation, Melnitzer saw the pesky Van Moorsel again, this time in a civil courtroom in Toronto, where Melnitzer was required to appear by the court order issued by Justice Keenan. There were no outbursts this time, however, as Melnitzer was busy defending himself against a battery of lawyers from several banks. They included his former associate from the Grand Bend beach trial, Russell Raikes, who was representing the interests of Cohen, Delanghe, Highley, Vogel and Dawson.

The bank lawyers were seeking to extend the freeze on assets. Melnitzer argued it should be lifted enough to at least provide him with money to live on and to hire a lawyer. Baltman sat near him in the court.

"I would like to have some essential protection from the court for living expenses and representation," he asked the presiding judge, Justice Dennis O'Leary. Melnitzer obtained a promise of $3000 a month living expenses and assurance that reasonable legal expenses would be covered. A payment not exceeding $3000 would be made to his mother, because her source of funds, Melfan, was tied up by the freeze.

Chris Osborne, now acting for both the National Bank and Coopers and Lybrand, warned the receiver might have to borrow money to make those payments. "I have a problem," he conceded. "At the moment there is no cash in the estate."

It was a shocking revelation about a man the National Bank had believed was worth $77 million just a few days earlier.

Melnitzer also persuaded O'Leary to seal the transcript of

a six-hour interview he had given Coopers and Lybrand two days earlier in which he confessed his crimes and helped the receiver locate and identify his assets. The judge agreed its release in civil court might prejudice Melnitzer's trial in criminal court. Arguing against the sealing order was Raikes, who said release of the transcript was "essential for the continued viability of our firm. We're prepared to have the chips come out, fall where they may."

The same day Melnitzer was in the Toronto courtroom, another *London Free Press* reporter located his mother in Montreal. In a brief telephone interview, Fanny Melnitzer told Alison Uncles she couldn't believe the events of the last few days.

"I don't know what to say," she began in her thick accent. "That such a brilliant man, such a wonderful human being which he was . . . could have done it. My husband told [our sons] the cheque which goes back [bounces], he wants to die. That's the way they were brought up . . . My son was brought up in a most respectable family . . . that the name is the first thing."

Obviously distraught, she added a plea: "What's in the family stays in the family and doesn't have to be publicized . . . surely it affects us."

Fanny Melnitzer went on to say her son "was famous and he reached the top," but what she was reading in the newspaper "is a very bad portrait."

When Melnitzer learned the paper had contacted his mother, he was enraged.

The press continued to dig into the case with gusto. The charge against Melnitzer was the talk of the town in London and across Ontario. Members of the legal community swapped their favorite Melnitzer stories and speculated on what had prompted his troubles.

Within days, reporter Uncles tracked down Archie Gibbs at his booth on the Grand Bend beach, where he was charging visitors $5 a day for parking on his property. Gibbs said many passers-by and his friends had been quizzing him about the man who won the beach for him. But he remained loyal to Melnitzer.

"I still would consider him a friend," Gibbs said. "He's just a likable person. He's an exceptionally good lawyer, it's hard to imagine such a thing could happen. Someday, I will speak to him. I would like to hear what he has to say after the pressure is off."

Pressure was being felt in many quarters. On August 9, Melnitzer's former law firm laid off nine of its support staff. Dawson said it was a belt-tightening move to cope with the expected revenue decline prompted by the expulsion of their top dollar-earner. The loss reduced the total staff complement to 70. The jobs affected were in the marketing and general administration areas.

Dawson said no clients had left the firm in the first two weeks despite the adverse publicity, and he predicted few would jump ship.

Also on August 9, the Royal Bank of Canada filed a lawsuit in London seeking the return of the nearly $2.5 million Melnitzer had obtained from it. But the same day in Toronto, Justice O'Leary extended the freeze on Melnitzer's assets. A side effect of this action was that Melnitzer could not be sued while his affairs were in the hands of a court-appointed receiver. As soon as they learned of the activities in Toronto, the red-faced London lawyers for the Royal immediately discontinued the action. All the bankers could do now was wait to see what assets the receiver could turn up and hope there would be enough to pursue once the freeze was off.

When he saw the thoroughness of the investigations being undertaken by the court-appointed receiver and the Mounties, Melnitzer developed another concern. He had believed that by co-operating he might exercise some control over the digging into his financial affairs. By bargaining with the few moves available to him, he hoped he could exert some leverage over the unfolding of events. But he soon discovered his leverage was minimal.

He was particularly anxious that his payments to Calla Reid not become public. His wife didn't know of the affair, and if she found out and reacted poorly, he could be back in jail. As the person who had posted his bail, she was, in effect, his jailer. Melnitzer warned the Mounties that if they made Reid's existence public, he would recant his confession and put them through a grinding and lengthy trial.

On August 16, Geoffrey Foster was in his office at the CIBC when he received a call about 1:45 p.m. It was Melnitzer. Surprised but keeping his wits about him, Foster grabbed a pen and began scribbling down the strange conversation that followed.

"Geoff, this is Julius. I saw Peter Lockyer [lawyer for the CIBC] and I told him I would call you. What can I say, Geoff? I am terribly sorry. Geoff, I am truly sorry and I don't know what I can do to make it up to you.

"It all started with my divorce," Melnitzer said, speaking slowly, his tone subdued. "I could not bear to see my wife walk away with very little. I overstated my assets at least three times and overpaid my wife in the divorce settlement. Millions also went into the law firm, as whenever the firm was short, I put the money in. In essence, the money went into the partners' pockets. I also purchased the $2.5 million of Champion Chemtech stock, and I was burned by Allan Richman as I was frequently borrowing from him at a 20- to 30-percent interest rate."

The lawyer went on to tell the banker whose faith he had abused that he had purposely created the impression of great wealth. Melnitzer said the art and other assets were purchased to support the fiction about his affluence.

"It looks like I'll be going away to jail for a long time. Once again, Geoff, I'm sorry."

Foster, still shaken at having been so thoroughly conned

by Melnitzer, was also angry that the CIBC's loss stood at nearly $8.4 million. The bank couldn't sue because of the freeze order imposed at the request of the National Bank. He was frustrated at his lack of options, and the extraordinary apology from a con man was cold comfort. He turned his notes of the conversation over to the Mounties.

Coopers and Lybrand continued the investigation of Melnitzer's assets and liabilities in preparation to return to civil court late in August. The picture was looking grim, much worse than originally thought.

In court, the receiver gave a preliminary tally that showed the lawyer's liabilities outstripped his assets by more than 10 to one. Debts and claims on Melnitzer's estate totalled more than $30 million, while his assets were calculated at less than $3 million. Among the major obligations were $14.15 million to Allan Richman for various investments and $5.5 million to investors in the Singapore Deal. And the banks wanted their millions back.

Meanwhile, Melnitzer's claim of assets, large and small, was being disputed. Baltman was claiming half the artwork, then valued at $2 million; his former law firm challenged the assertion Melnitzer had $716,000 invested there; Toronto lawyer John Bogart insisted he felt no obligation to repay the $100,000 Melnitzer had advanced him for introductions to potential clients, saying the damage to his reputation far exceeded that amount. Melnitzer's assets were relatively few.

The receiver had begun liquidating Melnitzer's legitimate shareholdings but was still stuck with the problem of little cash in the estate. Coopers and Lybrand was permitted by the court to borrow up to $200,000 to continue its work. Under terms of the first court order, the receiver would be paid for its labors in advance of all other creditors. Chris Osborne, lawyer for the receiver, complained the investigation was hampered by Melnitzer's poor record-keeping. He said Coopers and Lybrand needed another month to complete its tally of assets and liabilities.

Baltman was represented in court by her own lawyer, who argued the freezing order effectively cut her off from funds needed to survive. The court was told she earned little from acting and was unable to sell off assets the receiver had seized. She was granted a one-time payment of $3000 until the matter returned to court. Baltman began looking for work as a lawyer to support herself and her now dependent husband.

Throughout August, the Mounties interviewed Melnitzer, the banks and others to determine the full scope of his fraudulent behavior. By his next appearance in court on September 3, they were ready with a fat sheaf of new charges. So were the reporters and cameras.

As he entered the London courthouse, the beige-suited Melnitzer balked when he saw a horde of television cameras. He broke into a run when they spotted him, and when one cameraman got too close, he grabbed the camera lens with his hand. Inside the building, he pushed away the microphone a radio reporter had thrust in his face.

In court, a total of 56 new charges were filed, running to 23 pages. After conferring briefly with Michael Epstein, Melnitzer agreed to waive the reading of the highly detailed counts, thereby reducing his appearance time by more than an hour.

The charges dated back to 1985 and the forged Vanguard Trust shares. In all, there were five counts of forging publicly traded shares; 29 counts of uttering false documents to obtain lines of credit from the CIBC, the National Bank of Canada, the Royal Bank of Canada and the Bank of Montreal; three counts of attempting to defraud the Toronto Dominion Bank, the Hongkong Bank and Mutual Trust; 20 counts of defrauding the Singapore investors, Richman and Richman's companies.

The forgery charges related to stock certificates that, if valid, had a face value of $1.03 billion. The fraud charges involving the banks totalled $61.1 million; the attempted fraud charges totalled another $33 million; the fraud charges naming individuals totalled $14.7 million. The Mounties issued a press release that put the actual loss to banks at $12.35 million; to individuals, the full $14.7 million.

The case was clearly one of unprecedented proportion. The bank fraud and attempted bank fraud charges totalled $94.1 million, with individuals stung for nearly $15 million more.

Never before in Canada, possibly in North America, had an individual fraudulently obtained so much money from banks and others for his personal use. The case made headlines across the continent.

Melnitzer was ordered to return to court October 1. His bail was increased from $10,000 to $250,000, in recognition of the new array of charges now facing him. Once again, the money was pledged by Baltman, rather than formally paid in court. The police were satisfied that, as Melnitzer's spouse, Baltman had at least that amount of money available in her share of the joint assets. And despite the mind-boggling sums now involved in the case, the prosecutors were sure Melnitzer wouldn't flee the jurisdiction. Another term of his release was that he live at the Roxborough home or at Baltman's family cottage near Bracebridge, about two hours north of Toronto.

As he left the court, the strain on Melnitzer was apparent, and he again lashed out at the media. He warned a newspaper reporter who approached him, "If you come any closer to me, that's an assault." A television cameraman who ventured too close paid the price. Melnitzer ripped off a rubber lens cover and viewfinder. When the camera operator complained the action was an assault, the burly Melnitzer replied, "Charge me."

Many of the reporters on hand this day had been welcomed guests in his house eight months before on the night of the Grand Bend beach victory party. They had helped spread the word of his greatest triumph. Now as they witnessed his plunge, they were the enemy.

Julius Melnitzer's world had turned upside down.

13

An
Empty
Cookie Jar

"You stand disgraced in the public eye."

W ITHIN DAYS OF THE NEW charges being brought
against Melnitzer, it was learned that two of
his former colleagues were leaving the freshly renamed law
firm. Ron Delanghe and Ken McGill were bailing out of
Cohen, Delanghe, Highley, Vogel and Dawson. Delanghe and
his wife had been stung by Melnitzer for a total of $2,425,000
($1.5 million of that was what Delanghe owed Glen Sifton,
of Sifton Properties, whom he'd brought in on the deal),
while McGill and his wife had lost $150,000.

Delanghe would be joining Lerner and Associates,
London's largest law firm. Ironically, it was Lerner's that
Melnitzer had tried to emulate and planned to surpass.
Delanghe, the real estate and development specialist, would
be taking with him many of his better clients, including the

still-faithful builder, Sifton. McGill, a corporate specialist, was starting his own practice.

The remaining partners at Melnitzer's former firm were not happy with the news. At a time when it was important to pull together and prove to the community that it was business as usual, the departures were a setback. The firm was renamed yet again.

Jaime Watt, Melnitzer's former marketing whiz, acted as spokesperson to confirm the departure of Delanghe and McGill and tried to put the best public face on it. "Given the economy, given the Julius situation, it just seems that the best course of action for now is to pull back a bit," Watt said. "It may be that another one or two partners will leave still." He also confirmed the scuttlebutt on the street that the firm no longer planned to lease the top two floors of One London Place. Watt used the words "retrenchment and consolidation" to describe the game plan for Cohen, Highley, Vogel and Dawson. "Of course revenue is down," he conceded. "Julius isn't there anymore. Revenues are not down across the firm. They are down only as it relates to Julius's practice itself."

Observers were beginning to wonder, however, how the partnership could continue without major cutbacks. The loss of Melnitzer's revenue was compounded by the departure of Delanghe and his major clients.

The Canadian Imperial Bank of Commerce, which had been victimized for $8.4 million, was uncomfortable with the upstart National Bank's arranging for the court-appointed receiver. The receivership blocked any other lawsuits by individuals or banks Melnitzer had defrauded. With five times the loss of the smaller bank, the CIBC began exploring ways to get its own oar in the legal waters.

The bank's lawyers went after Melfan Investments, Deena Baltman and Melissa Melnitzer. The bank sued Melfan for the $8.4 million, noting Melnitzer had used guarantees from Melfan as security for his indebtedness. It also sought an injunction preventing Melfan from disposing of its assets until the lawsuit was settled.

The bank was determined to pursue anything and anyone it could in the belief that any recovery of funds was better than none. It sought a $100,000 guaranteed investment certificate in Melnitzer's name held at the Bank of Montreal. In separate lawsuits, the CIBC demanded Baltman and Melissa Melnitzer turn over the cars Melnitzer had purchased for them with money he had fraudulently obtained. Baltman's was a 1991 Acura sports sedan her husband purchased in May for $25,886. The bank sought an equal amount in damages. A similar claim was made against Melissa Melnitzer for the 1990 Mazda Miata sports car her father had given her as a gift. He had paid $28,465 for it about a year earlier with a series of CIBC cheques. The same amount in damages was also sought. The lawsuits are expected to take years to sort out.

As summer slipped into fall, developments were unfolding on several fronts. On September 17, the Law Society of Upper Canada charged Melnitzer with conduct unbecoming a lawyer. The disciplinary body based the charge on his presentation of forged certificates to the National Bank. Since this was not perpetrated while Melnitzer was acting in his capacity as a lawyer, "professional misconduct" did not apply. The charge carries a penalty ranging from a reprimand, fine or suspension to disbarment. A spokesperson for the society said a six-week investigation revealed there was no need to await the outcome of the criminal trial before laying the charge. Melnitzer advised the society he had voluntarily quit practising law after his arrest.

The London Free Press was unsuccessful in a bid to unseal the transcript of Melnitzer's self-incriminating interview with the court-appointed receiver. Justice Gordon Killeen, before whose London court all civil matters relating to Melnitzer were now to be brought, ruled that preserving the lawyer's right to a fair trial was a more important consideration than freedom of the press.

On September 26, the receiver returned to court to report its progress in liquidating Melnitzer's assets and unscrambling his tangled affairs. Chris Osborne and Jennifer Badley, acting on behalf of Coopers and Lybrand and the National Bank of Canada, were among 13 lawyers on hand for what was becoming an increasingly complicated case.

After his initial appearance when he'd sought a living allowance, Melnitzer did not appear in court on the receivership matters. Representing him this day and on all further civil proceedings was veteran Toronto litigator Donald Jack.

Osborne filed with the court the latest report on Melnitzer's affairs, which still showed liabilities of more than $30 million and assets of less than $3 million. The Coopers and Lybrand report noted that it appeared the lawyer's main assets were heavily encumbered. The artwork, it concluded, was valued at $2 million, but only for insurance purposes. It was probably worth much less, and Baltman was claiming half of it. Attempts to determine its value had thus far failed because the collection was so eclectic that no single appraiser felt comfortable undertaking the job. Melnitzer's main asset appeared to be his $2.5-million investment in Champion Chemtech, but CIBC officials were claiming their bank owned the shares, because Melnitzer had purchased them with a fraudulently obtained cash advance. It would turn out that 808756 Ontario Limited, the investment firm established for the Singapore Deal investors, and Grand Canyon Properties were also claiming shares in Champion.

Coopers and Lybrand had uncovered many such claims against nearly everything Melnitzer owned. The lawyer was clearly insolvent, the report concluded. No money had been located offshore, and Melnitzer had insisted in his interview with the accountants that he hadn't stashed any money away in case he was caught. The cookie jar did indeed seem to be empty. "It is clear . . . that these claims will be extensive and legally complex," the report said.

Osborne said Coopers and Lybrand was prepared to continue its work, the bill for which was in the "hundreds of thousands of dollars." To be on the safe side, however, Osborne had prepared a draft petition in bankruptcy in case other creditors preferred the protections afforded them under the federal Bankruptcy Act.

After some discussion outside court, the CIBC decided to spearhead a move to force the bankruptcy. The bank arranged with Peat Marwick Thorne to act as trustee in bankruptcy. The bank guaranteed the accounting firm a fee of $50,000 for its work.

Faced with that development, Osborne agreed to have Killeen declare Melnitzer bankrupt. He said Coopers and Lybrand would cease its investigation and produce a final report on its activities as soon as possible.

The Bankruptcy Act is a complex piece of legislation difficult for the average citizen to understand. It primarily involves the federal department of consumer and corporate affairs, which provides an official receiver to determine the cause of bankruptcy, arranges a meeting with creditors and attempts to ensure creditors are dealt with equitably, based on what money may be recoverable. A person who has been declared bankrupt cannot be sued until a discharge is registered (within a year of bankruptcy being declared), incur further debts or become a director of any company. After being discharged, a bankrupt person's problems are not over, however. One section of the Bankruptcy Act warns that a discharge does not release an individual from "any debt or liability for obtaining property by false pretenses or fraudulent misrepresentation." Once Melnitzer was discharged as a bankrupt, the fraud claims against him could be pursued.

On the same day bankruptcy was declared, Baltman's lawyer Robert Barnes sought a monthly living allowance of $5000 because her assets had been tied up by the freeze order. He urged Killeen to authorize the allowance because she was unemployed and unemployable. "She can't find employment in her qualified field because of her association with Julius Melnitzer," Barnes argued. But the judge rejected

Baltman's request. Not long afterward, Baltman obtained a temporary position with a Toronto law firm at a salary of $1300 a week.

The income would prove inadequate for the formerly globe-trotting couple. Money had never before been a problem for them. Now, they chafed at the drastic change in their financial situation. On November 13, Baltman's thirty-third birthday, lawyers for Baltman and Melnitzer were back in court, looking for money. Baltman wanted $28,000 for legal fees she had already incurred and $6000 to maintain their homes in Toronto and London. In an affidavit supporting her request, she described her quandary.

"Until August 1991, I believed Julius Melnitzer was a wealthy man. I believed Julius earned a substantial income from the practice of law and from investments. In August 1991, I learned for the first time that these beliefs were erroneous." She said she would have been earning $80,000 annually if she'd stayed in law, but since June had been pursuing a full-time acting career and had little income.

Melnitzer's lawyer sought $10,000 for his client's legal fees, an unspecified amount for future legal costs and a monthly allowance of $1500. In an affidavit, Michael Epstein said that "without $1500 a month to meet his living expenses, [Melnitzer] will have no means of paying such expenses, and that it is very unclear how, if at all, he will be able to provide himself with necessities."

In court, Baltman and Melnitzer received little sympathy from their creditors or Peat Marwick Thorne, the trustee in bankruptcy. Joseph Steiner, lawyer for the trustee, suggested Baltman should consider selling some of her $300,000 worth of jewelry before applying to the court for financial help. Steiner also said it was clear that Melnitzer, a man with no assets or income, could apply for Legal Aid to meet his court expenses. The Legal Aid plan provides financial help based on need, and an area director advised the court that after reviewing Melnitzer's financial picture, he was probably eligible.

Steiner went on to report that it appeared Melnitzer's might be a "no asset" bankruptcy, because Peat Marwick Thorne had been unable to locate any assets without claims on them. In a brief overview report, the accountants suggested his actual assets could be as little as $170,000 before the deduction of the estimated $400,000 in receivership fees and expenses. At the most, his assets might be $3.5 million.

After considering the request for allowances, Justice Killeen issued a 12-page decision rejecting it. He noted that, although Melnitzer was unemployed and relying on his wife for support, she was earning $1300 a week, or $67,600 annually.

"I would have thought that the family-unit income of the Melnitzers would suffice," Killeen wrote. He was more sympathetic to another situation, which he described as "a very sensitive matter." He agreed to Melnitzer's request that a supplementary final report filed by Coopers and Lybrand be sealed from the public. Killeen said its release might prejudice a fair trial. The report, which remained sealed for nearly four months, dealt exclusively with Melnitzer's payments to Calla Reid. Killeen also agreed to seal the documents from an upcoming formal interview with the official receiver in bankruptcy. Questions about Reid, and possibly about Interfaces, the New York escort agency, would be asked at that session, Melnitzer was sure.

In Toronto, the law society announced that a second charge of conduct unbecoming a lawyer had been laid against Melnitzer. This count related to the money he fraudulently raised from the Singapore Deal investors. Society lawyer Gavin MacKenzie said the investigation was continuing and he was monitoring criminal proceedings closely.

Within days, there was a new development on that front. When Melnitzer again appeared in a London criminal courtroom, he appeared relaxed, smiling and chatting with other lawyers. He even spoke briefly to a couple of representatives of the media, politely denying their requests for comment before entering. The change in demeanor was dramatic. In the courtroom, before a provincial-division judge, 13 of the 57 counts against Melnitizer were dropped. He then waived his right to have a preliminary hearing on any of the remaining charges and agreed to stand trial before a judge and jury at a later date. (A preliminary hearing is an inquiry to see if there is sufficient evidence to warrant sending an accused person to trial. It is also an opportunity for both defence and prosecution lawyers to test the strength of their cases and witnesses.)

Something was up, but no one was saying exactly what. Prosecutor Scott Hutchison of Toronto offered no explanation in court for the charge withdrawals, nor did Melnitzer offer any for why he'd chosen to bypass a hearing.

Melnitzer's smile hid the fact that a deal was being worked out behind the scenes that was expected to benefit both him and the prosecution. He would plead guilty to the remaining charges, and in exchange the prosecution would agree to a sentence Melnitzer felt he could live with, something around nine or ten years. The arrangement would shorten proceedings and Melnitzer could begin serving his sentence much sooner and, therefore, be back on the street sooner. With a nine-year sentence, for instance, he would be eligible for day parole after 18 months and full parole after three years. The prosecution would be saved the time and expense of a complicated and lengthy trial. Dropping the 13 counts was not a major concession, because they were all of uttering forged documents and were, in effect, a duplication of offences already covered in the other charges.

In a bit of legal housekeeping, Hutchison amended one of the charges relating to Singapore victim Glen Sifton, replacing his name with that of Ron Delanghe, to acknowledge that Sifton had invested his $1.5 million with Delanghe, rather than directly with Melnitzer.

Hutchison was thorough. At 29, he was one of the bright young stars in the 40-lawyer Crown law office of the Ontario attorney general. Called to the bar in 1989, he had already distinguished himself with work on special prosecutions and criminal appeals. He was comfortable in the rarefied atmosphere and pressure of the Ontario Court of Appeal where complex legal points are argued. Part of his training had been with the Appeal Court, where he had articled as a law clerk. He had also argued cases in the Supreme Court of Canada. The most recent was one in which he had delved into constitutional issues and the division of power between provincial and federal governments. In his research, he had uncovered the celebrated *Boggs vs. Regina*, the suspended-driving case that had given Melnitzer his first big win at the Supreme Court about a decade earlier. In his case, however, Hutchison had argued the opposite proposition to that advanced by Melnitzer. And he had won.

Aside from his ability to come to grips with complex issues, Hutchison was developing a reputation as a budding legal scholar. He had published three books in his short career, one on search-and-seizure, another on the presumption of innocence and a third on the Highway Traffic Act.

His office was located on Bay Street, just a few blocks north of the address where, 18 years earlier, the lawyer he was now prosecuting had likewise made a promising start with a big law firm.

As a member of the elite group of Ontario government lawyers who represent the public interest in major cases, Hutchison wouldn't ordinarily have been called upon to prosecute at a criminal trial unless a local prosecutor called for help. His introduction to the Melnitzer case was by pure fluke. Hutchison and George Gunn, the RCMP sergeant, had been trying for some time to unravel a particularly complicated fraud. So Hutchison wasn't surprised when Gunn called him on August 2. But Gunn wanted to talk about something even bigger; he was seeking advice on the just-breaking Melnitzer investigation. The young lawyer immediately pitched in and helped draft the first search warrant that same day. He was there for Melnitzer's first appearance in court three days later, a major feat considering he was in the midst of final preparations for his August 8 wedding to fellow lawyer Cathy Bellinger.

Throughout October, November and December, Hutchison spent a lot of time discussing the Melnitzer case with Michael Epstein. Joining Epstein for Melnitzer's defence was well-known Toronto lawyer Brian Greenspan. Together they meticulously studied the charges and evidence the Mounties had assembled, to ensure a guilty plea was in Melnitzer's best interests. Being in Toronto, Greenspan could communicate more effectively with Hutchison and have more immediate access to Melnitzer than Epstein could in London.

The prosecution and defence lawyers agreed to enter Melnitzer's pleas before the end of the year. A judge from outside the London and Toronto areas would be found to consider them.

The end of November brought the news of another consequence of Melnitzer's financial treachery. Ron Delanghe declared insolvency and filed a proposal with the bankruptcy office that he hoped would save him from bankruptcy.

He produced documents showing his liabilities topped $2.6 million, primarily because he'd been swindled. His assets were $360,000. Delanghe and his wife met their creditors within a month and asked them to accept payment of about 17.5 cents on the dollar. If the proposal was rejected, the couple would be forced to declare bankruptcy. The major creditor was client and friend Glen Sifton. Delanghe owed the builder's Glen Sifton Holdings $500,000 and Sifton's firm, Awata Ltd., another $1 million. The creditors approved the payout plan.

Meanwhile, Melnitzer was wrestling with his own bankruptcy concerns. A bankrupt person is required by law to meet with the official receiver in bankruptcy, an officer with the federal Department of Consumer and Corporate Affairs. The interview, designed to determine the cause of bankruptcy and review the actions of the bankrupt individual, is usually required within 21 days of a declaration of bankruptcy. Melnitzer's interview had been delayed several times by his civil and criminal lawyers who, wishing to keep the matters raised in it confidential, were seeking to have its report sealed by court order. Questions relating to Calla Reid and Interfaces were expected. In mid-September, despite legal intervention by the media, Justice Killeen upheld an earlier court order directing the Coopers and Lybrand report relating to Reid and the upcoming bankruptcy interview be sealed. But the judge ruled the documents couldn't remain sealed forever; they could be unsealed by subsequent court order, presumably after Melnitzer's criminal matters had been dealt with.

Once assured his answers to the bankruptcy official's questions would be kept secret, at least for the foreseeable future, Melnitzer agreed to the interview. On December 5, he met with senior bankruptcy officer John Everett, at Everett's London office. The official receiver had compiled a list of 87 questions for Melnitzer, the first 42 of them *pro forma* queries asked of any bankrupt person. The remainder dealt specifically with Melnitzer and his transactions. Over the course of several hours, Everett methodically worked through his questions, reading from the left side of a typed sheet and scrawling Melnitzer's answers, given under oath, in a column to the right. Excerpts are as follows:

Question 15: "What are the causes of your bankruptcy?"
Answer: "Not enough money."

Question 16: "When did you first become aware of your bankruptcy?"
Answer: "Late 1990 — early 1991."

Question 35: "How do you account for the deficit created by the business after deducting the personal debts?"
Answer: "I spent, or my business spent, more than I earned. The vast majority of shortfall is due to excessive

interest payments, the bulk of which relates to investments with Allan Richman and his various companies."

Everett saved the most personal questions for the end of the
interview. The eighty-third was: "What is your involvement
with a company called Interface [sic] and how much have
you spent or invested in this in the last three years?"
Melnitzer objected strenuously to that question, visibly irritated, and complained it was outside the scope of Everett's
mandate. He didn't want anything about Interfaces showing
up in Everett's report, sealed or not. After the unexpected
outburst and the spirited exchange that followed, Everett
agreed to let the matter drop.

Everett's replacement question dealt with the series of
cheques made out to Calla Reid. Melnitzer, knowing this was
dealt with earlier in the already sealed supplementary report
of Coopers and Lybrand, offered no objection when Everett
asked him to elaborate on the payments. His response as
recorded by Everett was: "With respect to all those payments,
there was no consideration received by me."

Everett's next question was whether Melnitzer had intended
to abscond from Canada with Miss Reid, but he opted to cross
it off his list. The bankruptcy official then wanted to know if
Melnitzer had any assets at Reid's residence. Melnitzer replied
that he did not. Three more unrelated questions and the
interview was terminated. Not long afterward, the transcript
and official report were placed in a sealed envelope.

Melnitzer was relieved to get the obligatory bankruptcy
interview out of the way. He viewed it as a nuisance and felt
it wasn't going to change things one way or another. At the
time, he was also engaged in far more important discussions
with his lawyer about his criminal charges. Those talks
would have a much more significant impact on his future,
both immediate and long term.

December 19 was a clear, cold day. A record overnight low
of minus 21 degrees Celsius had been set in London. Outside

the downtown courthouse, a freezing gaggle of cameramen awaited the arrival of Julius Melnitzer. They had been told he might be admitting his crimes this day. Stamping their feet to keep warm, they staked out the two entrances the lawyer had used in the past.

Shortly before 10 a.m., Melnitzer, wearing dark sunglasses, slipped into the building virtually unnoticed through a third entrance, frustrating the media. He was on his way to an appearance before Justice William Maloney, a senior member of the Ontario Court, general division, who had flown in from his base in northern Ontario. Maloney's greatest expertise was in civil, not criminal law, but he had a reputation for fairness. With his full jowls, bushy eyebrows and half-glasses, he bore more than a passing resemblance to Winston Churchill. Melnitzer had never appeared before him, although Maloney said that in his 17 years on the bench, he had certainly heard of the lawyer's good reputation.

On the fourteenth floor, courtroom 21 was late convening. Defence and prosecution lawyers were meeting with Maloney in his chambers to explain the background of the case and how they hoped to proceed. Melnitzer would be pleading guilty to all charges against him, but wanted to delay sentencing for about six weeks so he could get his affairs in order.

As spectators milled around waiting for court to start, Melnitzer, in a charcoal-colored wool suit, stayed close to Baltman, who wore an expensive-looking dark green suit and matching Italian-made shoes. They kept to themselves and seemed anxious to get the appearance over with.

Among the lawyers and others who dropped by was an accused murderer, Guy Paul Morin, who took a break from his protracted trial in the next courtroom. The 32-year-old Morin, of Queensville, near Toronto, was charged with first-degree murder in the 1984 stabbing death of a nine-year-old girl who'd lived next door. His case had been moved to London because of intense publicity in the Toronto area. It was Morin's second trial on the charge; after he was acquitted at the first, prosecutors successfully appealed and won a new trial. Morin was curious to see the lawyer whose case was pushing his out of the headlines. He waited patiently for proceedings to get started, but after 20 minutes, was called away by his own pressing legal concerns.

Court convened nearly an hour later than scheduled, and Hutchison's first move was to file a fresh indictment, the formal listing of all charges. He explained there were 43 counts, one less than on the last court appearance, because two charges of creating forged stock certificates had been combined into one for simplicity. The prosecutor said Melnitzer would be pleading guilty to all counts and was dispensing with the need for a jury. He suggested a reading of the charges could be waived because Melnitzer was a lawyer and "a sophisticated individual" who fully understood each count.

With Epstein and Greenspan at either elbow and Baltman sitting behind him, Melnitzer rose to confirm what the prosecutor was saying. "I'm pleading guilty to all of them," he said in his best courtroom voice.

But Maloney, out of an abundance of caution, opted to read each and every charge. After each count, he asked Melnitzer how he was pleading. "Guilty," Melnitzer replied 43 times.

After Maloney recorded the pleas, Hutchison rose to begin his recitation of the facts. He produced and filed as an exhibit a booklike 88-page statement of fact compiled with the agreement of defence counsel.

Hutchison touched on the highlights, explaining how Melnitzer's lifestyle had increased his voracious appetite for money, which prompted him to commit forgery and fraud. He described the first forgeries on the Vanguard and Melfan shares and how they had gone undetected. Then, he said, Melnitzer concocted the Singapore Deal, which led to forging the stock certificates and his eventual detection by the National Bank. The prosecutor included excerpts from Melnitzer's statements to police and bankers in which he claimed his problems started with his divorce and admitted every document he had ever given to any bank was forged.

The prosecutor recited many other highlights on Melnitzer's "slippery slope" of deceit. He concluded that the lawyer had cashed in on the reputation he had worked so hard to attain. "The value of reputation and standing in the community — that's what Mr. Melnitzer traded on. Reputation is everything."

Hutchison said Melnitzer operated so smoothly that the professional lenders were completely duped. "It's hard to believe banks would advance $21 million based on some pieces of paper," he said.

Hutchison and Greenspan each took care to point out that Sterling Marking Products, the printer of the certificates, was not involved in any wrongdoing. Hutchison said Sterling officials had taken great pains to keep the printing job stored safely because they were "concerned about them falling into the wrong hands. Little did they know they were delivering them into the wrong hands."

After listening to Hutchison's lengthy presentation of the facts and Greenspan's assurance that they were accepted by Melnitzer, Maloney entered convictions on each of the 43 counts. Melnitzer was ordered to return to court February 10 for sentencing and was permitted to remain free on the $250,000 bail posted by Baltman.

There would be no skiing holidays in Utah this Christmas season, or Mediterranean cruises or trips to the Far East. Even if he could have afforded it, Melnitzer wasn't permitted to leave the country under terms of his bail. The disgraced lawyer turned his attention to getting his affairs in order and encouraging his lawyers to make the best arrangements they could to ensure his sentencing went smoothly.

Just after Christmas, Justice Killeen rendered his decision in bankruptcy court on the payment of bills presented by Coopers and Lybrand, National Bank lawyers McMillan Binch and by eight other lawyers who had appeared in the receivership proceedings. All were looking to be paid for their services from Melnitzer's estate.

After reviewing the amounts claimed and the time sheets submitted by the accounting firm and the lawyers, Killeen awarded fees and disbursements totalling $491,276. Of that amount, $230,495 was allocated to Coopers and Lybrand and $171,889 to the National Bank lawyers. The remainder was split among the other eight.

The judge went on to praise the work of Coopers and Lybrand, which was conducted "with high skill and expertise at every stage of their stewardship." He said the receiver's weighty final report "set out both the sad background to this financial debacle and their skilled efforts to control the assets and take all reasonable efforts to protect the estate for possible claimants and creditors.

"The receiver had an incredibly complicated task to perform," Killeen said, dismissing one creditor's claim that Coopers and Lybrand had accomplished too little. "The receiver had to perform a detailed archaeological expedition into a tangled web of fraud going back at least to 1985 . . . Within narrow and pressing time constraints no stone was left unturned, and all appropriate protective measures were taken to ensure that identifiable assets were protected or controlled."

The judge's order stipulated that the nearly $500,000 was to be paid before claims from any of the financial institutions or individuals who had been swindled would be considered. Some of the other lawyers' fees had already been paid, such as those for representing Melnitzer in criminal court, but the balance would have to await the time-consuming review being undertaken by the trustee in bankruptcy, Peat Marwick Thorne.

Meanwhile, the Roxborough Street East home in Toronto was sold by the Toronto Dominion Bank because Melnitzer was in default on the $1.5-million mortgage. The trustee in bankruptcy registered a receiving order on the title, but the sale price barely exceeded the mortgage amount and no proceeds were realized for the estate.

After admitting his crimes, Melnitzer began contacting his old friends and associates, asking if they would send letters of character reference that might assist him at his sentencing. His plan was to present to the court many signs of support from across the community. Greenspan and Epstein wanted to stress the positive aspects of Melnitzer's personality and the contributions he had made, to point out that despite his terrible deception, a man of many admirable qualities lay beneath the surface, one who was a good candidate for rehabilitation. They hoped the letters would also work in Melnitzer's favor when the National Parole Board considered their client's first bid for parole.

Melnitzer was frank when he contacted his associates, freely admitting his offences and talking about a future in jail. He said he knew he was asking a big favor, but could a letter be sent that might help him at sentencing? The responses were mostly positive and letters began to stream in. A total of 25 would eventually be filed in court.

One of them was from John D. Arnup, a retired justice from the Ontario Court of Appeal. Years earlier, he had been treasurer of the Law Society of Upper Canada, a quaint title to denote the elected head of the governing body of the province's lawyers. He said Melnitzer had appeared before him on a number of criminal appeals during his tenure on the bench.

"Mr. Melnitzer made a favorable impression on the court," Arnup wrote. "He was always well prepared, accurate in his statement of the facts, and realistic and fair in his submissions as to sentence . . . He had a promising future as a counsel and was already one of the more competent counsel appearing before us."

Another example of high-level support came in a letter from Stuart Thom, a senior and very respected lawyer from Toronto. Like Arnup, Thom was also a former treasurer of the law society. In the mid-1980s, he had conducted

Ontario's inquiry into residential tenancies, before which Melnitzer appeared as counsel for landlords. Thom said the lawyer's conduct had always been exemplary and he had been looking forward to a "long-term association" with him.

Letters of support even came from two of Melnitzer's victims — his former marketing man, Jaime Watt, and law-school classmate, Jules Fleischer. Both expressed sadness at the turn of events but said Melnitzer had many good qualities that shouldn't be forgotten.

"When I look back," Watt wrote, "I begin to see that all the people in Julius's life came to expect far too much from him. Each of us came to believe that he was superhuman and could do anything and we adjusted our expectations accordingly. In short, we came to expect that of Julius which was both unreasonable and unfair. Unfortunately, he didn't have it within him to let us know that he was incapable of meeting our expectations and couldn't bring himself to let us down."

Fleischer wrote he couldn't understand how Melnitzer's usually high standards had deserted him at the time of the Singapore Deal on which he lost $200,000. "Like the classic Shakespearean tragic hero," Fleischer suggested, "he, too had a fatal flaw."

Ian Hunter, a law professor at the University of Western Ontario in London, stressed Melnitzer's willingness to assist in legal education and his abilities as a tough but fair adversary in court.

Martha Henry, artistic director of London's Grand Theatre, praised the lawyer's philanthropy and offered her own unique insight. "I believe that Mr. Melnitzer has a huge potential as a human being. He's one of these giant personalities about which books are written and films are made. He has a mind that works too fast for his character. Blessed, or cursed, with incredible ambition, he seems to me — rather than wanting to be destructive — to simply want to be somebody extraordinary."

But not everyone Melnitzer contacted was as willing to help. One day in late January, Goderich lawyer Dan Murphy returned to his office to find a message that Melnitzer had called. Murphy had represented the village of Grand Bend in the Archie Gibbs beach case, during which he had crossed swords with Melnitzer on countless occasions. Warily, he returned the call.

Melnitzer seemed cheerful enough when he told Murphy he would be going to jail and could use some help. He asked the small-town lawyer if he would send a support letter for the upcoming sentencing. Murphy, taken aback at the unexpected request, said he didn't think that would be appropriate. He reminded Melnitzer that he was a bencher (an elected director) at the law society, and as such he didn't want to exert any undue influence on the panel of benchers that would conduct Melnitzer's upcoming disciplinary hearing.

Melnitzer pushed Murphy gently, saying one of the letters of support he had already obtained came from Stuart Thom, who not only had been a bencher, but a former law society treasurer. "I'm not going to fight disbarment, you know," Melnitzer said.

Murphy said he wouldn't change his mind. Suddenly, he realized that Melnitzer's pitch for high-level support might also be aimed at paving the way for Melnitzer's eventual return to law.

"Julius, if you're thinking of reinstatement at some point, you better start laying the groundwork now," he advised.

Melnitzer wouldn't reveal his plans, but accepted Murphy's decision with good humor, saying he understood the lawyer's position.

Just as Murphy was marvelling at the somewhat surrealistic quality of this conversation, Melnitzer dropped another bombshell, showing his ego was still intact despite his travails.

"Did you realize, Murph, that this is the largest fraud carried out by anybody in North America?" he asked in partial response to Murphy's comment about reinstatement.

Murphy was at a loss for an answer. He couldn't believe his ears. Not only did Melnitzer not sound upset about going to jail, but he seemed almost proud of the scope of his crime. Months later, Murphy told a longtime friend he'd never forget that call. "It was unbelievable."

A report from Toronto psychiatrist Hans J. Arndt, whom Melnitzer had been seeing since shortly after his arrest, was also filed at the sentencing. In a letter to Greenspan just before the sentencing date, Arndt recounted their first meeting.

"Mr. Melnitzer initially presented himself as an exhausted, drawn and very depressed man, who frequently was in tears during the first interview. It was clear that he had been suffering from severe emotional problems for an extended period of time. However, only the most recent events and, in particular, his arrest in reference to the fraud charges, finally allowed him to actively seek psychiatric help." Arndt went on to say he had seen Melnitzer on 45 occasions for a total of 50 hours. "The frequency of these contacts was dictated by both his current emotional difficulties and the complexity of the underlying problems."

The psychiatrist said Melnitzer was taking Prozac, an anti-depressant medication, which was helping his therapy. He recommended both the drug and therapy be continued in prison. He then turned to the background of his patient.

"Mr. Melnitzer is emotionally a rather disturbed person. It is this severe emotional disturbance which underscores and provides some explanation why a highly respected and motivated lawyer became involved in the criminal activity which led to his arrest . . .

"Mr. Melnitzer's background, both [sic] his youth, his formative years and educational background, have been fully and candidly provided to me . . . He grew up in a rather conflicted environment, which propelled him into a highly motivated frame of mind in which he sought both success and recognition of his achievements. However, this also caused him to exaggerate his financial success and led to self-destructive behavior and the exaggerated need for public recognition and adulation.

"The underlying positive features of his personality . . . led him to extreme generosity with his time and money, a sense of decency and compassion for people less fortunate than he and to the numerous contributions he made to his community in a non-professional capacity."

In preparing for his impending loss of freedom, Melnitzer travelled to Kingston, Ontario, where he discussed his situation with prison authorities at what would likely be his new home. He learned that while day parole would not be available until he had served at least 18 months on a nine-year sentence, there were provisions relating to earlier temporary releases. Melnitzer discovered he could apply for educational day passes if he decided to take university courses. He began inquiring about the availability of business programs. By osmosis, he had already picked up much knowledge of business from his banking and investment activities. A business degree, he figured, shouldn't be too difficult, and it would get him started on a new career path if a return to law was denied him. Besides, attending university would keep him away from the bad guys for a few hours each day. He also began some early paperwork relating to his eventual classification as an offender to promote his placement in a minimum-security institution as soon as possible.

Finally, judgment day, February 10, arrived. Melnitzer travelled to London with his wife and daughter, who sat immediately behind him in court. Wearing a dark blue pin-striped suit, Melnitzer seemed more relaxed than on previous appearances. He joked briefly with Greenspan and Epstein before court convened, assured that Justice Maloney would likely accept the nine-year term agreed to by the prosecutor. The courtroom was packed with more than 70 spectators, many of them lawyers, friends and other associates of the once high-flying lawyer.

Prosecutor Hutchison was on his feet first, asking that Maloney order Melnitzer to repay his victims. He requested that compensation orders be issued for most of the defrauded parties. He sought $1.5 million for Ron Delanghe, and $925,000 for Ron and Bonnie Delanghe; $450,000 for Barry Parker, the Sifton Properties executive; $100,000 for Ivana Klouda, the former Cohen, Melnitzer office manager; $100,000 for Fletcher Dawson; $150,000 for Ken and Margaret McGill; $50,000 for Paul Vogel; and $250,000 for Melnitzer's friends, Hyman Goldberg and Laurie Seaman. Hutchison said he had been in touch with all those victims and they wanted compensation. He had been unable to contact Jules Fleischer and so was unable to seek a similar order on his behalf for $200,000.

Epstein interrupted to say Melnitzer had no opposition to having Fleischer added to the list of those he must repay. Maloney added Fleischer's name. Neither Allan Richman nor Jaime Watt, the remaining two individual investors who had lost $1.8 million and $25,000 respectively, were included. No explanation was given.

In addition, Hutchison sought orders to compensate the Canadian Imperial Bank of Commerce for $8,392,629, Grand Canyon Properties for $4 million, and Forward Properties for $4 million. The National, Toronto Dominion and Royal banks did not seek orders, although they were entitled to.

The compensation orders totalled $3.725 million for the private investors and $16.392 million for the CIBC and Allan Richman's real estate firms — for a grand total of $20.1 million.

Greenspan, who would make all the defence submissions this day, then rose to put the best face possible on Melnitzer and his crimes. In his half-hour speech, Greenspan said his client agreed that "what he had done was monstrous, but he was not a monster." He said Melnitzer was the product of Holocaust survivors and had created his own "financial holocaust. This is not a man of bravado at this stage of his life. He understands the charges and he feels shame and remorse." An example of that remorse was his willingness to co-operate with the authorities and save a lengthy and expensive trial, the defence lawyer said. The speed with which everything had been resolved was almost unprecedented.

Greenspan said Melnitzer's accomplishments were many, but "his life is now in a shambles. His career as a lawyer is over." He referred to the psychiatric report by Arndt and said it was clear Melnitzer must continue taking medication and treatment while in prison if his rehabilitation was to be successful.

He said Melnitzer became embroiled in a nightmare of his own making that was bound to fail. "It was a treadmill from which he was unable to extricate himself. He even expresses his gratitude that the end came, that it was shot down."

The lawyer then read excerpts from several of the letters filed as exhibits. Maloney interrupted at one point to say he had "great respect" for the retired Justice Arnup, whose letter was in the stack. Maloney also marvelled at the forgiving nature of Fleischer's letter of support. "The loss of $200,000 would destroy most people," he observed.

Greenspan concluded by reminding the court that the compensation orders were an integral part of Melnitzer's punishment and will "exist forever" until they are satisfied. He suggested a nine-year prison term be imposed, the second-highest penalty ever recorded for fraud in Ontario.

The lanky Hutchison took over and immediately confirmed that he agreed with the nine-year term. He said Melnitzer's crimes were "committed on such a scale that is almost unrivalled. It is hard to find a crime to compare to this." He said the only prison term longer was the 15-year sentence imposed on William Player, for his $330-million defrauding of Seaway, Greymac and Crown trusts.

Hutchison said Maloney had to remember Melnitzer's victims "have suffered serious, indeed devastating losses . . . some of them have lost the accumulated wealth of a lifetime. And there is relatively little chance of these monies ever being realized from the compensation orders." The prosecutor said that Melnitzer created an "enormous mess" and that civil claims would probably be pursued against him for years. "Much of the money went to maintain a lifestyle that was virtually unrivalled . . . He has enjoyed the luxury of the good life for the past five or six years on money he stole. I have no reason to believe there is a significant amount of money out there."

He said the Mounties, the banks, the receiver and trustee had looked for money that might have been stashed "but nobody's found any. If there is money out there, however, these compensation orders will be enforceable for the balance of Mr. Melnitzer's life."

He urged Maloney not to place too much emphasis on the letters of support from people who described Melnitzer's many accomplishments. "Reputation is what allowed Mr. Melnitzer to commit these offences," he pointed out. The faith others placed in him "is what allowed him to steal this enormous amount of money." He rejected assertions by some of the letter writers that Melnitzer had simply made mistakes. "These were deliberate, knowing acts committed by a man with intimate knowledge of what is right and what is wrong. He chose to do wrong."

At the end of his 15-minute pitch, however, Hutchison conceded that Melnitzer's co-operation with police was "unprecedented" and had averted a complex and lengthy investigation and trial. That was why, he said, he was agreeing to a nine-year term.

Maloney withdrew to consider the submissions and impose sentence. Under Canadian law, a judge is not bound by any sentencing agreement between the prosecution and defence. If the judge feels it is not in the public interest, he or she can impose a different penalty.

Court was adjourned for nearly three hours while Maloney reviewed the situation. It was nail-biting time for Melnitzer. Was the delay because the judge was wrestling with the joint submission?

When Maloney returned to the bench, his bushy eyebrows framed a frown. He asked Melnitzer to stand.

"Mr. Melnitzer, in 20 years at the bar and in now nearly 17 years as a judge presiding all over Ontario, I can't recall being involved in a case, or knowing of a case, where the man in the [prisoner's] dock was a man of the intelligence and the attainments that are so well recognized in you. For that reason, any lecture from the bench, from me, would be redundant, and I don't propose to expose you to that.

"No matter what the sentence of the court today, no matter what it is, it will be perceived differently depending on one's point of view. You and your family and your friends, for natural reasons, might think it unduly severe . . . The general public, particularly the skeptics and the cynics, especially those many people who unfortunately hold a negative view of lawyers and the legal system, might well consider it unduly lenient."

The courtroom was hushed; Melnitzer's head was slightly bowed.

Maloney said he wasn't going to tell Melnitzer about the principles of sentencing. The man before him knew them well and had undoubtedly lectured judges about them from the counsel table.

"You've already destroyed yourself, certainly insofar as the practice of your chosen profession is concerned, a profession to which you have dedicated so much of your life. In years of training and then in years of successful practice, you achieved an enviable reputation as a leader at the bar, at the leading edge of the litigation process . . . I knew you by reputation as a leader of the bar. And that's a reputation you don't gain without a lot of effort. All that's gone now."

Maloney went into the need to deter others who would consider fraud, before he returned to the man before him.

"You've no doubt brought a great deal of anguish upon yourself, your family and to your friends. You stand disgraced in the public eye, certainly in this vicinity. You have hurt many people, the victims particularly, but others as well. You know what you've really done, and I hope you are sensitive to this, you have really dealt a blow to your peers."

He reminded Melnitzer that the compensation orders had the force of court judgments, which would survive his bankruptcy. "Accordingly, you will have those debts and the compensation orders which I have just made, over your head for the rest of your life. I want the community at large to know that you will be saddled with legally enforceable debts in that vast amount, so that really you will not likely ever escape the consequences of your criminal conduct."

Then, as he finished his brief commentary, Maloney raised his bushy brows and got to the part Melnitzer and his lawyers had been waiting for.

"I regard the penalty which was the subject matter of the joint submission as being both substantial and appropriate. And so, Mr. Melnitzer, you are sentenced to serve a term of imprisonment of nine years.

"Will you remove the prisoner, please."

Melnitzer showed no emotion as he was led out of the courtroom by security officers. He didn't return the pained looks from his wife and daughter.

With Melnitzer gone, the always meticulous Hutchison had one last piece of legal housekeeping. He asked Maloney to endorse the court record to show 43 sentences of nine years each, all to be served concurrently.

The judge complied and added a recommendation that Melnitzer continue to receive psychiatric treatment "to the extent possible while he's confined."

It was over. Six months after his scheme of deceit had unravelled, Melnitzer became an inmate in federal prison. His fall had been fast and hard.

Defence lawyers declined comment on the sentencing, but Hutchison obliged reporters by joining them on the chilly, windswept courthouse steps. The prosecutor was asked if he thought Melnitzer could ever rebound from prison and the crippling compensation orders.

"He's a remarkable man," Hutchison replied simply. "There's not a lot that would surprise me about his abilities."

14

Fallout

*"The creditors are big boys who can take care
of themselves."*

SHORTLY AFTER MELNITZER WAS sent to prison, the
home on Tallwood Road was listed for sale at
$429,900. Montreal Trust put it on the market because he was
in default on the mortgage, the balance of which stood at
$192,000.

The trustee in bankruptcy hoped the sale would provide
some much-needed cash for Melnitzer's estate, but Baltman
was claiming half the house, so it was unclear how much of
that scarce commodity the sale would produce. At best, the
trustee calculated the net proceeds at almost $100,000.

The house was a sorry sight. It looked as though someone
had moved out in a great hurry months before, which is
exactly what had happened. The backyard swimming pool
and hot tub were solid ice because no one had bothered to
drain them. The furnishings had been removed but a few
personal items remained. In the spacious en suite bathroom,
an oversized wineglass was filled with matchbooks gathered
on the couple's travels around the world. Soap was still in
the soap dishes. In the kitchen, a collection tin for the Jewish
National Fund was half-filled with change. The ceilings had
numerous water stains and the walls where the art collection

once hung so proudly were bare except for dozens of plastic anchor plugs. A wall in the pink-wallpapered master bedroom displayed fist-sized holes.

In the basement, the exercise room was barren, save for its mirrored wall. Tucked away in a far corner of the basement, several cardboard boxes contained items that had been abandoned, among them law texts, legal files and books for pleasure reading, including quite a few nonfiction works relating to crime.

One box held several large scrapbooks chronicling Melnitzer's legal career. Included were brief newspaper clippings from his first cases in the 1970s, announcements of Fletcher Dawson and Paul Vogel joining Cohen, Melnitzer and of the firm's relocation. There was coverage of Melnitzer's big cases, including the Belvedere Hotel killing, programs for legal seminars at which he spoke, thank-you letters from their organizers and congratulations from well-respected lawyers on his greatest victories. Here were the benchmarks of Melnitzer's relentless drive to the top of his profession. They had been treasured mementoes, something to someday show his grandchildren.

After his sentencing, Melnitzer was taken to Millhaven Penitentiary, near Kingston, for processing and assessment. After a few weeks, he was transferred to the Beaver Creek Correctional Institution near Gravenhurst, about 160 kilometres north of Toronto, in the heart of Ontario's vacation land and not far from the cottage where he and Baltman had found seclusion following his arrest. The 120-inmate, minimum-security institution is the next best thing to being back on the street. Built during the Second World War as a training base for Norwegian pilots, Beaver Creek was expanded over the years, but it remains a collection of small wooden buildings resembling a summer camp in the bush. Inmates are drawn from all walks of life and are viewed by Correctional Service of Canada officials as worthy of trust, neither a danger to the public nor likely to attempt escape.

There are no bars or barbed wire at Beaver Creek. It is the kind of facility inmates in maximum-security institutions spend years hoping to qualify for, and prison officials can use it as a reward for good behavior. Because of his knowledge of the system and his efforts to be classified before sentencing, Melnitzer made it there from Millhaven in a little over a month.

Inmates are able to upgrade their education and learn various skills, and are expected to take part in forestry work, plantation maintenance, land-clearing projects and the like. Beaver Creek provides volunteers to assist the handicapped and senior citizens in the area and to help in the maintenance of such public facilities as arenas, parks and cemeteries. Prisoners, who have keys to their own rooms, can join drug and alcohol support groups and take part in a variety of organized sports, fishing, golfing, theatre and similar recreational and cultural activities. Melnitzer could have done a lot worse.

The day after he was sentenced, news of Melnitzer's involvement with Calla Reid became public when the *London Free Press* splashed it all over the front page. The newspaper had failed earlier in its legal challenge to overturn the sealing orders covering the Coopers and Lybrand report dealing with Reid and the interview with official receiver John Everett. On the eve of Melnitzer's sentencing, the newspaper had resumed its bid, arguing that the main reason advanced in support of the sealing order was about to evaporate. To obtain the order, Melnitzer's lawyers had said the release might prejudice his right to a fair trial. But upon completion of the sentencing procedure, Melnitzer's "trial" was over. When they learned the newspaper was renewing its fight to obtain the sensitive information, Melnitzer's lawyers realized it was hopeless to oppose the unsealing bid. Faced with the prospect of his wife's reading about his expensive liaison in the press or hearing about it directly, Melnitzer told Baltman about the other woman, assuring her it was history. While no one other than the couple themselves was privy to Baltman's reaction to learning of her husbands betrayal, one reaction she didn't demonstrate was vindictiveness. She easily could have revoked her bail promise, a move that would have immediately put Melnitzer behind bars. But she didn't. She could have abandoned him when he needed her most in his last days of freedom. She chose not to, however, remaining supportive throughout. Baltman stayed close to him on sentencing day, sitting in the front row in court, providing support and encouragement, not only to Melnitzer but to his daughter, Melissa.

Melnitzer's lawyers agreed not to argue against the move to unseal the documents providing the newspaper agreed to delay publication of the contents until February 11, the day after sentencing. Melnitzer wanted to be on his way to prison and Deena and Melissa back in Toronto before the news of the mistress hit the media. He was anxious to save his wife and daughter further embarrassment than they had already suffered. It proved a wise move, because while the *Free Press* agreed to the plan, it made the most of the information it had pried loose. The headline about the payments to Reid was larger than the one about Melnitzer's nine-year jail term.

At the end of February in London, the many creditors of Julius Melnitzer again gathered in bankruptcy court.

Peat Marwick Thorne reported to Justice Killeen that so little money had been found in the estate it couldn't afford to continue looking for more. The trustee in bankruptcy sought permission to conclude its work and apply for Melnitzer's formal discharge.

In a report and appendices filling more than 400 pages, the accounting firm concluded that after various claims on the estate were settled, its net value was anywhere from a deficit of $268,800 to a surplus of $2 million. And little of the nearly $500,000 Killeen awarded earlier as part of the receivership proceedings had been paid. Formal claims filed under the Bankruptcy Act totalled a further $42.5 million, the report said.

Peat Marwick Thorne's lawyer, Joseph Steiner, was blunt

when he addressed the court: "There is virtually no cash in the estate." The trustee, he said, had used up the $50,000 it had been guaranteed for fees and incurred a further $55,000 in disbursements. Steiner said that there were a few assets the trustee might conceivably chase, but that their value was limited and couldn't be realized without costly and time-consuming court action. "The trustee is not in a position to pursue any of the litigation that would be required."

Therefore, Steiner said, he was seeking permission to wrap up Peat Marwick Thorne's work and had tentatively scheduled Melnitzer's discharge from bankruptcy for late March. He said the various banks and the inspectors in charge of the estate had already agreed to the plan. The only opponent was 808756 Ontario Limited, the firm created for the investors in the Singapore Deal. Steiner said 808756 was insisting the trustee continue chasing assets at the trustee's own risk. He said he wasn't happy with that position and accused the numbered company of seeking "a free ride" so it wouldn't have to track down assets itself. "The creditors are big boys who can take care of themselves," he said, noting they were few in number and were owed substantial amounts. Steiner asked Killeen to disregard the objections from the numbered company.

Tony Van Klink, the lawyer representing 808756, rose to explain his client's position. He said Peat Marwick Thorne was pulling out too soon and had not yet fulfilled its legal requirement to locate and sell off Melnitzer's assets. He said the trustee had found more than $100,000 on top of what Coopers and Lybrand uncovered, so it had enough money to fund further work. Besides, he argued, a lack of funding was not sufficient to relieve the trustee of its legal obligations.

Among other failings, he said, the trustee had made little attempt to evaluate or chase the string of properties in Quebec owned by Melfan. Melnitzer retained a 20-percent interest in Melfan, so that was something of potential value. Van Klink said the numbered company was not convinced all Melnitzer's holdings had been uncovered. "It's quite conceivable there are assets out there," he said, urging Killeen to order Peat Marwick Thorne to redouble its efforts and look for more.

The judge replied that he didn't think creditors could force the trustee representing their interests to sue another party in order to collect a possible receivable.

Ian Wallace, the lawyer for the Canadian Imperial Bank of Commerce, which had pushed for the appointment of the trustee in the first place, argued that there had to be some limit on how far the trustee should be expected to chase assets. He said the bank and the other creditors overseeing the estate were satisfied Peat Marwick Thorne had done a good job. The trustee should be permitted to conclude its search and withdraw.

After considering the arguments, Killeen decided he wouldn't press Peat Marwick Thorne to look for more assets. The trustee could begin winding up its work.

The trustee's weighty report filed with the court contained no major revelations. It reported Melnitzer's art collection had finally been appraised. The value placed on it was $369,000, one-sixth of the amount Melnitzer had claimed. But Baltman was asserting ownership of many major pieces, and two banks said the collection had been pledged to them as security. The report uncovered $137,000 in shares in London-based Cableshare Inc., a further $14,000 in registered retirement savings plan certificates and an outstanding bill of $20,000 that a Toronto lawyer said he owed for work Melnitzer performed many months before; he planned to pay the money.

The report also revealed an ongoing squabble between the trustee and Melnitzer's former law firm. Peat Marwick Thorne wanted to know what had happened to the $1.1 million Melnitzer had deposited to the account of Cohen, Melnitzer on July 31, 1991. The money had been obtained from the Royal Bank, which now wanted it back. The law firm maintained it couldn't provide any information without violating client confidentiality and it didn't have permission to discuss the matter.

Other correspondence from the law firm disputed the receiver's earlier assertion that Melnitzer's May 1990 payment of $1.1 million was on behalf of Archie Gibbs for the Grand Bend case. Russell Raikes wrote to Peat Marwick Thorne that the facts were as follows: "Melnitzer advised our office manager, Ms. Klouda, that he was expecting funds in from the CIBC and would require a cheque in the same amount as soon as those funds were received. The funds were transferred to our general account, according to bank statements, and a cheque was issued to Melnitzer on the same date, May 18, 1990, for $1.1 million. Enclosed is a copy of the cheque."

The partners also took exception to Melnitzer's claim that he had $715,000 in his former firm's capital account. The partners argued that their potential claims against him more than offset the amount. Given that position, the trustee concluded that the only possibility of obtaining any money there would be through legal action.

The trustee had also uncovered $100,000 sitting in a trust account in the name of the Fair Rental Policy Organization of Ontario, the group for which Melnitzer had been counsel and, more recently, chairperson. Investigation revealed the organization was making no claim on the money, which Melnitzer admitted he had obtained from Allan Richman. However, Richman wanted the money back.

Once discharged from bankruptcy, Melnitzer would regain control of his financial affairs. While bankrupt, a person cannot borrow money without declaring he is bankrupt. Failure to disclose that fact is an offence under the Bankruptcy Act. After discharge, a person can borrow funds free from this requirement. And any money earned from that point on goes to the individual, not his estate. Regardless, credit bureaus keep track of bankrupts for seven years, and a person discharged from bankruptcy can be sued for debts incurred on the road to financial ruin. He is no longer protected from such litigation by his bankrupt status. As well as having the $20 million in compensation over his head, Melnitzer could face further lawsuits launched by his many creditors.

Peat Marwick Thorne's arrangements to apply for Melnitzer's discharge were short-circuited when Melnitzer took an unusual step. He filed a waiver with the bankruptcy court that would relieve the trustee of that task. Seldom is such a waiver filed, because it means the bankrupt person is responsible for applying for his or her own discharge and must incur the costs and aggravations associated with preparing reports and legal fees connected with the application. Still, this step gave him the right to exercise some control over his affairs. He could decide when to go for discharge and in which jurisdiction.

Since his prison term was being served in central Ontario, he could consider applying for discharge at the bankruptcy office in Toronto, for instance, giving him the benefit of accomplishing the task in relative anonymity, far from prying eyes in London, particularly the media's. And he could obtain the discharge when he felt it would be to his best advantage. Under law, a trustee in bankruptcy must file for the discharge within 12 months of the declaration of bankruptcy. When a waiver is filed, that requirement evaporates. Melnitzer could choose to remain bankrupt for the rest of his life if he wanted. Whatever his motive, filing the waiver gave him back a measure of control, something Melnitzer had always valued.

On March 3, Melnitzer's case was the subject of a disciplinary hearing at the Law Society of Upper Canada. He did not appear personally and was represented by his Toronto civil lawyer, Donald Jack. Discussions with the society and its senior counsel, Gavin MacKenzie, had been going on for many months. At one point, Melnitzer had offered to be the subject of a brief videotape to be shown to law students to demonstrate how much trouble lawyers can get into. About 10 such tapes have been prepared in the past featuring other lawyers who have run into trouble. The tapes are considered valuable teaching aids to dramatize the sorts of problems real-life lawyers can get into if they don't keep to the moral high ground. It is unclear whether Melnitzer was motivated by a continuing dedication to legal education or by the thought that such an offer might prove helpful in his criminal proceedings or later when dealing with parole officials. In any event, the offer was declined.

Three of the 40 elected benchers of the law society conducted the disciplinary hearing, which was chaired by Toronto lawyer Paul Copeland. The two counts of conduct unbecoming a lawyer, relating to the forged certificates and the Singapore Deal, had been replaced with a single, identical count, based on his pleas of guilty to the 43 charges and his sentencing the previous month.

Jack advised the hearing he was admitting guilt on behalf of Melnitzer. MacKenzie then filed the same 88-page statement of fact compiled by prosecutor Hutchison in the criminal case, noting Melnitzer had agreed to the facts set out in the document. Jack filed the same letters of support entered as exhibits at the sentencing and read several aloud. MacKenzie said disbarment was essential because of the great shame Melnitzer had brought to the profession. Jack stressed Melnitzer's positive record as a lawyer, teacher and first-rate advocate.

After hearing the submissions, Copeland delivered the decision on behalf of the committee.

"We agree with Mr. MacKenzie . . . that disbarment is required in this case, having regard to the seriousness of the offences, the number of offences and the relevance of the status of the stature of the solicitor in London to his ability to have committed these offences . . . a long series of fraudulent acts committed over six years involving staggering quantities of money. The nine-year sentence imposed was at the very high end of the range for sentences for fraud."

Copeland briefly reviewed the forgeries, the frauds and attempted frauds Melnitzer committed, adding that "for each category of offence the solicitor exploited his reputation not only in London, but in the province of Ontario as a prominent and competent lawyer." He went on to say that "the actions of the solicitor and the widespread publicity connected to his actions have had an impact on the general reputation of lawyers in the province . . . Disbarment is required in this case in part to repair that damage done by the solicitor's criminal activities."

Copeland commented that the letters of support were impressive and he registered amazement that Jules Fleischer and Jaime Watt, two of the victims, were among the writers. He then returned to the man whose fate was in the committee's hands.

"It is apparent that a very bright, competent, personable and well-liked man has committed very serious offences over a long period of time for reasons this committee finds hard to comprehend. For the solicitor and his family, his public fall from grace is a significant personal tragedy. For the society, the solicitor is a convicted criminal, guilty of most significant property offences. In our view, no penalty short of disbarment would be appropriate."

Disbarment wasn't official until late March when the monthly meeting of law-society benchers approved the committee report and issued a press release.

There it was — the nightmarish end to one man's dreams of legal immortality. Melnitzer's name, enshrined in legal textbooks, was stricken from the rolls of the Ontario bar. His chances of reinstatement at some future date are predicted to be slim to nonexistent. Only a half-dozen lawyers have been reinstated after disbarment in the province, and they had to prove they were totally changed persons, their offences the result of problems that had been brought under control and for which they were still receiving help.

Not long after the disbarment proceedings, Deena Baltman resumed her acting career. Without a dependent husband, she could afford to leave the law firm where she'd been working.

Another woman might have already left her spouse under circumstances of such thorough deception. On top of learning that Melnitzer had misled her for years about his business dealings were the revelations about the girlfriend in Toronto and the New York escort service. Much of what they had accumulated and shared was gone or else was the subject of what was expected to be protracted litigation. She had been particularly upset at the fight over her extensive jewelry collection, a substantial portion of which she had inherited from her late mother. It was clear there would be no speedy resolution to disputes such as her claims relating to the art collection.

But Baltman had stood by her husband of five years and partner of ten. She had calmed him when he became enraged; she dealt with others when he could not. She had posted bond for him. Baltman had helped him slip away from the reporters who congregated at his various court appearances. She had been stoic; she had been faithful. She obviously had no ulterior motives, because had she left him, her legal claims against their joint assets would have been stronger. But she chose to stick by him through the ordeal of his guilty plea and sentencing. People who knew the couple wondered, however, if her commitment could withstand the lengthy period of forced separation that lay ahead.

Her inner strength came as a surprise to some of the lawyers in London who didn't know her well. But not to Martha Henry, the artistic director of London's Grand Theatre, under whom she had studied. Henry's was one of the many letters of reference filed at Melnitzer's sentencing. She alone took the time to address some of her comments to the character of his wife.

"I have taught classes to Deena Baltman Melnitzer and I have found her to be good, honest and remarkably hardworking," Henry wrote. "You get to know someone well when you teach them; you have to get inside the head to see how they tick in order to help them learn. She is as straight as a die.

"Mrs. Melnitzer must have been devastated by the unfolding of the events over the past months. Still, she believes in the inherent goodness of her husband; she has stood beside him with every ounce of her being and has given up her own fledgling career as an actress to go back into a law firm where she can make ends meet and keep the marriage together. She has shown herself to be cut from the finest cloth; Julius would never betray her twice."

Cathy Melnitzer, remarried several years before, continued to live in Toronto, her lifestyle modest. Calla Reid spent months negotiating with the three banks that were after her condominium, car and money. All the while, she continued to search for a new job with another accounting firm.

Despite Melnitzer's prediction that his former law firm would flounder without him, the reorganized Cohen, Highley, Vogel and Dawson trimmed its expenses and survived. It wasn't easy during the first few months, with continuous media coverage about its cofounder's actions. The leaner law firm eventually did relocate in prestigious One London Place, but on a single floor, the eleventh, not the prized top two floors as originally planned. The firm rejected Melnitzer's claims he had any equity in it, arguing the damage he inflicted far exceeded the value of anything he might have left behind. Partners and associates were reluctant to discuss their situation or anything about the disgraced Big Guy. Harris Cohen declined to talk about his former partner, other than to say everyone at the firm wanted to put Melnitzer behind them, to get on with the business of law, and work to undo the harm he had caused them.

"He fooled everybody in the firm," Cohen said simply.

Allan Richman struggled to please his bankers and the handful of investors who had placed their money with him, money he had invested in Melnitzer's schemes. He felt completely betrayed by the man he had liked and respected, and his partner in a wide variety of ventures over the years. He couldn't believe his faith in Melnitzer had been so misplaced. After much negotiation, he advised the investors he would repay them in full, but it would take several years to do so. He said he felt responsible for their losses and would work hard to help them restore what, in some cases, had been life savings.

Being sent to prison is not the end of Melnitzer's problems. Any time after his discharge from bankruptcy, his many creditors can initiate lawsuits to recover their money. The first was filed by the National Bank of Canada at the time of his arrest. The other banks and individual victims were barred from initiating their own suits because of the receivership and later the bankruptcy.

Whether or not to sue will be a hard decision for the lawyers for the banks and the others. The compensation orders facing Melnitzer are judgments of a court and have priority over all other obligations. Creditors who launch lawsuits and win will have a long wait to collect, if ever. A successful lawsuit could result in a purely Pyrrhic victory. And to win a case of civil fraud, there is a major hurdle to overcome. The creditor must be able to identify clearly where the funds taken from it were placed. The claim fails if the funds were mixed with any other monies, ill-gotten or otherwise. Given Melnitzer's poor record-keeping, such a case will be difficult to make. The creditors may decide to cut their losses, abandon legal recourse and hope compensation is forthcoming.

The compensation order is truly burdensome for Melnitzer. Because it's collecting interest at 10 percent annually, the $20-million order will have risen to about $27 million after three years, about the time he can begin applying for full parole.

Melnitzer's spectacular fall rocked the entire Canadian legal community. It was featured as a cover story in the March 1991 edition of *Canadian Lawyer* magazine, which imposed a caricature of his face on a Monopolylike game board. The fictional game, titled Get Rich Quick, started at "Go. Borrow $200,000 As You Pass." Other spaces were marked "Court

Victory. Making Your Name," "Forge Securities," "Buy Art. Borrow More," "Busted! Go to Jail," and of course "Jail" — an entirely appropriate depiction of Melnitzer and his schemes.

In his editorial introducing the issue, Michael G. Crawford warned there were lessons to be learned from the Melnitzer case. "You think you know someone," he wrote. "He or she may have worked alongside you for years. It could be a partner, an ambitious young associate or an office administrator. And then, from out of the blue, the trust you shared is suddenly betrayed.

"It can happen in any relationship, of course. But there's something special about the trust that flows in a law office that makes betrayal even more painful than in other work settings. In many respects, trust is one of the pillars of day-to-day operations within the legal profession.

"But lately, it seems more and more practitioners, some very senior, have been willing to abuse and even prey upon that trust."

Crawford wrote that he had interviewed Melnitzer several times over the years. "While there's no excuse for what he did, what makes this story of a lawyer-gone-bad even more poignant is that the narcissistic trap he fell into may be one that could be lying out there for all of us."

Crawford put it another way later in a newspaper interview: "This really eats away at the fabric of the way law firms operate. Now law firm lawyers and partners have to cast a very suspicious eye on their colleagues."

Another observer, Michael Fitz-James, editor of the well-respected *Lawyers Weekly*, said lawyers across the country were "still shaking their heads" about the case. He said that less than one percent of lawyers engage in illegal activities. "A fraud of over $1 million in the legal community is pretty rare," he said. Shaking his own head, he added, "He was a top, top dog." But he suggested that despair, rather than shock, was the predominant reaction to Melnitzer's crimes. "Lawyers are used to dealing with the darker side of human nature, so they are not overly surprised when this sort of thing happens."

Melnitzer's crimes also had repercussions in the national and local banking communities. His fraud was acknowledged as the largest perpetrated by an individual against Canada's banks, and senior banking officials were embarrassed. They sent a flurry of directives to their managers reminding them to investigate thoroughly any security provided by customers seeking credit. Such procedures were already part of lending practices at all banks; it's just that they were often overlooked in dealings with familiar customers. Meanwhile, some lawyers reported their banks were becoming less generous in extending lines of credit and had begun demanding greater security.

Security chiefs at several major financial institutions conceded the Melnitzer fraud was extraordinary in terms of dollars. "It's a large hit, no doubt about it," said Sonny Saunders, chief of security at the Royal Bank. "It really does stand out. All bankers are now probably checking more closely stock certificates and other things offered as collateral." He said strict adherence to policies governing documentation would be the rule, rather than the exception, even for solid clients with proven track records.

Mike Ballard, vice-president of the Canadian Bankers Association, conceded the losses for fraud had been "horrifically high." He pointed out, however, that in terms of the billions of dollars handled by Canada's banks each year, it was a relative ripple. He said frauds such as Melnitzer's are "a rare occurrence," but because of their nature, he couldn't say they will never happen again. "The basic rule of banking is know your client," Ballard said, but he conceded even that wouldn't have stopped the canny lawyer. Melnitzer's bankers thought they knew him and had come to see him as "a pillar of the community," Ballard said. "This is what allowed him to perpetrate this kind of fraud. Unless you want to restructure the whole system, this kind of situation is pretty difficult to prevent."

The banking executive said one trend working against future Melnitzers was that soon all transfers of securities will be done by computer. That will eliminate the manual handling of stock certificates completely and allow lenders to confirm the validity of such collateral the moment it is pledged.

In London, Melnitzer's deceit sent shock waves through the banking community. The Royal Bank reassigned Colin Liptrot. No longer manager of its private banking centre, he became manager of business development, a move widely seen as a demotion.

About eight months after John Graham exposed Melnitzer as a fraud artist, he was fired as part of a reorganization at the National Bank. The move was unrelated to the Melnitzer affair, but it came as a shock to Graham, a father of three. Told to vacate his office the same day, Graham was informed the commercial lending centre in London was closing because of the depressed economy. He accepted the explanation and the fact that he would be joining the unemployed. Others in his office, including senior manager David Renwick, were offered transfers to Toronto.

At the time of Melnitzer's arrest, the National Bank had crowed about the "due diligence" its staff had exercised in detecting the forgeries. The bank didn't mention Graham's name at the time, but it was him they were talking about.

The abrupt sacking was a fine thank-you for the man who not only had saved his employer $15 million in potential losses — because he followed a hunch that never occurred to the three other bankers, all holding identical fake certificates — but saved four banks further potential losses of more than $50 million. Also let go in Toronto for similarly announced reasons was Ian Crook, the National's credit manager.

Meanwhile, at the CIBC, the bank that suffered the greatest loss at nearly $8.4 million, it's business as usual. The bank is still intent on overtaking the Royal Bank as the country's largest and apparently views the loss as one of the prices to pay for aggressive banking. Geoffrey Foster, who made the Melnitzer loans at the CIBC, remained Ontario vice-president.

With insurance covering most of the losses and the lawyer's crime merely a blip in the multibillion-dollar banking industry's ledgers, it is unlikely the bankers will learn much from the Melnitzer debacle. There is no real incentive to change a business as long as its profits are healthy.

Late in February 1992, the month Melnitzer began life in prison, Statistics Canada issued an interim report card on the state of the national economy. The bottom line for business in the last quarter of 1991 was worse than at any point of the recession a decade earlier, the agency reported. Operating profits for businesses over the year had plunged by 28 percent to $46.6 billion. The sole exception was the banking industry, which saw strong growth. Profits at the chartered banks rose by $863 million to $2.2 billion in the fourth quarter, well above their average quarterly profit of $1.2 billion in the previous three years.

With bottom-line numbers like that, no one was clamoring to "restructure the whole system," as Mike Ballard of the Canadian Bankers Association had put it.

Ironically, despite the banks' best efforts to eliminate trust in their dealings with the vast majority of their customers, it was trust — and some greed — that proved to be the Achilles heel for the bankers with whom Melnitzer dealt.

And a repeat is entirely possible.

Epilogue

MANY MEMBERS OF THE legal community are troubled by aspects of the Melnitzer case. Some are wary of the lawyer from past legal tangles in which he bested them. Aside from the obvious questions about what motivated him to turn to crime, many can't believe he committed a crime that was so easy to detect. And appreciative of Melnitzer's acute intelligence, they can't understand how he could apparently wind up with nothing from his multimillion-dollar schemes.

Some believe that Melnitzer had to know he would be tripped up and was preparing his nest for that eventuality. They point to the fact that he kept a heavy mortgage on the Roxborough Street home in Toronto. If Melnitzer thought he could keep his scam going, why didn't he buy the Toronto home outright and eliminate a heavy monthly mortgage obligation? The answer, they suggest, is that it would be better to keep the money liquid, stashed away somewhere so it couldn't be as easily seized and liquidated if he was found out. And what reason could there be for the frantic pace of banking in July, other than that he knew the jig was almost up and was trying to grab as much cash as he could before fleeing? It has been noted that Melnitzer was a prolific traveller with favorite destinations in the Caribbean, Europe and the Far East. It would have been relatively easy for him to squirrel money away from the Canadian authorities, so this line of thinking makes a degree of sense. For Melnitzer, once able to leave Canada, could take along a stout briefcase and pay visits to the banks where his money is stashed. Then he'd be up and running again.

These suspicions are fed by the fact that neither the court-appointed receiver nor the trustee in bankruptcy had much success tracking funds outside the country. The receiver was making some headway in that regard when it was pulled off the trail. The trustee was never adequately funded to pursue offshore funds because its fees were limited to a quarter of those of the receiver.

Aside from the suspicions is the question of arithmetic. On the face of it, a large amount of money appears to be unaccounted for. In Melnitzer's statement of affairs filed under oath with the official receiver in bankruptcy, he claimed assets of $7.3 million and liabilities of $28.5 million. That would mean he had somehow disposed of $21.2 million. The trustee in bankruptcy estimated the value of his estate at a little more than $2 million, while the official claims filed against it totalled $42.5 million, which leaves more than $40 million that cannot be traced.

Melnitzer claimed he had very little to show for his money and that most of it had been used to support his flashy lifestyle designed to fool the bankers. He had spent much to impress others, as well, lavished gifts on Baltman and was also making heavy interest payments to Richman and the banks. But observers feel, to dispose of that kind of money, he would have had to be burning it. Or "burying" it in faroff places.

Flying in the face of the stashed-money theory, however, is the meticulous work of Coopers and Lybrand. The court-appointed receiver, which drew judicial praise for the thoroughness of its efforts, was unable to locate anything outside Canada, aside from the money spent at Interfaces, the New York escort agency.

A combination of good luck and Melnitzer's ability to deflect questions conspired to keep that potentially embarrassing connection from becoming public. Coopers and

Lybrand had just unearthed the Interfaces cheques when they were pulled off the case to be replaced by an underfunded bankruptcy trustee unable to explore the matter. When police asked Melnitzer about Interfaces, he provided the same innocent explanation he gave the accounting firm — that he had paid the funds to a New York City art dealer and that Interfaces was probably one of the dealer's other businesses through which the cheques had been funneled. Yet, inexplicably, Melnitzer wouldn't provide even that answer during his mandatory interview under oath with the official receiver in bankruptcy, preferring to challenge the validity of the question, successfully turning it aside. The relationship with Interfaces was never fully explored by anyone, and Melnitzer clearly preferred it that way.

In its aborted search for money, however, Coopers and Lybrand had relied to some extent on Melnitzer's statement about offshore funds. During his interview with the firm, Melnitzer denied he had anything hidden outside Canada or that he had anticipated being caught. When asked specifically about the overseas deposits to which he had referred in his earlier dealings with the banks, Melnitzer was adamant that there were none.

"I have never, ever tried to protect myself or my wife or my kid in any way," he said. "You will never find — if you go through every cheque — you will never find large cash withdrawals . . . You will find no cheques written outside the jurisdiction of Canada, except for cheques that I may have written for purchases on holidays or for art which I bought all over the world . . . I never made any attempt, you know, to protect myself in case this all fell apart, or to hide anything so that in the end I'd have somewhere to run to."

The investigating Mounties don't believe there is any money hidden in other countries, although they'd be the first to admit they didn't have the resources to dig into such a possibility. But many of Melnitzer's peers, like those of lawyer Alvin Ashley in New York City now doing time for fraud, remain unconvinced.

The cynics insist Melnitzer also conned the legal system. He arranged to serve his time in a relatively pleasant institution and was never pressed very hard about money he might have hidden. It will be a few years yet before the contradictory views are either silenced or vindicated. Ironically, the lack of sufficient acclaim and recognition from his peers was one of the factors that helped push Melnitzer to a life of crime. Now when he doesn't want it, they are giving him credit for something he specifically denies.

Whatever the truth, Melnitzer wasn't prepared to talk after he pleaded guilty. He shunned all press interviews. At one point, however, he was reportedly attempting to interest book publishers in his story. He was looking for a sizable advance, reflecting his continued "think big" approach to life. But he found no takers.

In 1991, a total of 75,773 individual Canadians or businesses declared bankruptcy or were petitioned into it. Their total indebtedness was more than $10.3 billion, for an average of $135,500 each. Melnitzer's $43-million bankruptcy was instrumental in boosting both figures.

Bankruptcy is a terrible experience, as anyone who has had to undergo it will attest. It's an admission of failure. There is humiliation in having one's affairs taken over by a trustee and watching sometimes prized assets sold off at fire-sale prices to satisfy creditors.

One would think those unable to keep their assets greater than their liabilities would find it difficult to borrow money again. Not so. With liabilities wiped clean, just-discharged bankrupt persons have an attractive asset-to-debt ratio. This means bankers will likely be interested in them as prospective customers. Federal government figures show that is exactly what happens. On average, 10 to 12 percent of those persons who become bankrupt are doing so for a *second* time. Someone, somewhere, is lending these people money. If the lenders are out there, Julius Melnitzer will no doubt find them.

Melnitzer is paying his debt to society and time will tell if he can repay the debts to his lenders. But he has taken much more from the people close to him, and it's doubtful he will ever be able to repay them for his total breach of their faith.

Fanny Melnitzer learned that her son was a liar and a cheat. He smeared the family name and undid decades of work to achieve respect. She is probably relieved Alexander died before seeing the shame that befell his family. She can no longer brag about her oldest son, the famous lawyer who had "reached the top."

Her son's treachery has also embroiled the family firm, upon which she relies for an income, in what could be a protracted legal battle. Melfan Investments is the financial nest egg so carefully crafted by Alexander Melnitzer to ensure the continued well-being of his family. Any threat to it can also have implications for Rudy and Roslyn, who are otherwise too far removed, in San Francisco and in Western Canada, respectively, to be deeply affected by the fallout from their brother's acts.

Melissa Melnitzer resumed her studies at the University of Toronto with the knowledge that the family name was sullied and that the man she looked up to is a criminal who used her name to carry out his massive deceit. His actions ensnared her in his legal tangles and resulted in one of the banks scooping the sports car he'd given her.

Melnitzer remains devoted to her. In early June, four months after he was sentenced, Melnitzer secured an escorted pass from Beaver Creek to attend graduation ceremonies at U of T's Victoria College where Melissa collected her bachelor of science degree.

Deena Baltman has suffered in her front-row seat. Everything she shared with Melnitzer has collapsed around her. The travel is gone, as well as the fine homes, the furniture, the art and a privileged lifestyle. And some of the friends they shared. Her pursuit of acting must now be tempered by certain economic realities. The safety net provided by her husband's resources is gone, which may make progress more difficult in her chosen field. She's been forced into a leading role in a play she doesn't care for because of its unpleasant plot twist.

Harris Cohen, unlike others in the law firm he founded with Melnitzer, was fortunate not to be stung in the Singapore Deal. His conservatism, his cautious outlook, stood him in good stead yet again. But the actions of a man who had been his closest friend and confidant caused him extreme stress. When the firm had to retrench, Cohen, as well as the others, suffered financially. He will likely never get over the terrible betrayal by a man he thought he knew and upon whom he relied. And he feels terrible for the other partners who were victimized, sometimes blaming himself for what happened. He wonders if he should have detected warning signs earlier and challenged Melnitzer before things got out of control.

Other members of the law firm remain bitter, knowing their losses will set back their accumulation of capital for years. Some will never again be willing to place their full trust in a colleague. They are paying the price emotionally as well as financially.

Mountie Ray Porter was finally able to take his much-delayed vacation once the Melnitzer business was behind him. Then it was back to probing into the murky and never-ending world of commercial crime. He was barely able to savor the satisfaction a police officer derives from knowing a con man has been stopped and is serving time. In fact, professional as always, the sergeant was modestly describing the landmark case as "just another file." Despite his heavy workload, Porter was able to take upgrading courses and apply for the rank of inspector. Promotion is in his future.

Prosecutor Scott Hutchison returned to the Crown law office in Toronto, where he continues to tackle the grab bag of cases he is assigned. He had dealt with other frauds, but much of his time is spent on appeal work, running the gamut from fraud to murder.

As for Julius Melnitzer, he is a resilient man and may still accomplish much with his life, despite the crushing compensation orders. He is relatively young and no stranger to hard work. No doubt he will want to prove himself all over again.

Within a few months of his incarceration, Melnitzer began applying for unescorted temporary absences from Beaver Creek. He had been studying the parole regulations and learned passes could be attained for a variety of reasons, among them the need to continue psychiatric treatment.

But on September 2, about seven months after he was sentenced, Melnitzer's well-crafted plans suffered a setback. A dispute with another inmate earned him a black eye and a trip to Warkworth, a medium-security prison about two and a half hours to the southeast. His antagonist was Nicolas Canizares, the only other former lawyer serving time at Beaver Creek. Canizares, 40, had been sentenced in 1989 to 12 and a half years after pleading guilty to trafficking in cocaine with a street value of $1.4 million. A divorced father of one, Canizares was an extremely intelligent man who had much in common with Melnitzer. Until he was captured on police videotape transacting coke deals from his Toronto law office, Canizares had enjoyed the good life. He had a penchant for silk suits, drove a gold-colored BMW and owned a home in Rosedale, the same swank section of Toronto as Melnitzer's Roxborough Street home. Like Melnitzer, Canizares was also working the parole system for everything he could while at Beaver Creek. He'd won unescorted three-day passes and was mere months away from a transfer to a halfway house from which he would have day parole.

Prison officials refused to discuss the incident, citing confidentiality provisions in the federal Privacy Act. But they conceded that Melnitzer's move to Warkworth was a disciplinary measure. The altercation apparently brought no punishment for Canizares; weeks later he was still being referred to as a model prisoner. For Melnitzer, however, the implications of his scrape with Canizares were significant. Another inmate told an outsider that Melnitzer had "screwed himself" in the episode, for a move to Warkworth is dreaded by inmates. The dreary, 600-prisoner facility can be an unpleasant environment: as many as two-thirds of its prisoners are sex offenders, and many of the rest are prone to violence. The move to medium security will likely delay by many months Melnitzer's plans for early release. He'd expected that by August 1993, 18 months after he was sentenced, he would be granted day parole from a halfway house and probably be attending school. He was hoping for full parole by February 1995. But those time frames are bound to change because of the black mark on his record his tangle with Canizares earned him. Somehow Canizares had awakened in Melnitzer the combative spirit with which Melnitzer had trounced so many of his legal adversaries in the courtroom.

When, eventually, Melnitzer is eligible to apply for full parole, his freedom will allow him to do many things — including indulge his passion for travel. If he does, it is certain those who hold the compensation orders will be most interested to know if his itinerary will include Switzerland, the Cayman Islands or other destinations with secretive banks.

It is clear the last chapter about Julius Melnitzer has yet to be written.

Appendix

The 43 criminal charges to which Julius Melnitzer pleaded guilty:

Stock Forgery
1) Stock certificates of BCE Inc., International Business Machines Corporation, Exxon Corporation, Canadian Pacific Limited and McDonald's Corporation.

Bank Frauds
2) Canadian Imperial Bank of Commerce: personal line of credit of $20 million.
3) Canadian Imperial Bank of Commerce: revolving reducing demand loan of $8.85 million.
4) Canadian Imperial Bank of Commerce: corporate line of credit of $2.5 million for Grand Canyon Properties Limited.
5) Royal Bank of Canada: personal line of credit of $8 million.
6) Royal Bank of Canada: personal line of credit of $3 million.
7) National Bank of Canada: personal line of credit of $15 million.
8) National Bank of Canada: revolving reducing demand loan of $2 million.
9) Toronto Dominion Bank: mortgage of $1.5 million.

10) Bank of Montreal: personal line of credit of $250,000.

Attempted Fraud on Banks, Trust Companies

11) Toronto Dominion Bank for proposed personal line of credit of $21 million.
12) Hongkong Bank of Canada for proposed personal line of credit of $6 million.
13) Mutual Trust Company for proposed personal line of credit of $6 million.

Frauds against Individuals

A. *Allan Richman and his investors*

14) Allan Richman, London investor, and Forward Properties: $4 million.
15) Allan Richman and Grand Canyon Investments: $2.5 million.
16) Allan Richman and Grand Canyon Investments: $1 million.
17) Allan Richman and Grand Canyon Investments: $1 million.
18) Allan Richman, $450,000.
19) Allan Richman, $200,000.

B. *The Singapore Deal*

20) Allan Richman: $1.8 million.
21) Ronald Delanghe, law partner: $1.5 million.
22) Ronald Delanghe and Bonnie Delanghe: $925,000.
23) Barry Parker, property firm executive: $450,000.
24) Ivana Klouda, law-firm administrator: $100,000.
25) Fletcher Dawson, law-firm partner: $100,000.
26) Ken McGill, law partner, and Margaret McGill: $150,000.
27) Paul Vogel, law partner: $50,000.
28) Jules Fleischer, longtime friend: $200,000.
29) Jaime Watt, marketing man: $25,000.
30) Hyman Goldberg, dentist friend, and Laurie Seaman: $250,000.

Plus: 13 other counts of forging documents, including stock certificates, financial statements and other material used in the above frauds.

The Totals

Amount defrauded from banks:	$61.1 million
Amount defrauded from individuals:	$14.7 million
Total defrauded:	$75.8 million
Attempted fraud:	$33.0 million
Actual Loss to Banks:	$12.35 million
Actual Loss to Individuals:	$14.7 million
Total Loss	$27.05 million

Index

advertising, and legal profession, 68; *see also*
    Cohen, Melnitzer, advertising and
    promotion
Advocates Society, 103
Allard, Brian, 207-208
Allen and Overy, 133
Anders, Debbie, 87
Arndt, Hans J., 236-37, 239
Arnup, John D., 233, 239
Ashley, Alvin, 176-78, 263
Aur Resources Inc., 189-90
Awata Corporation, 135, 226

Badley, Jennifer, 195-96, 198, 220
Ballard, Mike, 257-58, 259
Baltman, Deena
    acting career of, 99, 101, 104, 124, 142, 214,
        252, 265-66
    bank's seeking of damages against, 218-19
    called to the bar, 95
    claim of artwork against, 220, 248
    claims of assets by, 243
    expensive taste of, 97, 111
    financial arrangements with Julius, 100-101
    freezing of assets of, 213, 214
    gifts to, from Julius, 102, 262
    income and fees sought by following Julius's
        bankruptcy, 221-21
    inner strength of, 253-54
    interest in fitness, 124
    introduction to Julius, 95
    jewelry collection of, 253
    joining of Cohen, Melnitzer, 95, 123
    reaction regarding Julius's affair with Calla
        Reid, 212
    moving in with Julius, 95
    position of husband in marriage, 100-101
    posting of bail for Julius, 203, 215, 231
    return to legal profession by, 214, 222
    supportiveness of, 209, 229, 230, 237, 242,
        245-46, 252-53
    travels with Julius, 7, 98, 116, 126, 160, 185-86
    wedding to Julius, 99-100

Bank of Montreal, 107-108, 113, 125, 126, 166,
    171-72, 186, 192, 194, 214, 219
Bank of Nova Scotia, 166
banking community
    effects of Julius Melnitzer's crimes on, 257
bankruptcies, number of, 264; *see also* Julius
    Melnitzer, bankruptcy of
Bankruptcy Act, 221
banks, *see also* Bank of Montreal, Bank of Nova
    Scotia, Canadian Imperial Bank of
    Commerce, National Bank of Can-
    ada, Royal Bank of Canada, Toronto
    Dominion Bank
    bad loans by, 166
    and changes within industry, 171
    compared with trust companies, 166-67,
        169
    competition among, 171
    and confidentiality, 164
    credit-card frauds against, 166
    deregulation of (U.S.), 165
    failures of, 164-65
    frauds, others perpetrated on, 169-71
    insurance covering losses of, 259
    profit-making of, 163, 166, 259
    robberies of, 166
    savings-and-loans (U.S.), 165, 166
    and small- vs. big-time borrowers, 161-64
Barnes, Robert, 221-22
BCE Inc. shares, 9, 13, 15, 27, 154, 157, 159, 182,
    191
Beaver Creek Correctional Institution, 244-45
Bell Canada, 9
Bell, Del, 65-66
Belvedere Hotel case, 50-54, 60, 93, 244
Blaney, Pasternak, Smela, Eagleson and Watson,
    43-44
Bogart, John, 144, 213
Boggs case, 54-57, 59, 111, 225
Bradnam, Susan, 88-89
Bronfman family, 167
Buchanan, Jerry, 25
Byer, David, 38

Cableshare, 151, 189, 248
Canada Pension Plan, 140-41
Canada Trust, 42, 166, 167
Canadian Bankers Association, 257
Canadian Lawyer, 255-56
Canadian Imperial Bank of Commerce, 93, 113,
    126, 133, 143, 158, 166, 169-70, 172,
    173, 175, 180-82, 183, 185, 187, 189,
    190, 192, 201, 212-13, 214, 218-19,
    220, 221, 238, 248, 249, 258-59
Canadian Bankers' Association, 165, 257, 259
Canadian Pacific Limited shares, 6, 9, 13, 14, 15,
    27, 154, 157, 159, 182, 191
Canizares, Nicolas, 267-68
Champion Chemtech Limited, 124, 129, 149,
    150, 151-52, 181, 182, 184, 212, 220
Champlain Meat Packers Ltd., 38
Chilcott, Justice W. Daniel, 74, 75, 78-79, 81-82,
    83, 84, 85, 86
Cohen, Delanghe, Highley, Vogel and Dawson,
    206, 209, 211, 213, 217
Cohen, Donna, 69
Cohen, Elliot, 42
Cohen, Harris
    background of, 42
    betrayal of Julius Melnitzer, effect on, 266
    billings of, 64, 122-23
    early friendship with Julius Melnitzer, 41-43
    embarrassed by Julius Melnitzer, 64, 124
    formation of Cohen, Melnitzer, 45, 46
    friendship with Julius Melnitzer, 42-43, 64
    lack of interest in investment schemes, 122-
        23, 132, 266
    later relationship with Julius Melnitzer, 122-
        23, 254
    presentation of Stradivarius, 118
    professional relationship with Julius
        Melnitzer, 63-64

Cohen, Highley, Vogel and Dawson, 217, 218,
    254
Cohen, Jerome, 42
Cohen, Melnitzer; *see also* Melnitzer, Julius,
    cases of
    advertising and promotion of, 3, 68-70, 88, 118
    bankers of, 173, 180
    billings of, 64, 85-86; *see also* Melnitzer,
        Julius, billings of
    contributions to Grand Theatre, 69, 117
    Deena Baltman's joining, 95
    effects of recession on, 111
    expansion of, 54, 63-64, 68, 106-107, 121-22,
        181
    expulsion of Julius Melnitzer, 205
    formation of, 45, 46
    launch of Singapore Deal at, 129-32
    partners, 25-26, 29-30, 31, 54, 85-86, 107,
        112, 122, 175
    reaction and response to arrest of Julius
        Melnitzer, 204-205, 206
    renaming of firm, 206
    search of offices of, 24-29, 197, 199-200
    squabble with Peat Marwick Thorne, 248
    status in London of, 2, 69, 121-22
    working relationship with Sterling Marking
        Services, 154
Cohen, Nicky, 42

Cohen, Rochelle, 42
Cohen, Rose, 42
Cohen and Watt, 69, 80; *see also* Watt, Jaime
Coopers and Lybrand, 198-99, 209-10, 213-14,
    219-21, 223, 227, 228, 231-32, 245,
    247, 262-63
Copeland, Paul, 251-52
Copps, Sheila, 22-23
Crawford, Michael G., 255-56
Crook, Ian, 195-96, 198, 258
Crown Trust, 167, 168, 239
Cudmore, Gordon, 66-67

Dawson, Fletcher, 25, 54, 58, 62, 112, 132, 206,
    208-209, 211, 238, 244
Dawson, Janine, 25-28
Defence Lawyer's Trial Book (Melnitzer and
    Dawson), 62
Delanghe, Bonnie, 31, 32, 132, 217, 226, 238
Delanghe, Ron, 26, 27, 28-29, 30-32, 33, 118, 126,
    132, 135, 136, 144, 186, 187, 190,
    217, 218, 224, 226, 238
Devonshire Financial Group Limited, 145
Doxtator, Isaac William, 50-53
Driver, Alan, 199, 202

Eagleson, Alan, 44
Ehler, Kelly, 147-48
Epstein, Michael, 26, 28, 29, 201, 214, 222, 226,
    230, 233, 237, 238
Ernst and Young, 103, 104, 149
Everett, John, 227-28, 245
Exxon Corporation shares, 6, 9, 15, 27, 154,
    157-58, 159, 182, 191

Fair Rental Policy Organization, 114, 121, 142,
    144, 206, 249
Fitz-James, Michael, 256-57
Fleischer, Jules, 133, 190, 192, 204, 234, 238,
    239, 252
Forward Properties, 108, 125, 149, 185, 238
Foster, Geoffrey M., 133, 135, 180-81, 182, 183,
    212-13, 259

General Motors Diesel Division, 42
Gibbs, Charles, 76
Gibbs, Archie, 71, 72-77, 85, 87-88, 210-11, 235
    legal fees of, 80, 84, 85-86, 124-25, 127, 141,
        190, 248-49
    on witness stand, 79-80
Gibbs, Harold, 72
Gibbs case, *see* Grand Bend beach case
Goldberg, Hyman, 133, 135, 238
Gorman, Joseph, 22-23
Gorman, Constable Steve, 18-19
Graham, Howard, 83
Graham, John, 184, 186, 195, 197
    firing of, 258
    meeting with Julius Melnitzer, 1-11, 191
    meeting with David Renwick, 11-14
Grand Bend beach case (Gibbs versus the Corpo-
    ration of the Village of Grand Bend)
    celebration of outcome, 86-87, 216
    decision, 86
    historical background of, 71-73
    legal fees of participants, 80; *see also* Gibbs,
        Archie

media attention to, 74-75, 80, 87-89
referral to Cohen, Melnitzer, 72-73
trial, 74-85, 123
Grand Theatre (London, Ont.), 69, 101, 117, 234, 253
Grand Canyon Investments, 109
Grand Canyon Properties, 11, 125, 143, 149, 159, 182, 184, 185, 220, 238
Green, Harold, 74
Greenspan, Brian, 226, 230, 231, 233, 237, 238-39
Gretzinger, Harold, 117-18, 119
Gretzky, Wayne, 152
Greymac Trust, 167, 168, 239
Gunn, Sergeant George, 21, 25-28, 196-98, 200, 225

Hassan, Hamoody, 155
Hassan, Sam, 154-56, 157, 179-80, 186, 189, 203-204
Hedden, Pat, 50
Henderson, Constable John, 19-20
Henry, Martha, 101, 234, 253-54
Highley, Frank, 206
Home-Stake Production Company swindle, 140
Hongkong Bank of Canada, 146, 147, 148, 150, 151, 152, 214
Hubley, Corporal Mike, 26, 196-97, 200
Hunter, Ian, 234
Hutchison, Scott, 224-26, 230-31, 237-38, 239-40, 242, 266

IBM Corporation shares, 6, 9, 15, 27, 154, 157, 159, 182, 191
Imasco Limited, 167
Interfaces escort agency, 104-105, 223, 227, 228, 262-63

J.C. Penney, 151
Jack, Donald, 220, 250

Kahnert, Tom, 180, 182, 189
Keenan, Justice Harry, 24, 198-99, 209
Kent, Andy, 195
Khan, Peter, 203-204
Killeen, Justice Gordon, 219, 221, 223, 227, 231-232, 246, 248
Klouda, Ivana, 132, 238, 249
Klym, Peter, 40

Labatt's Breweries, 42
Lambden, David, 77-78, 82
landlord and tenant matters, Ontario, 59-61; see also Fair Rental Policy Organization; Thom Commission of Inquiry into Residential Tenancies
Lang Michener, 205-206, 207
Lanza, Joseph, 118-19
Laskin, Chief Justice Bora, 58
law, conduct of, 67-68
Law Reform Commission of Canada, 62
Law Society of Upper Canada, 67, 68, 205-206, 208, 219, 223, 233, 250
lawyers, breach of trust by, 175-78
lawyers, testosterone levels of, 102
Lawyer's Weekly, 256-57
Legal Aid plan, 222

Lerner, Michael, 156
Lerner and Associates, 217-18
line of credit, defined, 108
Liptrot, Colin, 172-73, 174-75, 190-91, 193, 258
Lockyer, Peter, 212
London City Press Club, 65-66
London Foundation, 117
London Free Press, 65, 80, 88-89, 208, 210, 219, 245, 246
London Furniture, 42
London Life Insurance Company, 4, 42, 121
London, Ont.
  cultural community in, 3, 99
  description of, 42, 45
  Jewish community in, 42, 45, 49, 174
  law scene of, 47
London Psychiatric Hospital, 94
Lonergan, Paul, 174
Los Angeles Kings, 152
Lovell, Frederick, 50, 52

MacDonald, Corporal Al, 18, 20
MacDonald, John Allen, 52-53
MacKenzie, Gavin, 208, 223, 250, 251
Maloney, Justice William, 229, 230, 231, 237-38, 239, 240-42
Marcus and Associates, 185
Mason, Fraser, 149-50
Mayer, Uri, 118
McDonald's Corporation shares, 9, 15, 27, 154, 157, 159, 182, 191
McGee, Patricia, 88
McGill, Ken, 132, 217, 218, 238
McGill, Margaret, 132, 238
McMillan Binch, 194-95, 197, 198, 231
McNall, Bruce, 152
Melfan Investments Ltd., 3-4, 107, 110, 112, 113, 114, 127, 133, 143, 153, 171, 176, 182, 183, 184, 185, 186, 191, 202, 209, 218-19, 230, 247, 265
Melnitzer, Alexander, 35, 36-37, 38, 39, 110, 114, 192, 265
Melnitzer, Cathy
  depression, signs of, 93
  early years of in London, Ont., 49, 59, 92, 107
  loan guarantees by family of, 92, 94, 95, 96, 107, 111
  marriage breakup and separation of, 93, 94, 95-96
  marrying Julius Melnitzer, 41
  meeting Julius Melnitzer, 39, 91
  nursing studies and career of, 45, 49, 94. 97
  qualities of, 91-92
  remarriage of, 97, 254
  separation and divorce settlements of, 96, 97, 111, 212, 231
Melnitzer, Deena, see Baltman, Deena
Melnitzer, Fanny, 35, 36, 38, 209, 210, 265
Melnitzer, Julius
  accounting material forged by, 184-85, 186
  admission to London Psychiatric Hospital, 94
  affair with Calla Reid, revelation of to wife, 245-46
  appearances, need to keep up, 115, 117
  arrest of, 104, 183, 201-203
  art collection of, 3, 98, 115-17, 184, 212, 213, 220, 243-44, 248

assets and liabilities statement prepared by, 184-85, 186; *see also* worth of
bail posted for, 203, 215
banking community, effects of crimes on, 257
bankruptcy of, 221-22, 226-28, 231-32, 246-47, 249-50, 255, 264
billings, fees, salary of, 3, 64, 80, 82, 84, 85-86, 96, 107, 111, 122, 218; *see also* Gibbs, Archie; Grand Bend beach case
birth of daughter, Melissa, 43
cases of; *see* Belvedere Hotel case, Boggs case, Szpyt case, Grand Bend beach case
character reference requests made by, 233-36, 239, 240
charges laid against, 32-33, 201, 214-15, 219, 223, 224, 230, 251, 269-71
childhood years of, 35-38
civil litigation cases, interest in, 58-59
claim to have written "Hotel California," 63
co-authorship of *The Defence Lawyer's Trial Book*, 62
compensation sought by victims of, 238, 255
competitive nature of, 37-38
conduct unbecoming charges laid against, 219, 223, 251
confession of, 201-202, 209-10, 212, 229
threat to recant, 212
conviction of, 105
courtroom manner of, 2, 52-53, 56, 58, 61, 76-80, 81-85
credit-card bills of, 115
creditors of, prospects for, 255
criminal cases of, early, 46-54
Criminal Code challenges made by, 54-58, 62
criminal law
early interest in, 47
loss of interest in, 58
defence submissions at trial of, 238-39
disbarment of, 235, 251-52
divorce of, 96-97, 111, 113, 212, 231
dog support paid by, 96
dogs of 98-99
and educational video, offer to be subject of, 250-51
escort agency, cheques of written to; *see* Interfaces
expulsion of from Cohen, Melnitzer, 205
Fair Rental Policy Organization
named chairman of, 121
resigned from, 206-207
false information provided to Mutual Trust, 149-51
fictitious accounts of, 123, 190
forgeries, first perpetrated by, 111-12, 113, 114; *see also* BCE Inc.; Canadian Pacific Limited; Exxon Corporation; IBM Corporation; McDonald's Corporation; Melnitzer, stock holdings of
forgery charges, total laid against, 214; summarized, 269
formation of Cohen, Melnitzer, 45, 46
fraud charges, total laid against, 214; summarized, 269-71

freezing of assets of, 198, 209, 211
gifts from, 102, 103-104, 105, 262; *see also* Baltman, Deena; Melnitzer, Melissa; Reid, Calla
gold and silver investments of, 107, 110-11, 149, 151
and Harris Cohen, friendship with
degeneration of, 64
early, 41, 42-43
high school
suspension from, 40
and university years of, 38-40
hockey boasts of, 63
homes of
London, 3, 20, 21, 49-50, 59, 92-93, 95, 96, 97-98, 110, 184, 243
Montreal childhood, 35-36, 39
Toronto, 5, 21, 41, 101, 122-23, 142-44, 159, 182, 184, 199, 232-33
imprisonment of, 244-45, 265, 266-68
obtaining pass to attend daughter's graduation, 265
interest payments of, 172
investments, early, 59
investment schemes of, *see* Cableshare; Champion Chemtech; Forward Properties; gold and silver investments of; Grand Canyon Properties; Melfan Investments; Prenor Trust; Singapore Deal; Vanguard Trust
landlord and tenant matters, involvement in, 3, 59-61, 95, 114, 121, 206-207; *see also* Fair Rental Policy Organization; Thom Commission of Inquiry into Residential Tenancies
law firms of, *see* Blaney, Pasternak, Smela, Eagleson and Watson; Cohen, Melnitzer; Torkin, Manes, Cohen and Arbus
Law Reform Commission paper written by, 62
law school years of, 40-43
lawsuits filed against, 196
lawyers acting for, *see* Epstein, Michael; Greenspan, Brian; Jack, Donald
legal community's view of, 48, 53, 61, 65, 70, 80, 87, 210, 255-57, 261
lines of credit, total, 187, 193
loan guarantees made by inlaws, 92, 94, 95, 96, 107, 111
marriage; *see also* Baltman, Deena; Melnitzer, Cathy
breakup and separation of, 93, 94, 95-96; *see also* separation and divorce settlements of
role in, 100-101
media
publicity courted by, 3, 49, 53, 56, 58, 65-66, 74-75, 80, 87-89, 118-19
publicity not courted by, 200, 207, 208, 209, 210, 214, 215-16, 223-24, 229, 245, 246
scuffles with, 208, 214
Montreal Junior Canadiens, 63
mortgages of, *see* homes of
music, interest in, 38, 63
nightclub venture of, 112

obscenity rendered by following Robinette submission, 61
Ontario Court of Appeal cases, 54-55, 58, 59-61
parole eligibility of, 233, 237, 267, 268
philanthropy of, 3, 117
physical qualities of, 7, 90, 97, 124
plea of to charges, 224, 229, 230
and police, co-operation with following arrest, 240
preliminary hearing, waiving of rights to, 224
prison dispute involving, 267-68
professional ethics of, 61, 89
psychiatric report about, 236-37, 239
psychiatric treatment recommended for, 242, 267
psychiatry, interest in, 41
real estate investments, transactions, 5, 10, 63, 107, 109, 110, 111, 114, 127; see also homes of; investment schemes of
receiver appointed for, 196, 198-99; see also Coopers and Lybrand
recognition and acceptance, desire for, 49, 54, 62-63, 65-67, 88, 106, 114
record-keeping of, 123, 213
relationships, extramarital, 93-94, 95, 97, 102, 103-104; see also Baltman, Deena; Reid, Calla
religious background of, 36
sentencing of, 224, 229, 237-42, 244
separation and divorce settlements of, 96, 97, 212
social manners of, 91
sports and fitness, interest in, 63, 81, 91, 124, 144
standards instilled in, 36-37, 38
stashing of funds, speculation about, 220, 240, 261-64
stockbroker of, 154
stock holdings of
    actual, 189
    fraudulent, 6, 8-16, 24-29, 32-33, 153-57, 180, 183-84, 187, 189; see also BCE Inc.; Canadian Pacific Limited; Exxon Corporation; IBM Corporation; McDonald's Corporation
Stradivarius, purchase by, 118-19, 185
stuffed toy collection of, 98
Supreme Court cases of, 54, 56-58
surrender of, 32
Szirt, Cathy; see Melnitzer, Cathy
temperamental nature of, 2-3, 5, 123, 125
Torkin, Manes, Cohen and Arbus
    made associate counsel of, 142
    removal from, 207
travels of, 7, 98, 116, 126, 160, 185-86, 261-62, 268
University of Western Ontario, involvement with, 61, 234
vegetarian habits of, 98
victims of schemes; see Bank of Montreal; Canadian Imperial Bank of Commerce; Dawson, Fletcher; Delanghe, Bonnie; Delanghe, Ron; Fleischer, Jules; Forward Properties; Goldberg, Hyman; Grand Canyon Properties;

Hongkong Bank of Canada; Klouda, Ivana; McGill, Ken; McGill, Margaret; Mutual Trust Company; National Bank of Canada; Parker, Barry; Richman, Allan; Royal Bank of Canada; Seaman, Laurie; Toronto Dominion Bank;; Vogel, Paul; Watt, Jaime.
    view of legal profession, 69
    wedding to Deena Baltman, 99-100
    worth of, 2, 3, 175, 185, 186, 209, 213, 220, 223, 247, 262
Melnitzer, Melissa, 13, 15 43, 45, 49, 92, 95, 96, 97, 100, 102, 107, 153, 154, 157, 201, 203, 218-19, 237, 242, 246, 265
Melnitzer, Roslyn, 35, 36, 37, 107, 265
Melnitzer, Rudy, 35, 37, 265
Merrill Lynch, 149, 150
Molony, Brian, 169-71
Montreal (1950s), 34-35
Montreal Trust, 13, 14-15, 98, 243
Morden, Judge John, 60
Morin, Guy Paul, 229-30
Murphy, Dan, 75, 76, 78, 234-36
Mutual Trust Company, 146, 147-51, 152, 214

National Basketball Association, 151, 152
National Bank of Canada, 1-16, 19, 21, 24, 28, 32, 114, 166, 175, 184-85, 186, 187, 188, 191, 195, 196, 197, 198, 201, 207-208, 209, 212, 214, 218, 219, 230, 231-32, 238, 255, 258
National Ballet of Canada, 117, 172
natives, legal treatment of, 51
Nicholas, Peter Louie, 50
Northland and Canadian Commercial bank failures, 164-65

O'Grady, Gerald, 77
O'Leary, Justice Dennis, 209, 211
"Oklahoma" technique, 168-69
Orchestra London, 100, 118-19
Osborne, Chris, 194-97, 198, 209, 213-14, 220-21

Parker, Barry, 132, 238
Peat Marwick Thorne, 206, 221, 222-23, 232-33, 246-48, 249, 250
Peel, Constable, Joe, 18
Pilzmaker, Martin, 205-206
Player, William, 168-69, 239
Pollock, Helen, 26
Polzl, Diethard, 15
Ponzi, Charles, 137-40, 141, 188
Ponzi scheme, 136-41, 164, 176, 188; see also Ashley, Alvin; Canada Pension Plan
Porter, Nancy, 20-21
Porter, Sergeant Ray, 17-29, 32, 197-98, 200-203, 266
Prenor Trust Company of Canada, 125, 149
Price Waterhouse, 110, 125

Quebec (1950s), 34

Raikes, Russell, 26, 75, 80, 82, 86, 87, 123, 209, 210, 249
Ranger, Maurice, 208
Reid, Calla, 103-104, 192, 212, 223, 227, 228, 245, 254

Rent Review Advisory Committee, 114
Renwick, David, 6, 8, 10-14, 175, 184-85, 186, 195, 197, 258
Residential Tenancy Commission, Ontario, 59-61
Richman, Allan, 10, 108-110, 113, 114, 119, 125, 127, 132-33, 145-46, 149, 176, 182, 185, 190, 209, 212, 213, 214, 228, 238, 254-55, 262
Robinette, J.J., 60-61
Ross, F. Donald, 72, 84
Royal Bank of Canada, 114, 158, 164, 166, 172-75, 179, 180-81, 185, 187, 190-91, 193, 201, 211, 214, 238, 248, 257, 258
Royal Trust, 15, 166, 167
Royal Canadian Mounted Police; see also Gunn, Sergeant George; Hubley, Corporal Mike; Porter, Sergeant Ray
    London detachment, 17-29, 196, 201, 204, 208, 214
    Toronto detachment, 19, 21, 22-23, 24

San Antonio Spurs, 151, 152, 159
Saunders, Sunny, 257
Schram, Bob, 156
ScotiaMcLeod Inc., 152, 154, 190
Seaman, Laurie, 133, 135, 238
Seaway Trust, 167, 168, 239
Segal, Murray, 56
Sharen, Bob, 84
Shea, Ed, 14-15
Shewchuk, Inspector Dave, 19
Shore, Gary, 158-60
Siegal, Fogler, 43
Sifton, Glen, 31, 135-36, 144, 217, 218, 224, 226
Sifton Holdings Limited, 135, 226
Sifton Properties Ltd., 31, 132, 135, 217, 238
Singapore Deal, 7, 10, 24, 29-32, 33, 128-36, 143, 144-45, 150, 160, 176, 185, 186- 88, 190, 192, 202, 204-205, 209, 213, 220, 223, 224, 230, 234, 247, 251, 266
    forged documentation regarding, 133-34
Slipacoff, Lennie, 118, 119
Steiner, Joseph, 222-23, 246-47
Sterling Marking Products, 154-58, 179-80, 183, 186, 189, 201, 203-204, 231
Suske, Stephen, 145-47, 152
Sutcliffe, Brad, 12-16, 195-96, 197
swindles, examples of, 136-41; see also Ashley, Alvin; Molony, Brian; Oklahoma technique; Player, William; Ponzi scheme
Szirt, Katalin (Catherine), see Melnitzer, Cathy
Szpyt case, 57-58

Thom, Stuart, 233-34, 235
Thom Commission of Inquiry into Residential Tenancies, 114, 233-34
Thompson, Corporal Henry, 18
Thompson, Norman, 126
Tod, Ian, 207
Torkin, Manes, Cohen and Arbus, 142, 144, 207
Toronto Dominion Bank, 8, 113, 143, 158-60, 166, 179, 182, 187, 189, 193, 201, 214, 232-33, 238
Trilon Financial Corp., 167
Trippet, Robert S., 140
trust companies, see also Canada Trust, Crown Trust, Greymac Trust, Montreal Trust, Mutual Trust, Royal Trust, Seaway Trust,
    collapses of, 167
    compared with banks, 166-67, 169
    defined, 165
    and fraud, 168-69
    ownership of, 167
    services offered by, 166
Tutt, Corporal Al, 26

Uncles, Alison, 210
University of Toronto Law School, 40, 41
University of Western Ontario, 61, 101, 234

Van Klink, Tony, 247-48
Van Moorsel, Greg, 208, 209
Vanguard Trust, 111, 112, 113, 125, 127, 149, 152, 153, 160, 171, 182, 214, 230
Vogel, Paul, 54, 75, 81, 87, 132, 238, 244

Walker, Judge Douglas, 25, 26
Wallace, Ian, 248
Watt, Jaime, 69, 88, 132, 218, 234, 238, 252; see also Cohen and Watt
Wells Fargo Bank, 151, 152
Wickett, Tom, 75, 78, 81, 83-84

Young, Jim, 159